RESTful Java Web Services

Second Edition

Design scalable and robust RESTful web services
with JAX-RS and Jersey extension APIs

Jobinesh Purushothaman

BIRMINGHAM - MUMBAI

RESTful Java Web Services
Second Edition

First published: November 2009

Second edition: September 2015

Production reference: 1160915

Published by Packt Publishing Ltd.
Livery Place
35 Livery Street
Birmingham B3 2PB, UK.

ISBN 978-1-78439-909-2

www.packtpub.com

This book is an update to *RESTful Java Web Services* by *Jose Sandoval*.

Credits

Author
Jobinesh Purushothaman

Reviewers
Erik Azar
Giuliano Araujo Bertoti
Ludovic Dewailly
Debasis Roy

Commissioning Editor
Nadeem N. Bagban

Acquisition Editor
Harsha Bharwani

Content Development Editor
Amey Varangaonkar

Technical Editors
Novina Kewalramani
Shiny Poojary

Copy Editors
Tani Kothari
Angad Singh

Project Coordinator
Suzanne Coutinho

Proofreader
Safis Editing

Indexer
Tejal Soni

Graphics
Jason Monteiro
Abhinash Sahu

Production Coordinator
Manu Joseph

Cover Work
Manu Joseph

About the Author

Jobinesh Purushothaman works with Oracle as a consulting solutions architect. In his current role, he is involved in the design and architectural decisions of various products that use Java EE and Oracle Application Development Framework technologies. Occasionally, he speaks at industry conferences, such as JavaOne and the Oracle Technology Network Developer Day. Jobinesh authored his first book, *Oracle ADF Real World Developer's Guide*, in 2012 for Packt Publishing. You can find his blog at http://www.jobinesh.com.

He holds a master of science (MSc) degree in computer science from Bharathiar University, India, and a master of business administration (MBA) degree from Indira Gandhi National Open University (IGNOU), India. After completing his MSc in computer science, Jobinesh started his career in 1999 with MicroObjects Private Limited, India. His career has taken him to different countries and various companies, where he has worked as a developer, technical leader, mentor, and technical architect. Jobinesh joined Oracle India Private Limited in 2008. Prior to joining Oracle, he worked as a senior software engineer at Emirates Group IT, Dubai from 2004 to 2008, where he was part of an IT strategy and architecture team.

Jobinesh currently lives in Bangalore, India, with his wife, Remya, son, Chinmay, and daughter, Ameya.

Acknowledgments

First and foremost, I would like to thank my parents, Mr. Purushothaman M.R and Mrs. Ratnam K.N, for allowing me to realize my own potential. All the support and encouragement they have provided me over the years were the greatest gifts that anyone has ever given me. I would like to thank my elder brother, Mr. Biju P Manakkattil, with all my heart for all the support he gave me throughout my life.

A thank you to my lovely wife, Remya, for her love, care, understanding, and sacrifices. Thanks to my son, Chinmay, for being my true inspiration for this work. Thanks to my sweet little daughter, Ameya, for filling my life with fun and joy. I could not have done this without their support.

Thanks to my nephews, Devadathan and Dhananjay, and sister-in-law, Mrs. Kavitha Biju, for all their support and well wishes. Thanks to my parents-in-law, Mr. Mohanan P.C and Mrs. Presanna P.N, for their love and care.

I sincerely thank and appreciate the team at Packt Publishing for their unconditional support, professionalism, and commitment through this project. Special thanks to Amey Varangaonkar, Harsha Bharwani, and Nadeem Bagban for all their support throughout this project. Thanks to all the technical reviewers for ensuring the quality of this book. They include Erik Azar, Ludovic Dewailly, Giuliano Araujo Bertoti, and Debasis Roy.

Special thanks to my managers at Oracle—Sharad Medhavi, who is a senior director at Oracle, and Chris Tonas, vice president at Oracle—for their support throughout this project. Thanks to Rekha Mathew, the technical manager at Oracle, for her help with *Appendix, Useful Features and Techniques*, in this book. Thanks to Vinay Agarwal, the principal product manager at Oracle, for his valuable insights on the REST metadata formats.

Thanks to the members of the Java EE, Jersey framework, and Apache Olingo communities for their timely responses to the questions that I raised in the discussion forums and mailing lists. A special thanks to all my friends for their encouragement and unconditional support throughout my life.

About the Reviewers

Erik Azar has been a professional software architect and developer for over 20 years. He has worked in diverse positions for companies ranging from start-ups to Fortune 500 companies, developing software such as systems and network management platforms, enterprise business applications in the insurance industry (specializing in healthcare, both personal and commercial), and benefit management.

He's currently a senior technical architect at Availity, LLC. He works with a small core team, developing Availity's next-generation healthcare REST API platform. He currently resides in Jacksonville, Florida, USA, with his partner, Rebecca; their three teenage children, Patrick, Kyra, and Cassandra; and their three dogs.

In his spare time, Erik enjoys exploring various open source operating systems, such as Haiku (BeOS). He has been a Linux hobbyist since the days of the original Slackware and Debian distros in the early 90s. Today, he's most interested in embedded devices and building REST APIs to manage IoT devices on the cloud. When he's not behind a computer, you can find him out riding his Harley, out with friends enjoying the local Jacksonville music scene, or working with non-profit organizations to help them understand how they can use technology to help market, fundraise, and manage their information.

I would like to use this opportunity to extend a special acknowledgement to my family for their support during the course of this book's development.

And I'd also like to acknowledge Suzanne Coutinho from the Packt Publishing team for her support in dealing with my challenging workload and schedule with my job during the development of this book.

Giuliano Araujo Bertoti is a master of science in electronics and computer engineering from the Aeronautics Institute of Technology (ITA), Brazil. He teaches software engineering and human-computer interaction disciplines at FATEC, which is an institute of technology in Brazil. In his free time, he walks with his beautiful wife and son in the gardens and plays soccer.

I would like to thank my mom, dad, grandma, son, and wife for their support at all times.

Ludovic Dewailly is a senior hands-on software engineer and development manager with over 12 years of experience in designing and building software solutions on platforms ranging from resource-constrained mobile devices to cloud computing systems. He is currently helping FancyGiving.com (`https://www.fancygiving.com/`), which is a social shopping, wishing, and gifting platform, to architect and build their system. His interests lie in software architecture and tackling the challenges of the web scale. He is the author of *Building a RESTful Web Service with Spring*, *Packt Publishing*.

I would like to thank my fiancée, Gaia, for helping me find the time to review this book during a very busy period.

Debasis Roy is working as a senior software engineer for NewsCred, in their Dhaka office. He has more than 8 years of professional experience in Java/C++/web-relevant technologies. He is enthusiastic about application architecture.

Currently, he is working on the development of the content marketing system for NewsCred. Previously, he worked at Vizrt. There, he was involved in the development of their sports analysis tool called Viz Sports (also known as LiberoVision), and the Viz Online Suite (also known as Escenic).

He has also worked on *RESTful Java Web Services Security* and *PostgreSQL Administration Essentials*, both published by Packt Publishing.

I would like to thank Packt Publishing for giving me the opportunity to review this wonderful book and for helping me learn new things.

www.PacktPub.com

Support files, eBooks, discount offers, and more

For support files and downloads related to your book, please visit www.PacktPub.com.

Did you know that Packt offers eBook versions of every book published, with PDF and ePub files available? You can upgrade to the eBook version at www.PacktPub.com and as a print book customer, you are entitled to a discount on the eBook copy. Get in touch with us at service@packtpub.com for more details.

At www.PacktPub.com, you can also read a collection of free technical articles, sign up for a range of free newsletters and receive exclusive discounts and offers on Packt books and eBooks.

https://www2.packtpub.com/books/subscription/packtlib

Do you need instant solutions to your IT questions? PacktLib is Packt's online digital book library. Here, you can search, access, and read Packt's entire library of books.

Why subscribe?

- Fully searchable across every book published by Packt
- Copy and paste, print, and bookmark content
- On demand and accessible via a web browser

Free access for Packt account holders

If you have an account with Packt at www.PacktPub.com, you can use this to access PacktLib today and view 9 entirely free books. Simply use your login credentials for immediate access.

Table of Contents

Preface   **ix**

Chapter 1: Introducing the REST Architectural Style   **1**

The REST architectural style   **1**

Introducing HTTP   **4**

HTTP versions   4

Understanding the HTTP request-response model   5

Uniform resource identifier   7

Understanding the HTTP request methods   8

Representing content types using HTTP header fields   9

HTTP status codes   10

The evolution of RESTful web services   12

The core architectural elements of a RESTful system   **14**

Resources   14

URI   15

The representation of resources   16

Generic interaction semantics for REST resources   16

The HTTP GET method   18

The HTTP POST method   21

The HTTP PUT method   22

The HTTP DELETE method   23

Hypermedia as the Engine of Application State   25

Description and discovery of RESTful web services   **26**

Java tools and frameworks for building RESTful web services   **27**

Summary   **28**

Chapter 2: Java APIs for JSON Processing   **29**

A brief overview of JSON   **29**

Understanding the JSON data syntax   30

Basic data types available with JSON   31

A sample JSON file representing employee objects   32

Processing JSON data   **32**

Using JSR 353 – Java API for processing JSON   **34**

Processing JSON with JSR 353 object model APIs   34

Generating the object model from the JSON representation   35

Generating the JSON representation from the object model   39

Processing JSON with JSR 353 streaming APIs   41

Using streaming APIs to parse JSON data   41

Using streaming APIs to generate JSON   44

Using the Jackson API for processing JSON   **45**

Processing JSON with Jackson tree model APIs   46

Using Jackson tree model APIs to query and update data   47

Processing JSON with Jackson data binding APIs   48

Simple Jackson data binding with generalized objects   48

Full Jackson data binding with specialized objects   49

Processing JSON with Jackson streaming APIs   50

Using Jackson streaming APIs to parse JSON data   50

Using Jackson streaming APIs to generate JSON   52

Using the Gson API for processing JSON   **53**

Processing JSON with object model APIs in Gson   54

Generating the object model from the JSON representation   54

Generating the parameterized Java collection from the JSON representation   55

Generating the JSON representation from the object model   56

Processing JSON with Gson streaming APIs   57

Reading JSON data with Gson streaming APIs   57

Writing JSON data with Gson streaming APIs   59

Summary   **61**

Chapter 3: Introducing the JAX-RS API   **63**

An overview of JAX-RS   **63**

JAX-RS annotations   **64**

Specifying the dependency of the JAX-RS API   65

Using JAX-RS annotations to build RESTful web services   65

Annotations for defining a RESTful resource   65

Annotations for specifying request-response media types   68

Annotations for processing HTTP request methods   70

Annotations for accessing request parameters   73

Returning additional metadata with responses   **82**

Understanding data binding rules in JAX-RS   **83**

Mapping the path variable with Java types   83

Mapping the request and response entity body with Java types   84

Using JAXB to manage the mapping of the request and response entity body to Java objects   84

Building your first RESTful web service with JAX-RS   **87**

Setting up the environment   87

Building a simple RESTful web service application using NetBeans IDE 88
Adding CRUD operations on the REST resource class 93
Client APIs for accessing RESTful web services **98**
Specifying a dependency of the JAX-RS client API 99
Calling REST APIs using the JAX-RS client 99
Simplified client APIs for accessing REST APIs 101
Summary **102**
Chapter 4: Advanced Features in the JAX-RS API **103**
Understanding subresources and subresource locators in JAX-RS **104**
Subresources in JAX-RS 104
Subresource locators in JAX-RS 105
Exception handling in JAX-RS **107**
Reporting errors using ResponseBuilder 107
Reporting errors using WebApplicationException 108
Reporting errors using application exceptions **110**
Mapping exceptions to a response message using ExceptionMapper 111
Introducing validations in JAX-RS applications **112**
A brief introduction to Bean Validation 113
Building custom validation constraints 115
What happens when Bean Validation fails in a JAX-RS application? 118
Supporting custom request-response message formats **118**
Building a custom entity provider 120
Marshalling Java objects to the CSV representation with MessageBodyWriter 121
Marshalling CSV representation to Java objects with MessageBodyReader 124
Asynchronous RESTful web services **126**
Asynchronous RESTful web service client **129**
Managing HTTP cache in a RESTful web service **131**
Using the Expires header to control the validity of the HTTP cache 131
Using Cache-Control directives to manage the HTTP cache 132
Conditional request processing with the Last-Modified HTTP
response header 134
Conditional request processing with the ETag HTTP response header 136
Conditional data update in RESTFul web services 138
Understanding filters and interceptors in JAX-RS **139**
Modifying request and response parameters with JAX-RS filters 140
Implementing server-side request message filters 140
Implementing server-side response message filters 143
Implementing client-side request message filters 144
Implementing client-side response message filters 145

Modifying request and response message bodies with
JAX-RS interceptors   146
    Implementing request message body interceptors   146
    Implementing response message body interceptors   147
Managing the order of execution for filters and interceptors   148
Selectively applying filters and interceptors on REST resources
by using @NameBinding   148
Dynamically applying filters and interceptors on REST resources
using DynamicFeature   150
Understanding the JAX-RS resource lifecycle   **151**
Summary   **153**
Chapter 5: Introducing the Jersey Framework Extensions   **155**
Specifying dependencies for Jersey   **156**
Programmatically configuring JAX-RS resources
during deployment   **157**
    A quick look at the static resource configurations   160
Modifying JAX-RS resources during deployment
using ModelProcessor   **160**
    What is Jersey ModelProcessor and how does it work?   160
        A brief look at the ModelProcessor interface   161
Building Hypermedia as the Engine of Application State
(HATEOAS) APIs   **163**
    Formats for specifying JSON REST API hypermedia links   164
    Programmatically building entity body links using JAX-RS APIs   166
    Programmatically building header links using JAX-RS APIs   168
    Declaratively building links using Jersey annotations   169
        Specifying the dependency to use Jersey declarative linking   169
        Enable Jersey declarative linking feature for the application   169
        Declaratively adding links to resource representation   170
        Grouping multiple links using @InjectLinks   172
        Declaratively building HTTP link headers using @InjectLinks   173
Reading and writing binary large objects using Jersey APIs   **174**
    Building RESTful web service for storing images   174
    Building RESTful web service for reading images   177
Generating chunked output using Jersey APIs   **178**
    Jersey client API for reading chunked input   181
Supporting Server Sent Event in RESTful web services   **182**
Understanding the Jersey server-side configuration properties   **187**
Monitoring RESTful web services using Jersey APIs   **189**
Summary   **190**

Chapter 6: Securing RESTful Web Services   191
Securing and authenticating web services   192
HTTP basic authentication   192
Building JAX-RS clients with basic authentication   194
Securing JAX-RS services with basic authentication   197
Configuring JAX-RS application for basic authentication   198
HTTP digest authentication   202
Securing RESTful web services with OAuth   203
Understanding the OAuth 1.0 protocol   204
Building the OAuth 1.0 client using Jersey APIs   206
Understanding the OAuth 2.0 protocol   210
Understanding the grant types in OAuth 2.0   213
Building the OAuth 2.0 client using Jersey APIs   214
Authorizing the RESTful web service accesses via the security APIs   218
Using SecurityContext APIs to control access   219
Using the javax.annotation.security annotations to control access with the Jersey framework   220
Using Jersey's role-based entity data filtering   222
Input validation   224
Summary   224

Chapter 7: The Description and Discovery of RESTful Web Services   225
Introduction to RESTful web services   226
Web Application Description Language   226
An overview of the WADL structure   226
Generating WADL from JAX-RS   228
Generating the Java client from WADL   232
Market adoption of WADL   233
RESTful API Modeling Language   233
An overview of the RAML structure   234
Generating RAML from JAX-RS   236
Generating RAML from JAX-RS via CLI   239
Generating JAX-RS from RAML   239
Generating JAX-RS from RAML via CLI   241
A glance at the market adoption of RAML   241
Swagger   242
A quick overview of Swagger's structure   242
An overview of Swagger APIs   244

Generating Swagger from JAX-RS 244
Specifying dependency to Swagger 246
Configuring the Swagger definition 247
Adding Swagger annotations on a JAX-RS resource class 248
Generating Java client from Swagger 251
A glance at the market adoption of Swagger 252
Revisiting the features offered in WADL, RAML, and Swagger 252
Summary 253
Chapter 8: RESTful API Design Guidelines 255
Identifying resources in a problem domain 256
Transforming operations to HTTP methods 256
Understanding the difference between PUT and POST 258
Naming RESTful web resources 258
Fine-grained and coarse-grained resource APIs 260
Using header parameter for content negotiation 261
Multilingual RESTful web API resources 262
Representing date and time in RESTful web resources 262
Implementing partial response 263
Implementing partial update 263
Returning modified resources to the caller 265
Paging resource collection 266
Implementing search and sort operations 267
Using HATEOAS in response representation 268
Hypertext Application Language 268
RFC 5988 – Web Linking 270
Versioning RESTful web APIs 272
Including the version in resource URI – the URI versioning 273
Including the version in a custom HTTP request header – HTTP header versioning 274
Including the version in a HTTP Accept header – the media type versioning 275
Hybrid approach for versioning APIs 276
Caching RESTful web API results 276
HTTP Cache-Control directive 277
HTTP conditional requests 277
Using HTTP status codes in RESTful web APIs 279
Overriding HTTP methods 282
Documenting RESTful web APIs 283
Asynchronous execution of RESTful web APIs 284
Microservice architecture style for RESTful web applications 285

Using Open Data Protocol with RESTful web APIs   **286**
    A quick look at OData   286
      URI convention for OData-based REST APIs   286
      Reading resources   287
      Querying data   287
      Modifying data   288
      Relationship operations   288
    Summary   **289**

Appendix: Useful Features and Techniques   **291**
    Tools for building a JAX-RS application   **291**
    Integration testing of JAX-RS resources with Arquillian   **293**
      Adding Arquillian dependencies to the Maven-based project   295
      Configuring the container for running tests   296
      Adding Arquillian test classes to the project   297
      Running Arquillian tests   299
    Implementing PATCH support in JAX-RS resources   **300**
      Defining the @PATCH annotation   300
      Defining a resource method to handle HTTP PATCH requests   300
    Using third-party entity provider frameworks with Jersey   **303**
      Transforming the JPA model in to OData-enabled RESTful
      web services   305
    Packaging and deploying JAX-RS applications   **307**
      Packaging JAX-RS applications with an Application subclass   308
      Packaging the JAX-RS applications with web.xml and an
      Application subclass   309
        Configuring web.xml for a servlet 2.x container   310
        Configuring web.xml for a Servlet 3.x container   310
      Packaging the JAX-RS applications with web.xml and without
      an Application subclass   311
        Configuring web.xml for the servlet 2.x container   311
        Configuring web.xml for the servlet 3.x container   312
    Summary   **313**
Index   **315**

Preface

Representational State Transfer (REST) is a simple yet powerful software architecture style that is meant for creating scalable web services. This book, RESTful Java web services, is a practical guide for developing RESTful web services using JAX-RS and Jersey extension APIs.

The book starts off with an introduction to RESTful web services and assumes that the reader has no prior knowledge of the RESTful architectural style. Each topic is explained with real-life use cases and code samples. This approach helps the reader in easily translating the theories into solutions for many kinds of real life use cases. In a nutshell, this is a practical guide on using JAX-RS and the Jersey framework extensions to build robust RESTful web services; it is not just about the theory of REST.

What this book covers

Chapter 1, Introducing the REST Architectural Style, covers the REST software architectural style and core architectural elements that form a RESTful system.

Chapter 2, Java APIs for JSON Processing, gives an overview of the JSON message format, and the popular tools and frameworks around JSON.

Chapter 3, Introducing the JAX-RS API, introduces JAX-RS APIs. This chapter will explain how to build RESTful web services with JAX-RS APIs.

Chapter 4, Advanced Features in the JAX-RS API, takes a deeper look into the advanced JAX-RS APIs, along with many real life use cases and code samples.

Chapter 5, Introducing the Jersey Framework Extensions, discusses some of the very useful Jersey framework extension APIs that are not yet a part of the JAX-RS standard.

Chapter 6, Securing RESTful Web Services, explores how to secure RESTful web services using the HTTP basic authentication and OAuth protocols.

Chapter 7, The Description and Discovery of RESTful Web Services, describes popular solutions that are available today for describing, producing, consuming, and visualizing RESTful web services.

Chapter 8, RESTful API Design Guidelines, discusses the best practices and design guidelines that developers will find useful while building RESTful web services. Learning the best practices will help you avoid common pitfalls that others might have faced before.

Appendix, Useful Features and Techniques, covers various useful features and techniques that we had deferred while discussing specific topics in this book. This section explores tools and techniques for building, testing, extending, and packaging JAX-RS web applications.

What you need for this book

The examples discussed in this book are built using the following software and tools:

- The Java SE Development Kit 8, or newer versions
- NetBeans IDE 8.0.2 (with the Java EE bundle), or newer versions
- The Glassfish Server 4.1, or newer versions
- Maven 3.2.3, or newer versions
- The Oracle Database Express Edition 11g Release 2, or newer versions
- The HR sample schema that comes with the Oracle database
- The Oracle database JDBC driver (ojdbc7.jar or newer versions)

Detailed instructions for setting up all the required tools to run the examples used in this book are discussed in the *Appendix, Useful Features and Techniques* section of this book.

Who this book is for

This book is for Java developers who want to design and develop scalable and robust RESTful web services with the JAX-RS and Jersey APIs. Contents are structured by keeping an eye on real life use cases from the RESTful API world and their solutions. Although the JAX-RS API solves many of the common RESTful web service use cases, some solutions are yet to be standardized as JAX-RS APIs. Keeping this in mind, a chapter is dedicated in this book for discussing Jersey extension APIs, which takes you beyond JAX-RS. This book also discusses the best practices and design guidelines for your REST APIs. In a nutshell, you will find this book useful while dealing with many real life use cases, such as dynamic resource configuration, message broadcasting with the server-sent event, HATEOAS, and so on.

Conventions

In this book, you will find a number of styles of text that distinguish between different kinds of information. Here are some examples of these styles, and an explanation of their meaning.

Code words in text are shown as follows: "Assume that we want to delete the Sales department from the data storage."

A block of code is set as follows:

```
{"departmentId":10,
"departmentName":"IT",
"manager":"John Chen,
"links": [ {
    "rel": "employees",
    "href": "http://packtpub.com/resources/departments/IT/
    employees"
} ]"}
```

When we wish to draw your attention to a particular part of a code block, the relevant lines or items are set in bold:

```
@Path("departments")
@Produces(MediaType.APPLICATION_JSON)
public class DepartmentResource{
//Class implementation goes here...
}
```

Any command-line input or output is written as follows:

```
mvn install -DskipTests
```

New terms and **important words** are shown in bold. Words that you see on the screen, in menus or dialog boxes for example, appear in the text like this: "Select **Local Domain** and click on **Next** to continue the wizard."

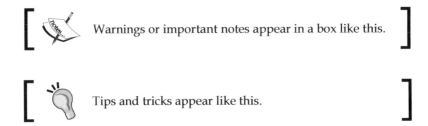

Warnings or important notes appear in a box like this.

Tips and tricks appear like this.

Reader feedback

Feedback from our readers is always welcome. Let us know what you think about this book—what you liked or may have disliked. Reader feedback is important for us to develop titles that you really get the most out of.

To send us general feedback, simply send an e-mail to feedback@packtpub.com, and mention the book title via the subject of your message.

If there is a topic that you have expertise in and you are interested in either writing or contributing to a book, see our author guide on www.packtpub.com/authors.

Customer support

Now that you are the proud owner of a Packt book, we have a number of things to help you to get the most from your purchase.

Downloading the example code

You can download the example code files for all Packt books you have purchased from your account at http://www.packtpub.com. If you purchased this book elsewhere, you can visit http://www.packtpub.com/support and register to have the files e-mailed directly to you.

Instructions for running examples are available in the README.md file present in the root folder of each project.

Errata

Although we have taken every care to ensure the accuracy of our content, mistakes do happen. If you find a mistake in one of our books—maybe a mistake in the text or the code—we would be grateful if you could report this to us. By doing so, you can save other readers from frustration and help us improve subsequent versions of this book. If you find any errata, please report them by visiting http://www.packtpub.com/submit-errata, selecting your book, clicking on the **Errata Submission Form** link, and entering the details of your errata. Once your errata are verified, your submission will be accepted and the errata will be uploaded to our website or added to any list of existing errata under the Errata section of that title.

To view the previously submitted errata, go to https://www.packtpub.com/books/content/support and enter the name of the book in the search field. The required information will appear under the **Errata** section.

Piracy

Piracy of copyright material on the Internet is an ongoing problem across all media. At Packt, we take the protection of our copyright and licenses very seriously. If you come across any illegal copies of our works, in any form, on the Internet, please provide us with the location address or website name immediately so that we can pursue a remedy.

Please contact us at copyright@packtpub.com with a link to the suspected pirated material.

We appreciate your help in protecting our authors, and our ability to bring you valuable content.

Questions

You can contact us at questions@packtpub.com if you are having a problem with any aspect of the book, and we will do our best to address it.

1
Introducing the REST Architectural Style

In this chapter, we will cover the **Representational State Transfer (REST)** software architectural style, as described in Roy Fielding's PhD dissertation. You may find a brief discussion on HTTP before getting into the details of REST. Once the base is set, we will be ready for the next step. We will then discuss the set of constraints, the main components, and the abstractions that make a software system RESTful. Here is the list of topics covered in this chapter:

- The REST architectural style
- Introducing HTTP
- The evolution of RESTful web services
- The core architectural elements of a RESTful system
- Description and discovery of RESTful web services
- Java tools and frameworks for building RESTful web services

The REST architectural style

REST is not an architecture; rather, it is a set of constraints that creates a software architectural style, which can be used for building distributed applications.

 You can read *Architectural Styles and the Design of Network-Based Software Architectures*, Roy Fielding, 2000, which talks about the REST architectural style by visiting http://www.ics.uci.edu/~fielding/pubs/dissertation/top.htm.

Fielding arrived at REST by evaluating all networking resources and technologies available for creating distributed applications. He observed that without any constraints, one may end up developing applications with no rules or limits that are hard to maintain and extend. After considerable research on building a better architecture for a distributed application, he ended with the following constraints that define a RESTful system:

- **Client-server**: This constraint keeps the client and the server loosely coupled. In this case, the client does not need to know the implementation details in the server and the server is not worried about how the data is used by the client. However, a common interface is maintained between the client and the server to ease the communication.

- **Stateless**: There should be no need for the service to keep users' sessions. In other words, each request should be independent of the others.

- **Cacheable**: This constraint has to support a caching system. The network infrastructure should support a cache at different levels. Caching can avoid repeated round trips between the client and the server for retrieving the same resource.

- **Uniform interface**: This constraint indicates a generic interface to manage all interactions between the client and the server in a unified way, which simplifies and decouples the architecture. This constraint indicates that each resource exposed for use by the client must have a unique address and should be accessible through a generic interface. The client can act on the resources by using a generic set of methods.

- **Layered system**: The server can have multiple layers for implementation. This layered architecture helps to improve scalability by enabling load balancing. It also improves performance by providing shared caches at different levels. The top layer, being the door to the system, can enforce security policies as well.

- **Code on demand**: This constraint is optional. This constraint indicates that the functionality of the client applications can be extended at runtime by allowing a code download from the server and executing the code. Some examples are the applets and the JavaScript code that get transferred and executed on the client side at runtime.

The following diagram illustrates a high-level architectural view of a RESTful system:

The preceding constraints do not dictate what kind of technology to use; they only define how data is transferred between components and the benefits of following guidelines. Therefore, a RESTful system can be implemented in any available networking architecture. More importantly, there is no need for us to invent new technologies or networking protocols. We can very well use the existing networking infrastructures, such as the **World Wide Web (WWW)**, or simply the Web, to create RESTful architectures. Consequently, a RESTful architecture is one that is maintainable, extendable, and distributed.

Before all REST constraints were formalized, we already had a working example of a RESTful system, the web. Now, you may ask why introduce these RESTful requirements to web application development when it is agreed that the Web is already RESTful.

Here is the answer: We need to first qualify what it means for the web to be RESTful. On the one hand, the static web is RESTful because static websites follow Fielding's definition of a RESTful architecture. For instance, the existing web infrastructure provides caching systems, stateless connection, and unique hyperlinks to resources, where resources are all of the documents available on every website and the representations of these documents are already set by files being browser readable (the HTML files, for example). Therefore, the static web is a system built in the REST-like architectural style. In simple words, we can say that REST leverages these amazing features of the web with some constraints.

On the other hand, traditional dynamic web applications have not always been RESTful because they typically break some of the outlined constraints. For instance, most dynamic applications are not stateless because servers track users through the container sessions or client-side cookie schemes. Therefore, we conclude that the dynamic web is not normally built in the REST-like architectural style.

> The REST architectural style is not specific to any protocol. However, as HTTP is the primary transfer protocol for the web today, REST over HTTP is the most common implementation. In this book, when we talk about REST, we refer to REST over HTTP unless otherwise stated.

Now, you may be curious to learn more about a RESTful system. The rest of the chapter will definitely help you to know the internals. However, the topics on the RESTful system, which we are going to discuss in the coming sections, may need some basic knowledge of HTTP. So, let's take a crash course on HTTP to learn some basics and then proceed with our discussions thereafter. You can skip the next section if you are already familiar with HTTP.

Introducing HTTP

Hypertext Transfer Protocol (HTTP) is the foundation of data communication for WWW. This protocol defines how messages are formatted, transmitted, and processed over the Internet. Let's have a quick recap of HTTP in this section.

HTTP versions

HTTP has been consistently evolving over time. So far, there are three versions. HTTP/0.9 was the first documented version, which was released in the year 1991. This was very primitive and supported only the GET method. Later, HTTP/1.0 was released in the year 1996 with more features and corrections for the shortcomings in the previous release. HTTP/1.0 supported more request methods such as GET, HEAD, and POST. The next release was HTTP/1.1 in the year 1999. This was the revision of HTTP/1.0. This version is in common use today.

HTTP/2 (originally named HTTP 2.0) is the next planned version. It is mainly focused on how the data is framed and transported between the client and the server.

> To learn more about HTTP, you can refer to the Wikipedia resources that you may find at http://en.wikipedia.org/wiki/Hypertext_Transfer_Protocol.

Understanding the HTTP request-response model

HTTP works in a request-response manner. Let's take an example to understand this model better.

The following example illustrates the basic request-response model of communication between a web browser and a server over HTTP. The following sequence diagram illustrates the request and response messages sent between the client and the server:

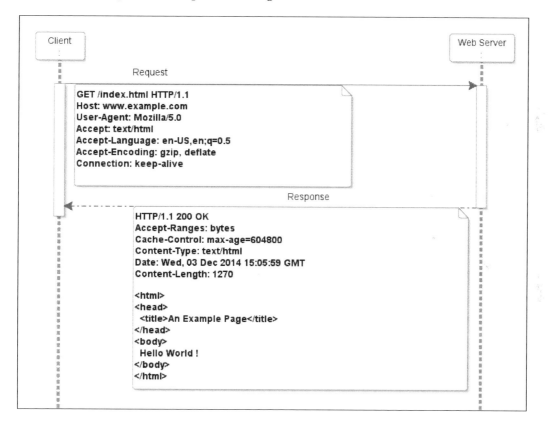

Here is a detailed explanation of the sequence of actions shown in the preceding diagram.

The user enters the following URL in the browser, `http://www.example.com/index.html`, and then submits the request. The browser establishes a connection with the server and sends a request to the server in the form of a request method, URI, and protocol version, followed by a message containing request modifiers, client information, and possible body content. The sample request looks like the following:

```
GET /index.html HTTP/1.1
Host: www.example.com
User-Agent: Mozilla/5.0
Accept: text/htmlAccept-Language: en-US,en;q=0.5
Accept-Encoding: gzip, deflate
Connection: keep-alive
```

Let's take a minute to understand the structure of the preceding message. The following code is what you see in the first lines of the request in our example:

```
GET /index.html HTTP/1.1
```

The general format for the request line is an HTTP command, followed by the resource to retrieve, and the HTTP version supported by the client. The client can be any application that understands HTTP, although this example refers to a web browser as the client. The request line and other header fields must end with a carriage return character followed by a line feed character. In the preceding example, the browser instructs the server to get the `index.html` file through the HTTP 1.1 protocol.

The rest of the information that you may see in the request message is the HTTP header values for use by the server. The header fields are colon-separated key-value pairs in the plain-text format, terminated by a carriage return followed by a line feed character. The header fields in the request, such as the acceptable content types, languages, and connection type, are the operating parameters for an HTTP transaction. The server can use this information while preparing the response for the request. A blank line is used at the end of the header to indicate the end of the header portion in a request.

The last part of an HTTP request is the HTTP body. Typically, the body is left blank unless the client has some data to submit to the server. In our example, the body part is empty as this is a GET request for retrieving a page from the server.

So far, we have been discussing the HTTP request sent by the client. Now, let's take a look at what happens on the server when the message is received. Once the server receives the HTTP request, it will process the message and return a response to the client. The response is made up of the reply status code from the server, followed by the HTTP header and a response content body:

```
HTTP/1.1 200 OK
Accept-Ranges: bytes
```

```
Cache-Control: max-age=604800
Content-Type: text/html
Date: Wed, 03 Dec 2014 15:05:59 GMT
Content-Length: 1270

<html>
<head>
  <title>An Example Page</title>
</head>
<body>
  Hello World !
</body>
</html>.
```

The first line in the response is a status line. It contains the HTTP version that the server is using, followed by a numeric status code and its associated textual phrase. The status code indicates one of the following parameters: informational codes, success of the request, client error, server error, or redirection of the request. In our example, the status line is as follows:

```
HTTP/1.1 200 OK
```

The next item in the response is the HTTP response header. Similar to the request header, the response header follows the colon-separated name-value pair format terminated by the carriage return and line feed characters. The HTTP response header can contain useful information about the resource being fetched, the server hosting the resource, and some parameters controlling the client behavior while dealing with the resource, such as content type, cache expiry, and refresh rate.

The last part of the response is the response body. Upon the successful processing of the request, the server will add the requested resource in the HTTP response body. It can be HTML, binary data, image, video, text, XML, JSON, and so on. Once the response body has been sent to the requestor, the HTTP server will disconnect if the connection created during the request is not of the `keep-alive` type (using the `Connection: keep-alive` header).

Uniform resource identifier

You may see the term **uniform resource identifier** (URI) used very frequently in the rest of the chapter. A URI is a text that identifies any resource or name on the Internet. One can further classify a URI as a **Uniform Resource Locator (URL)** if the text used for identifying the resource also holds the means for accessing the resource such as HTTP or FTP. The following is one such example:

```
https://www.packtpub.com/application-development
```

In general, all URLs are URIs. To learn more about URIs, visit
`http://en.wikipedia.org/wiki/Uniform_resource_identifier`.

Understanding the HTTP request methods

In the previous section, we discussed about the HTTP GET request method for retrieving a page from the server. More request methods similar to GET are available with HTTP, each performing specific actions on the target resource. Let's learn about these methods and their role in client-server communication over HTTP.

The set of common methods for HTTP/1.1 is listed in the following table:

Method	Description
GET	This method is used for retrieving resources from the server by using the given URI.
HEAD	This method is the same as the GET request, but it only transfers the status line and the header section without the response body.
POST	This method is used for posting data to the server. The server stores the data (entity) as a new subordinate of the resource identified by the URI. If you execute POST multiple times on a resource, it may yield different results.
PUT	This method is used for updating the resource pointed at by the URI. If the URI does not point to an existing resource, the server can create the resource with that URI.
DELETE	This method deletes the resource pointed at by the URI.
TRACE	This method is used for echoing the contents of the received request. This is useful for the debugging purpose with which the client can see what changes (if any) have been made by the intermediate servers.
OPTIONS	This method returns the HTTP methods that the server supports for the specified URI.
CONNECT	This method is used for establishing a connection to the target server over HTTP.
PATCH	This method is used for applying partial modifications to a resource identified by the URI.

We may use some of these HTTP methods, such as GET, POST, PUT, and DELETE, while building RESTful web services in the later chapters.

Continuing our discussion on HTTP, the next section discusses the HTTP header parameter that identifies the content type for the message body.

Representing content types using HTTP header fields

When we discussed the HTTP request-response model in the *Understanding the HTTP request-response model* section, we talked about the HTTP header parameters (the name-value pairs) that define the operating parameters of an HTTP transaction. In this section, we will cover the header parameter used for describing the content types present in the request and the response message body.

The `Content-Type` header in an HTTP request or response describes the content type for the message body. The `Accept` header in the request tells the server the content types that the client is expecting in the response body. The content types are represented using the Internet media type. The Internet media type (also known as the MIME type) indicates the type of data that a file contains. Here is an example:

```
Content-Type: text/html
```

This header indicates that the body content is presented in the `html` format. The format of the content type values is a primary type/subtype followed by an optional semicolon delimited attribute-value pairs (known as parameters).

The Internet media types are broadly classified in to the following categories on the basis of the primary (or initial) `Content-Type` header:

- `text`: This type indicates that the content is plain text and no special software is required to read the contents. The subtype represents more specific details about the content, which can be used by the client for special processing, if any. For instance, `Content-Type: text/html` indicates that the body content is `html`, and the client can use this hint to kick off an appropriate rendering engine while displaying the response.

- `multipart`: As the name indicates, this type consists of multiple parts of the independent data types. For instance, `Content-Type: multipart/form-data` is used for submitting forms that contain the files, non-ASCII data, and binary data.

- `message`: This type encapsulates more messages. It allows messages to contain other messages or pointers to other messages. For instance, the `Content-Type: message/partial` content type allows for large messages to be broken up into smaller messages. The full message can then be read by the client (user agent) by putting all the broken messages together.

- `image`: This type represents the image data. For instance, `Content-Type: image/png` indicates that the body content is a `.png` image.

- **audio**: This type indicates the audio data. For instance, `Content-Type: audio/mpeg` indicates that the body content is MP3 or other MPEG audio.

- **video**: This type indicates the video data. For instance, `Content-Type: video/mp4` indicates that the body content is MP4 video.

- **application**: This type represents the application data or binary data. For instance, `Content-Type: application/json; charset=utf-8` designates the content to be in the **JavaScript Object Notation (JSON)** format, encoded with UTF-8 character encoding.

 JSON is a lightweight data-interchange format. If you are not familiar with the JSON format, not to worry now; we will cover this topic in *Chapter 2, Java APIs for JSON Processing*.

We may need to use some of these content types in the next chapters while developing the RESTful web services. This hint will be used by the client to correctly process the response body.

 We are not covering all the possible subtypes for each category of media type here. To refer to the complete list, visit the website of **Internet Assigned Numbers Authority (IANA)** at `http://www.iana.org/assignments/media-types/media-types.xhtml`.

The next topic, a simple but important one, is on HTTP status codes.

HTTP status codes

For every HTTP request, the server returns a status code indicating the processing status of the request. In this section, we will see some of the frequently used HTTP status codes. A basic understanding of status codes will definitely help us later while designing RESTful web services:

- **1xx Informational**: This series of status codes indicates informational content. This means that the request is received and processing is going on. Here are the frequently used informational status codes:

    ○ `100 Continue`: This code indicates that the server has received the request header and the client can now send the body content. In this case, the client first makes a request (with the `Expect: 100-continue` header) to check whether it can start with a partial request. The server can then respond either with `100 Continue` (OK) or `417 Expectation Failed` (No) along with an appropriate reason.

- ○ `101 Switching Protocols`: This code indicates that the server is OK for a protocol switch request from the client.

- ○ `102 Processing`: This code is an informational status code used for long running processing to prevent the client from timing out. This tells the client to wait for the future response, which will have the actual response body.

- `2xx Success`: This series of status codes indicates the successful processing of requests. Some of the frequently used status codes in this class are as follows:

  - ○ `200 OK`: This code indicates that the request is successful and the response content is returned to the client as appropriate.

  - ○ `201 Created`: This code indicates that the request is successful and a new resource is created.

  - ○ `204 No Content`: This code indicates that the request is processed successfully, but there's no return value for this request. For instance, you may find such status codes in response to the deletion of a resource.

- `3xx Redirection`: This series of status codes indicates that the client needs to perform further actions to logically end the request. A frequently used status code in this class is as follows:

  - ○ `304 Not Modified`: This status indicates that the resource has not been modified since it was last accessed. This code is returned only when allowed by the client via setting the request headers as `If-Modified-Since` or `If-None-Match`. The client can take appropriate action on the basis of this status code.

- `4xx Client Error`: This series of status codes indicates an error in processing the request. Some of the frequently used status codes in this class are as follows:

  - ○ `400 Bad Request`: This code indicates that the server failed to process the request because of the malformed syntax in the request. The client can try again after correcting the request.

  - ○ `401 Unauthorized`: This code indicates that authentication is required for the resource. The client can try again with the appropriate authentication.

  - ○ `403 Forbidden`: This code indicates that the server is refusing to respond to the request even if the request is valid. The reason will be listed in the body content if the request is not a `HEAD` method.

  - ○ `404 Not Found`: This code indicates that the requested resource is not found at the location specified in the request.

- ° `405 Method Not Allowed`: This code indicates that the HTTP method specified in the request is not allowed on the resource identified by the URI.

- ° `408 Request Timeout`: This code indicates that the client failed to respond within the time frame set on the server.

- ° `409 Conflict`: This code indicates that the request cannot be completed because it conflicts with some rules established on resources, such as validation failure.

- `5xx Server Error`: This series of status codes indicates server failures while processing a valid request. Here is one of the frequently used status codes in this class:

  - ° `500 Internal Server Error`: This code indicates a generic error message, and it tells that an unexpected error occurred on the server and the request cannot be fulfilled.

 To refer to the complete list of HTTP status codes maintained by IANA, visit `http://www.iana.org/assignments/http-status-codes/http-status-codes.xhtml`.

With this topic, we have finished the crash course on HTTP basics. We will be resuming our discussion on RESTful web services in the next section. Take a deep breath and get ready for an exciting journey.

The evolution of RESTful web services

Before getting into the details of REST-enabled web services, let's take a step back and define what a web service is. Then, we will see what makes a web service RESTful.

A web service is one of the very popular methods of communication between the client and server applications over the Internet. In simple words, web services are web application components that can be published, found, and used over the web. Typically, a web service has an interface describing the web service APIs, which is known as **Web Services Description Language (WSDL)**. A WSDL file can be easily processed by machines, which blows out the integration complexities that you may see with large systems. Other systems interact with the web service by using **Simple Object Access Protocol (SOAP)** messages. The contract for communication is driven by the WSDL exposed by the web service. Typically, communication happens over HTTP with XML in conjunction with other web-related standards.

What kind of problems do the web services solve? There are two main areas where web services are used:

- Many of the companies specialized in Internet-related services and products have opened their doors to developers using publicly available APIs. For instance, companies such as Google, Yahoo, Amazon, and Facebook are using web services to offer new products that rely on their massive hardware infrastructures. Google and Yahoo offer their search services; Amazon offers its on-demand hosting storage infrastructure and Facebook offers its platform for targeted marketing and advertising campaigns. With the help of web services, these companies have opened the door for the creation of products that did not exist some years ago.

- Web services are being used within the enterprises to connect previously disjointed departments such as marketing and manufacturing. Each department or **line of business (LOB)** can expose its business processes as a web service, which can be consumed by the other departments.

  By connecting more than one department to share information by using web services, we begin to enter the territory of the **Service-Oriented Architecture (SOA)**. The SOA is essentially a collection of services, each talking to one another in a well-defined manner, in order to complete relatively large and logically complete business processes.

All these points lead to the fact that a web service has evolved into a powerful and effective channel of communication between a client and a server over a period of time. The good news is that we can integrate RESTful systems into a web service-oriented computing environment without much effort. Although you may have a fair idea about RESTful web services by now, let's see the formal definition before proceeding further.

What is a RESTful web service?

Web services that adhere to the REST architectural constraints are characterized as RESTful web services. Refer to the section, *The REST architectural style*, at the beginning of this chapter if you need a quick brush up on the architectural constraints for a RESTful system.

Remember that REST is not the system's architecture in itself, but it is a set of constraints that when applied to the system's design leads to a RESTful architecture. As our definition of a web service does not dictate the implementation details of a computing unit, we can easily incorporate RESTful web services to solve large-scale problems. We can even fully use RESTful web services under the larger umbrella of the SOA.

With this larger view of the SOA, we begin to see how REST has the potential to impact the new computing models being developed.

 The RESTful web API or REST API is an API implemented using HTTP and the REST architectural constraints. Technically speaking, this is just another term for a RESTful web service. In this book, we will use these terms interchangeably.

The core architectural elements of a RESTful system

Having learned the basics of a RESTful system, you are now ready to meet the more exciting concepts of REST. In this section, we will learn the core architectural elements that make a system RESTful.

A uniform interface is fundamental to the architecture of any RESTful system. In plain words, this term refers to a generic interface to manage all interactions between a client and a server in a unified way. All resources (or business data) involved in the client-server interactions are dealt with by a fixed set of operations. The following are core elements that form a uniform interface for a RESTful system:

- Resources and their identifiers
- Representations of resources
- Generic interaction semantics for the REST resources
- Self-descriptive messages
- Hypermedia as the engine of an application state

Let's look at these items in detail.

Resources

A RESTful resource is anything that is addressable over the Web. By addressable, we mean resources that can be accessed and transferred between clients and servers. Subsequently, a resource is a logical, temporal mapping to a concept in the problem domain for which we are implementing a solution.

Here are some examples of the REST resources:

- A news story
- The temperature in NY at 4:00 p.m. EST

- A tax return stored in the IRS database

- A list of code revision history in a repository such as SVN or CVS

- A student in a classroom in a school

- A search result for a particular item in a Web index, such as Google

Even though a resource's mapping is unique, different requests for a resource can return the same underlying binary representation stored in the server. For example, let's say we have a resource within the context of a publishing system. Then, a request for `the latest revision published` and a request for `revision number 12` will at some point in time return the same representation of the resource. In this example, the last revision is Version 12. However, when the latest revision published is increased to Version 13, a request to the latest revision will return Version 13, and a request for revision 12 will continue returning Version 12. This implies that in a RESTful architecture, each resource can be accessed directly and independently, and sometimes, different requests may point to the same resource.

As we are using HTTP to communicate, we can transfer a variety of data types between clients and servers as long as the data type used is supported by HTTP. For example, if we request a text file from CNN, our browser receives a text file. If we request a Flash movie from YouTube, our browser receives a Flash movie. The data is streamed in both cases over TCP/IP and the browser knows how to interpret the binary streams because of the `Content-Type` header present in the HTTP response header. Following this principle, in a RESTful system, the representation of a resource in the response body depends on the desired Internet media type, which is specified within the request header sent by the client.

URI

A URI is a string of characters used to identify a resource over the Web. In simple words, the URI in a RESTful web service is a hyperlink to a resource, and it is the only means for clients and servers to exchange representations.

The client uses a URI to locate the resources over Web and then, sends a request to the server and reads the response. In a RESTful system, the URI is not meant to change over time as it may break the contract between a client and a server. More importantly, even if the underlying infrastructure or hardware changes (for example, swapping the database servers) for a server hosting REST APIs, the URIs for resources are expected to remain the same as long as the web service is up and running.

The representation of resources

The representation of resources is what is sent back and forth between clients and servers in a RESTful system. A representation is a temporal state of the actual data located in some storage device at the time of a request. In general terms, it is a binary stream together with its metadata that describes how the stream is to be consumed by the client. The metadata can also contain extra information about the resource, for example, validation, encryption information, or extra code to be executed at runtime.

Throughout the life of a web service, there may be a variety of clients requesting resources. Different clients can consume different representations of the same resource. Therefore, a representation can take various forms, such as an image, a text file, an XML, or a JSON format. However, all clients will use the same URI with appropriate `Accept` header values for accessing the same resource in different representations.

For the human-generated requests through a web browser, a representation is typically in the form of an HTML page. For automated requests from the other web services, readability is not as important and a more efficient representation, such as JSON or XML, can be used.

Generic interaction semantics for REST resources

In the previous sections, we introduced the concepts of resources and representations. We learned that resources are mappings of the actual entity states that are exchanged between clients and servers. Further, we discussed that representations are negotiated between clients and servers through the communication protocol (HTTP) at runtime. In this section, we will learn about the generics of interaction semantics and self-descriptive messages followed for the client-server communication in a RESTful system.

Developing RESTful web services is similar to what we have been doing up to this point with our web applications. In a RESTful web service, resources are exchanged between the client and the server, which represent the business entities or data. HTTP specifies methods or actions for the resources. The most commonly used HTTP methods or actions are POST, GET, PUT, and DELETE. This clearly simplifies the REST API design and makes it more readable. On the other hand, in traditional application development, we can have countless actions with no naming or implementation standards. This may call for more development effort for both the client and the server, and make the APIs less readable.

In a RESTful system, we can easily map our **CRUD** actions on the resources to the appropriate HTTP methods such as POST, GET, PUT, and DELETE. This is shown in the following table:

Data action	HTTP equivalent
CREATE	POST or PUT
READ	GET
UPDATE	PUT or PATCH
DELETE	DELETE

In fact, the preceding list of HTTP methods is incomplete. There are some more HTTP methods available, but they are less frequently used in the context of RESTful implementations. Of these less frequent methods, OPTIONS and HEAD are used more often than others. So, let's glance at these two method types:

- OPTIONS: This method is used by the client to determine the options or actions associated with the target resource, without causing any action on the resource or retrieval of the resource

- HEAD: This method can be used for retrieving information about the entity without having the entity itself in the response

In their simplest form, RESTful web services are networked applications that manipulate the state of resources. In this context, resource manipulation means resource creation, retrieval, update, and deletion. However, RESTful web services are not limited to just these four basic data manipulation concepts. They can even be used for executing business logic on the server, but remember that every result must be a resource representation of the domain at hand.

A uniform interface brings all the aforementioned abstractions into focus. Consequently, putting together all these concepts, we can describe RESTful development with one short sentence: we use URIs to connect clients and servers in order to exchange resources in the form of representations.

Let's now look at the four HTTP request types in detail and see how each of them is used to exchange representations to modify the state of resources.

The HTTP GET method

The method, GET, is used to retrieve resources. Before digging into the actual mechanics of the HTTP GET request, we first need to determine what a resource is in the context of our web service and what type of representation we are exchanging.

For the rest of this section, we will use the example of a RESTful web service handling department details for an organization. For this service, the JSON representation of a department looks like the following:

```
{"departmentId":10,"departmentName":"IT","manager":"John Chen"}
```

The JSON representation of the list of departments looks like the following:

```
[{"departmentId":10,"departmentName":"IT","manager":"John Chen"},
{"departmentId":20,"departmentName":"Marketing","manager":"Ameya
  J"},
{"departmentId":30,"departmentName":"HR","manager":"Pat Fay"}]
```

With our representations defined, we now assume URIs of the form `http://www.packtpub.com/resources/departments` to access a list of departments, and `http://www.packtpub.com/resources/departments/{name}` to access a specific department with a name (unique identifier).

> To keep this example simple and easy to follow, we treat the department name as a unique identifier here. Note that in real life, you can use a server-generated identifier value, which does not repeat across entities, to uniquely identify a resource instance.

We can now begin making requests to our web service. For instance, if we wanted a record for the IT department, we would make a request to the following URI: `http://www.packtpub.com/resources/departments/IT`.

A representation of the IT department at the time of the request may look like the following code:

```
{"departmentId":10,"departmentName":"IT","manager":"John Chen"}
```

Let's have a look at the request details. A request to retrieve details of the IT department uses the GET method with the following URI:

```
http://www.packtpub.com/resources/departments/IT
```

Let's see what happens when a client requests for the IT department by using the preceding mentioned URI. Here is the sequence diagram for the GET request:

What is happening here?

1. A Java client makes an HTTP request with the GET method type and IT as the identifier for the department.

2. The client sets the representation type that it can handle through the Accept request header field. This request message is self-descriptive:

    ° It uses a standard method (the GET method in this example) with known semantics for retrieving the content

    ° The content type is set to a well-known media type (text/plain)

    ° This request also declares the acceptable response format

3. The web server receives and interprets the GET request to be a retrieve action. At this point, the web server passes control to the underlying RESTful framework to handle the request. Note that RESTful frameworks do not automatically retrieve resources, as that is not their job. The job of a framework is to ease the implementation of the REST constraints. Business logic and storage implementation is the role of the domain-specific Java code.

4. The server-side program looks for the IT resource. Finding the resource could mean looking for it in some data store such as a database, a file system, or even a call to a different web service.

5. Once the program finds the IT department details, it converts the binary data of the resource to the client's requested representation. In this example, we use the JSON representation for the resource.

6. With the representation converted to JSON, the server sends back an HTTP response with a numeric code of 200 together with the JSON representation as the payload. Note that if there are any errors, the HTTP server reports back the proper numeric code, but it is up to the client to correctly deal with the failure. Similar to the request message, the response is also self-descriptive.

All the messages between a client and a server are standard HTTP calls. For every retrieve action, we send a GET request and we get an HTTP response back with the payload of the response being the representation of the resource or, if there is a failure, a corresponding HTTP error code (for example, 404, if a resource is not found; 500, if there is a problem with the Java code in the form of an exception).

Getting a representation for all departments works the same way as getting a representation for a single department, although we now use the URI as http://www.packtpub.com/resources/departments and the result is the JSON representation, which looks like the following code:

```
[{"departmentId":10,"departmentName":"IT","manager":"John Chen"},
{"departmentId":20,"departmentName":"Marketing","manager":"Ameya
  J"},
{"departmentId":30,"departmentName":"HR","manager":"Pat Fay"}]
```

> The HTTP GET method should only be used to retrieve representations, not for performing any update on the resource. A GET request must be safe and idempotent. For more information, refer to http://www.w3.org/DesignIssues/Axioms.

For a request to be safe, it means that multiple requests to the same resource do not change the state of the data in the server. Assume that we have a representation, R, and requests happen at a time, t. Then, a request at time t1 for resource R returns R1; subsequently, a request at time t2 for resource R returns R2 provided that no further update actions have been taken between t1 and t2. Then, R1 = R2 = R.

For a request to be idempotent, multiple calls to the same action should not change the state of the resource. For example, multiple calls to create resource R at times t1, t2, and t3 mean that R will exist only as R and the calls at times t2 and t3 are ignored.

The HTTP POST method

The POST method is used to create resources. As we are creating a department, we use the HTTP POST method. Again, the URI to create a new department in our example is http://www.packtpub.com/resources/departments. The method type for the request is set by the client.

Assume that the Sales department does not exist in our list, and we want to add it to the list. The Sales data representation looks like the following:

```
{"departmentName":"Sales","manager":"Tony Greig"}
```

Now, the sequence diagram of our POST request looks like the following:

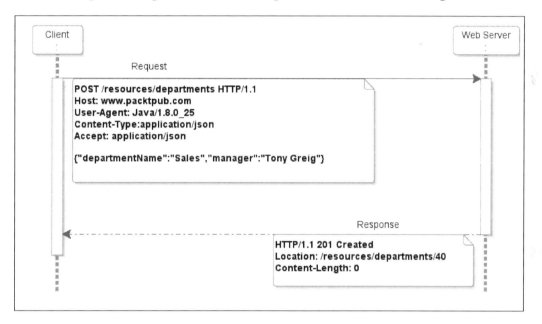

The series of steps for the POST request is as follows:

1. A Java client makes a request to the http://www.packtpub.com/resources/departments URI with the HTTP method set to POST.

2. The POST request carries the payload along with it in the form of a JSON representation of the Sales department.

3. The server receives the request and lets the REST framework handle it; our code within the framework executes the proper commands to store the representation, irrespective of which data persistence mechanism is used.

4. Once the new resource is stored, a response code, 2xx (representing a successful operation), is sent back. In this example, the server sends 201 Created, which implies that the server has fulfilled the request by creating a new resource. The newly created resource is accessible by traversing the URI given by a Location header field. If it is a failure, the server sends the appropriate error code.

The HTTP PUT method

The PUT method is used to update resources. To update a resource, we first need its representation in the client; secondly, at the client level, we update the resource with the new value(s) that we want; and finally, we update the resource by using a PUT request together with the representation as its payload.

In this example, let's add a manger to the Sales department that we created in the previous example.

Our original representation of the Sales department is as follows:

```
{"departmentId":40,"departmentName":"Sales","manager":"Tony
  Greig" }
```

Let's update the manager for the Sales department; our representation is as follows:

```
{"departmentId":40,"departmentName":"Sales","manager":"Ki Gee"}
```

We are now ready to connect to our web service to update the Sales department by sending the PUT request to http://www.packtpub.com/resources/departments/Sales. The sequence diagram of our PUT request is as follows:

The series of steps for the PUT request is as follows:

1. A Java client makes a PUT request to `http://www.packtpub.com/resources/departments/Sales` with the JSON payload representing the modified department details.

2. The server receives the request and lets the REST framework handle it. At this point, we let our code execute the proper commands to update the representation of the `Sales` department. Once completed, a response is sent back. The `204 No Content` response code indicates that the server has fulfilled the request but does not return the entity body.

The HTTP DELETE method

The DELETE method is used to delete the resource. In this example, we will delete a resource by making use of the same URI that we used in the other three cases.

Assume that we want to delete the `Sales` department from the data storage. We send a DELETE request to our service with the following URI: `http://www.packtpub.com/resources/departments/Sales`.

The sequence diagram for our DELETE request is shown in the following diagram:

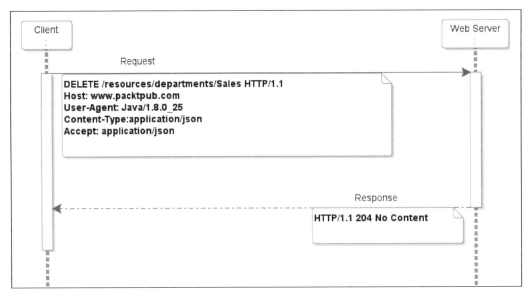

The series of steps for the DELETE request is as follows:

1. A Java client makes a DELETE request to `http://www.packtpub.com/resources/departments/Sales`.

2. The server receives the request and lets the REST framework handle it. At this point, the server code executes the proper commands to delete the representation of the `Sales` department.

3. Once completed, a response is sent back.

With this, we have covered all the major actions that can be carried out on resources in a RESTful web service. To keep things simple during our discussion, we did not talk about the actual implementation of the CREATE, READ, UPDATE, and DELETE operations on the resource. In all three examples, we presumed that we have a well-behaved web service that adheres to the RESTful guidelines and the client and the server communicate over HTTP. We use the communication protocol to send action requests, and our resource representations are sent back and forth through unchanging URIs. We will cover more detailed end-to-end examples later in this book.

 A point to note about our sequence diagrams is that we are assuming that all the underlying technologies are Java technologies (servers and clients). However, these are just components in the whole architecture and the explanations apply to any technology stack.

Hypermedia as the Engine of Application State

Hypermedia as the Engine of Application State (HATEOAS) is an important principle of the REST application architecture. The principle is that the model of application changes from one state to another by traversing the hyperlinks present in the current set of resource representations (the model). Let's learn this principle in detail.

In a RESTful system, there is no fixed interface between the client and the server as you may see in a conventional client-server communication model such as **Common Object Request Broker Architecture (CORBA)** and **Java Remote Method Invocation (Java RMI)**. With REST, the client just needs to know how to deal with the hypermedia links present in the response body; next, the call to retrieve the appropriate resource representation is made by using these dynamic media links. This concept makes the client-server interaction very dynamic and keeps it different from the other network application architectures.

Here is an example illustrating the HATEOAS principle. In this example, the `http://www.packtpub.com/resources/departments/IT` URI returns the following response to the client:

```
{"departmentId":10,
"departmentName":"IT",
"manager":"John Chen,
"links": [ {
        "rel": "employees",
        "href": "http://packtpub.com/resources/departments/IT/
employees"
    } ]"}
```

This is the current state of the system. Now, to get the employees belonging to the department, the client traverses the hyperlink present in the response body, namely `http://www.packtpub.com/resources/departments/IT/employees`. This URI returns the following employee list. The application state now changes into the following form (as represented by the response content):

```
[{"employeeId":100,
 "firstName":"Steven",
 "lastName":"King",
 "links": [ {
        "rel": "self",
        "href": "http://www.packtpub.com/resources/employees/100"
    }]
 },
 {"employeeId":101,
```

```
"firstName":"Neena",
"lastName":"Kochhar",
"links": [ {
        "rel": "self",
        "href": "http://www.packtpub.com/resources/employees/101"
    }]
}]
```

In this example, the application state changes from one state to another when the client traverses the hypermedia link. Hence, we refer to this implementation principle as Hypermedia as the Engine of Application State.

Description and discovery of RESTful web services

As you may know, WSDL is used for describing the functionality offered by a SOAP web service. For a SOAP web service, this is a widely accepted standard and is supported by many enterprises today. In contrast, for RESTful web services, there is no such standard and you may find different metadata formats used by various enterprises.

However, in general, you may see the following goals in common among all these metadata formats for RESTful APIs, although they differ in their syntax and semantics:

- Entry points for the service

- Resource paths for accessing each resource

- HTTP methods allowed to access these resources, such as GET, POST, PUT, and DELETE

- Additional parameters that need to be supplied with these methods, such as pagination parameters, while reading large collections

- Format types used for representing the request and response body contents such as JSON, XML, and TEXT

- Status codes and error messages returned by the APIs

- Human readable documentation for REST APIs, which includes the documentation of the request methods, input and output parameters, response codes (success or error), API security, and business logic

Some of the popular metadata formats used for describing REST APIs are **Web Application Description Language (WADL)**, **Swagger**, **RESTful API Modeling Language (RAML)**, **API Blueprint**, and **WSDL 2.0.** We will have a more detailed discussion on each of these items in *Chapter 7, The Description and Discovery of RESTful Web Services.*

Java tools and frameworks for building RESTful web services

Over the last few years, the REST architectural style has become very popular in the industry and many enterprises have accepted it as the current standard for building public web APIs, particularly when scalability and simplicity are major concerns for them. Today, one may see many tools and frameworks available on the market for building RESTful web services. In this section, we will briefly discuss some of the most popular Java-based frameworks and tools for building RESTful systems.

The Java API for RESTful web services (JAX-RS) is the Java API for creating RESTful web services following the REST architectural pattern discussed in this chapter. JAX-RS is a part of the **Java Platform Enterprise Edition (Java EE)** platform and is designed to be a standard and portable solution. There are many reference implementations available for JAX-RS today. Some of the most popular implementations are Jersey, Apache CXF, RESTEasy, and Restlet. At this juncture, it is worth mentioning that most of the frameworks in the preceding list, such as Jersey and Apache CXF, are not just limited to reference implementations of the JAX-RS specifications, but they also offer many additional features on top of the specifications.

Apart from the JAX-RS-based frameworks (or extensions built on top of JAX-RS), you may also find some promising nonstandard (not based on JAX-RS) Java REST frameworks on the market. Some such frameworks are as follows:

- One such framework is RESTX, which is an open source Java REST framework and is primarily focused on the server-side REST API development. This is relatively new on the market and simplifies the REST API development.

- Spark is another framework that falls into this category. It is a Java web framework with support for building REST APIs. Spark 2.0 is built using Java 8, leveraging all the latest improvements of the Java language.

- Play is another framework worth mentioning in this category. It is a Java (and Scala)-based web application framework with inherent support for building RESTful web services.

Discussing all these frameworks does not come under the scope of this book. We will focus on some of the most popular frameworks with many real-life use cases in mind. In the next chapters, you will learn JAX-RS as well as additional features available with the Jersey framework for building scalable and maintainable RESTful web services.

Summary

This chapter is intended to give an overview of RESTful web services. This is essential for an easy understanding of what we will learn in the rest of the book. As we have just started our topic, we have not covered any code samples in this chapter to keep it simple. In the following chapters, we will examine the most popular Java tools and frameworks available for building a RESTful web service along with many real-life examples and code samples.

In the next chapter, we will discuss the JSON representation of the REST resources and the Java APIs for JSON processing.

2
Java APIs for JSON Processing

In the previous chapter, you were introduced to the REST architectural style. Remember that REST does not prescribe any specific message format for client-server communication. One can use an appropriate format for representing messages as long as the chosen format is supported by HTTP. XML and JSON are the two most popular formats used by RESTful web services today. Out of these two formats, JSON has been widely adopted by many vendors because of it is simple and lightweight. In this chapter, you will learn more about the JSON message format and various processing tools and frameworks related to JSON.

The following topics are covered in this chapter:

- A brief overview of JSON
- Using the JSR 353 — Java API for processing JSON
- Using the Jackson API for processing JSON
- Using the Gson API for processing JSON

A brief overview of JSON

JSON is a lightweight, text-based, platform neutral, data interchange format in which objects are represented in the attribute-value pair format. Historically, JSON originated from JavaScript. However, nowadays, it is considered to be a language-independent format because of its wide adoption by all modern programming languages. In this section, you will learn the basics of the JSON format. You will also learn how to represent real-life business data in the JSON format.

Understanding the JSON data syntax

The JSON format is very simple by design. It is represented by the following two data structures:

- **An unordered collection of name-value pairs (representing an object)**: The attributes of an object and their values are represented in the name-value pair format; the name and the value in a pair is separated by a colon (:). Names in an object are strings, and values may be of any of the valid JSON data types such as number, string, Boolean, array, object, or null. Each name:value pair in a JSON object is separated by a comma (,). The entire object is enclosed in curly braces ({ }).

  For instance, the JSON representation of a department object is as follows:

  ```
  {"departmentId":10, "departmentName":"IT",
   "manager":"John Chen"}
  ```

  This example shows how you can represent various attributes of a department, such as departmentId, departmentName, and manager, in the JSON format.

- **An ordered collection of values (representing an array)**: Arrays are enclosed in square brackets ([ ]), and their values are separated by a comma (,). Each value in an array may be of a different type, including another array or an object.

  The following example illustrates the use of an array notation to represent employees working in a department. You may also see an array of locations in this example:

  ```
  {"departmentName":"IT",
    "employees":[
      {"firstName":"John", "lastName":"Chen"},
      {"firstName":"Ameya", "lastName":"Job"},
      {"firstName":"Pat", "lastName":"Fay"}
    ],
    "location":["New York", "New Delhi"]
  }
  ```

Basic data types available with JSON

While discussing the JSON syntax in the previous section, we glanced at some of the basic data types used in JSON. Let's take a detailed look at each item.

Here is the list of the basic data types available with JSON:

- **Number**: This type is used for storing a signed decimal number that may optionally contain a fractional part. Both integer and floating point numbers are represented by using this data type. The following example uses the decimal data type for storing `totalWeight`:

  ```
  {"totalWeight": 123.456}
  ```

- **String**: This type represents a sequence of zero or more characters. Strings are surrounded with double quotation marks and support a backslash escaping syntax. Here is an example of the string data type:

  ```
  {"firstName": "Jobinesh"}
  ```

- **Boolean**: This type represents either a `true` or a `false` value. The Boolean type is used for representing whether a condition is `true` or `false`, or to represent two states of a variable (`true` or `false`) in the code. Here is an example representing a Boolean value:

  ```
  {"isValidEntry": true}
  ```

- **Array**: This type represents an ordered list of zero or more values, each of which can be of any type. In this representation, comma-separated values are enclosed in square brackets. The following example represents an array of `fruits`:

  ```
  {"fruits": ["apple", "banana", "orange"]}
  ```

- **Object**: This type is an unordered collection of comma-separated attribute-value pairs enclosed in curly braces. All attributes must be strings and should be distinct from each other within that object. The following example illustrates an object representation in JSON:

  ```
  {"departmentId":10,
  "departmentName":"IT",
  "manager":"John Chen"}
  ```

- **null**: This type indicates an empty value, represented by using the word `null`. The following example uses `null` as the value for the `error` attribute of an object:

  ```
  {"error":null}
  ```

The example in the next section illustrates how you can use the JSON data types that we discussed in this section for representing the details of employees.

A sample JSON file representing employee objects

Here is a sample JSON document file called `"emp-array.json"`, which contains the JSON array of the `employee` objects. The content of the file is as follows:

```
[ {"employeeId":100,"firstName":"John","lastName":"Chen",
  "email":"john.chen@xxxx.com","hireDate":"2008-10-16"},
  {"employeeId":101,"firstName":"Ameya","lastName":"Job",
  "email":"ameya.job@xxx.com","hireDate":"2013-03-06"},
  {"employeeId":102,"firstName":"Pat","lastName":"Fay",
  "email":"pat.fey@xxx.com","hireDate":"2001-03-06"} ]
```

We will use this `emp-array.json` file as the input source for many examples that we will discuss later in this chapter.

By now, you should have a fairly good understanding of the JSON syntax. We will later learn various techniques for processing JSON data.

Processing JSON data

If you use Java RESTful web service frameworks, such as JAX-RS, for building RESTful web APIs, the serialization and deserialization of the request and response messages will be taken care of by the framework. However, understanding the JSON structure and tools for processing JSON will definitely help you when the default offering by the framework does not meet your requirements. The following diagram illustrates the role of the JSON marshalling and unmarshalling components in a typical Java RESTful web service implementation:

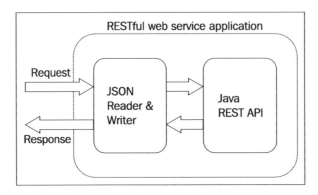

This section will teach you the various processing models for JSON data. By the term processing, we mean reading, writing, querying, and modifying JSON data. Two widely adopted programming models for processing JSON are as follows:

- **Object model**: In this model, the entire JSON data is read into memory in a tree format. This tree can be traversed, analyzed, or modified with the appropriate APIs. As this approach loads the entire content into the memory first and then starts parsing, it ends up consuming more memory and CPU cycles. However, this model gives more flexibility while manipulating the content.

- **Streaming model**: The term streaming is very generic in meaning and can be used in many aspects. In our discussion, this term means that data can be read or written in blocks. This model does not read the entire JSON content into the memory to get started with parsing; rather, it reads one element at a time. For each token read, the parser generates appropriate events indicating the type of token, such as the start or end of an array, or the start or end of the object and attribute values. A client can process the contents by listening for appropriate events. The most important point is that instead of letting the parser push the content to the client (push parser), the client can pull the information from the parser as it needs (pull parser). In this model, the client is allowed to skip or stop reading contents in the middle of the process if it has finished reading the desired elements. This model is also useful when you write contents to an output source in blocks.

You may want to consider using streaming APIs in the following situations:

- When the data is huge in size and it is not feasible to load the entire content into the memory for processing the content

- When the partial processing is needed and the data model is not fully available yet

We will revisit these two parsing models while discussing tools for processing JSON later in this chapter.

Using JSR 353 – Java API for processing JSON

There are many Java-based frameworks available today for processing JSON. In this section, we will learn about the APIs available on the Java EE platform for processing JSON. Java EE 7 has standardized the JSON processing APIs with **Java Specification Request (JSR)**, that is, **JSR 353 - Java API for JSON Processing**. This JSR offers portable APIs to parse, generate, transform, and query JSON data. The JSR 353 APIs can be classified into two categories on the basis of the processing model followed by the APIs:

- Object model API
- Streaming model API

We had a generic discussion on these two processing models in the previous section, *Processing JSON data*. In this section, we will see how these processing models are implemented in JSR 353.

 Dependencies for JSR 353 - Java API for JSON Processing are listed at https://jsonp.java.net/download.html.

Processing JSON with JSR 353 object model APIs

This category of APIs generates an in-memory tree model for JSON data and then, starts processing it as instructed by the client. This is conceptually similar to the **Document Object Model (DOM)** API for XML.

Here is a list of the frequently used classes in the object model API of the JSR 353 specification:

Class or interface	Description
javax.json.Json	This class is the main factory class for creating JSON processing objects such as JsonReader and JsonWriter.
javax.json.JsonReader	This interface reads the JSON content and generates a JSON object or array as appropriate.
javax.json.JsonWriter	This interface writes a JSON object or array to an output source.

Class or interface	Description
`javax.json.JsonObjectBuilder`	This interface offers APIs for generating `JsonObject` models from scratch.
`javax.json.JsonArrayBuilder`	This interface offers APIs for generating `JsonArray` models from scratch.
`javax.json.JsonValue`	This interface is the superinterface representing an immutable JSON value. The JSON value takes one of the following forms: • `javax.json.JsonObject` • `javax.json.JsonArray` • `javax.json.JsonNumber` • `javax.json.JsonString` • `javax.json.JsonValue.TRUE` • `javax.json.JsonValue.FALSE` • `javax.json.JsonValue.NULL`

The JSR 353 object model APIs are easy to use and rich in offerings.

> Refer to the complete list of the object model APIs available in JSR 353 at `http://docs.oracle.com/javaee/7/api/javax/json/package-summary.html`.

Generating the object model from the JSON representation

The example in this section illustrates the usage of the JSR353 object model APIs for building an object representation of the JSON data.

Downloading the example code

All the code examples that you may see in this chapter are downloadable from the Packt website link mentioned at the beginning of this book, in the *Preface* section. In the downloaded source, open the `rest-chapter2-jsonp` folder to access all the examples discussed in this chapter.

This example uses the JSON array of the `employee` objects stored in the `emp-array.json` file as an input source. The contents of this file are listed under the *A sample JSON file representing employee objects* section. Let's see how we can convert the JSON content present in the file into a Java object model by using the JSR353 object model API.

As you must have guessed, the first step is to read the JSON content from the `emp-array.json` file and store it in an appropriate data structure. The following code snippet illustrates the APIs for reading the JSON content from the file to `javax.json.JsonArray`:

```
//Import statements for the core classes
import java.io.InputStream;
import javax.json.JsonArray;
import javax.json.JsonReade;

//Get input stream for reading the specified resource.
InputStream inputStream =
    getClass().getResourceAsStream("/emp-array.json");
// Create JsonReader to read JSON data from a stream
Reader reader = new InputStreamReader(inputStream, "UTF-8");
JsonReader jsonReader = Json.createReader(reader);
// Creates an object model in memory.
JsonArray employeeArray = jsonReader.readArray();
```

Here is a brief description of the preceding code snippet. The `javax.json.Json` instance is the factory class that we use for creating JSON processing objects. We will use this JSON class to create the `javax.json.JsonReader` instance. After this, we need to read the JSON content into an appropriate object model. As the JSON data that we use in this example holds an array of `employee` objects, we call `readArray()` on the `JsonReader` instance to retrieve `javax.json.JsonArray`. The `JsonArray` instance contains an ordered sequence of zero or more objects read from the input source.

 If the input is a JSON object, you can call `readObject()` on `JsonReader` to retrieve the JSON object that is presented in the input source.

Now, let's see how to convert `JsonArray` elements into specific object types. In this example, we will convert each `JsonObject` present in `employeeArray` into the `Employee` object. The `Employee` class used in this example is shown here for your reference:

```
//All import statements are removed for brevity
public class Employee {
    private String firstName;
    private String lastName;
    private String email;
    private Integer employeeId;
```

```
private java.util.Date hireDate;
//Getters and Setter for the above properties are not
//shown in this code snippet to save space
}
```

 Currently, the Java EE platform lacks a binding feature, which does the automatic conversion of the JSON content into Java classes. There is a proposal, **JSR 367: JavaTM API for JSON Binding (JSON-B)**, to provide a standard binding layer for converting Java objects into/from JSON messages.

In this example, we create the `Employee` instance for each `JsonObject` present in `employeeArray`.

The following code snippet is a continuation of the previous example. This example converts `employeeArray` that we retrieved from the JSON input file into a list of `Employee` objects:

```
//import statements for the core APIs used in
//the following code snippet
import javax.json.JsonObject;
import javax.json.JsonValue;
import java.text.SimpleDateFormat;
import java.util.Date;

//Iterate over employeeArray(JsonArray)
//and process each JsonObject
List<Employee> employeeList = new ArrayList<Employee>();
for(JsonValue jsonValue : employeeArray) {
  //Get JsonObject and read desired attributes
  //and copy them to Employee object
  if(jsonValue.getValueType().equals
    (JsonValue.ValueType.OBJECT)){
      JsonObject jsonObject = (JsonObject) jsonValue;
      Employee employee = new Employee();
      employee.setFirstName(jsonObject.getString("firstName"));
      employee.setLastName(jsonObject.getString("lastName"));
      employee.setEmployeeId(jsonObject.getInt("employeeId"));
      //Converts date string (from JSON) to java.util.Date object
      SimpleDateFormat dateFormat =
        new SimpleDateFormat("yyyy-MM-dd");
      Date hireDate=
        dateFormat.parse(jsonObject.getString("hireDate"))
      employee.setHireDate(hireDate);
```

```
        employeeList.add(employee);
    }
}
```

The preceding code iterates over the `JsonArray` instance and builds the `Employee` instances. Let's take a closer look at the `JsonArray` object to understand how it stores JSON data.

A `JsonArray` instance contains one or more `javax.json.JsonValue` elements, each representing an item present in the input source. Remember that `JsonValue` is a top-level interface, and at runtime, it takes one of the following forms on the basis of the content type:

- `javax.json.JsonObject`: This form is an immutable JSON object value
- `javax.json.JsonArray`: This form is an immutable array representing an ordered sequence of zero or more JSON values
- `javax.json.JsonNumber`: This form is an immutable JSON numerical value
- `javax.json.JsonString`: This form is an immutable JSON string value
- `javax.json.JsonValue.TRUE`: This form represents the JSON TRUE value
- `javax.json.JsonValue.FALSE`: This form represents the JSON FALSE value
- `javax.json.JsonValue.NULL`: This form represents the JSON NULL value

By now, we have read the entire JSON content from the input file into the `Employee` objects. It is now time for some cleanup activities. The following code closes the `inputStream` and `jsonReader` objects after use. This lets the runtime release the system resources associated with the stream:

```
if (inputStream != null) {
  inputStream.close();
}
if (jsonReader != null) {
  jsonReader.close();
}
```

> Once you have finished using the `InputStream`, `OutputStream`, `JsonReader`, or `JSonWriter` objects, make sure that you close them to release the associated resources.

Generating the JSON representation from the object model

In the previous section, we discussed the APIs provided by JSR 353 to convert the JSON data into the Java object model. In this section, we will learn how to convert a Java object model into the JSON format, which is the opposite of the operation discussed in the previous section.

The very first step is to build an object model. You can use either of the following classes to generate the object model. The choice of the builder class depends on whether you want to generate a JSON object or a JSON array:

- **javax.json.JsonObjectBuilder**: This builder class is used for generating the JSON object model from scratch. This class provides methods to add the name-value pairs to the object model and to return the final object.
- **javax.json.JsonArrayBuilder**: This builder class is used for generating an array of the JSON objects from scratch. This class provides methods to add objects or values to the array model and to return the final array.

The builder classes can be created either from the `javax.json.Json` factory class or from the `javax.json.JsonBuilderFactory` class. You may go for `JsonBuilderFactory` if you want to override the default configurations for the generated objects (configurations are specific to vendors) or if you need to create multiple instances of the builder classes.

The following code snippet illustrates the use of the `JsonArrayBuilder` APIs for converting an array of the `employee` objects into the JSON array. The client builds the JSON objects by using `JsonObjectBuilder` and adds them to `JsonArrayBuilder`. Finally, when the client calls the `build()` method, `JsonArrayBuilder` returns the associated JSON array:

```
//import statements for the core classes used in this example
//Other imports are removed for brevity
import javax.json.Json;
import javax.json.JsonArray;
import javax.json.JsonArrayBuilder;
import javax.json.JsonObject;
import javax.json.JsonObjectBuilder;
import javax.json.JsonWriter;
import java.io.FileOutputStream;
import java.io.OutputStream;


// Creates a JsonArrayBuilder instance that is
```

```
// Build JsonArray
JsonArrayBuilder jsonArrayBuilder = Json.createArrayBuilder();

//Get a list of Employee instances.
// We are not interested in the implementation details of the
// getEmployeeList() method used in this example.
List<Employee> employees = getEmployeeList();

//Iterate over the employee list and create JsonObject for each item
for (Employee employee : employees) {

//Add desired name-value pairs to the JSON object and push
// each object in to the array.
  jsonArrayBuilder.add(
    Json.createObjectBuilder()
    .add("employeeId", employee.getEmployeeId())
    .add("firstName", employee.getFirstName())
    .add("lastName", employee.getLastName())
    .add("email", employee.getEmail())
    .add("hireDate", employee.getHireDate())
  );

}
//Return the json array holding employee details
JsonArray employeesArray = jsonArrayBuilder.build();

//write the array to file
OutputStream outputStream = new FileOutputStream
  ("emp-array.json");
JsonWriter jsonWriter = Json.createWriter(outputStream);
jsonWriter.writeArray(employeesArray);

//Close the stream to clean up the associated resources
outputStream.close();
jsonWriter.close();
```

The resulting file output content may look like the following:

```
[ {"employeeId":100,"firstName":"John","lastName":"Chen",
  "email":"john.chen@xxxx.com","hireDate":"2008-10-16"},
  {"employeeId":101,"firstName":"Ameya","lastName":"Job",
  "email":"ameya.job@xxx.com","hireDate":"2013-03-06"}]
```

Processing JSON with JSR 353 streaming APIs

This category of APIs supports the streaming model for both reading and writing the JSON content. This model is designed to process a large amount of data in a more efficient way. Conceptually, this model is similar to the **Streaming API for XML (StAX)** parser that you might have used while dealing with the XML data.

Streaming APIs are grouped in the `javax.json.stream` package in the JSR specification. In this section, we will see how we can use streaming APIs for efficiently processing JSON data.

Here is a list of the frequently used classes in the streaming API provided by the JSR 353 specification:

Class	Description
`javax.json.stream.JsonParser`	This class provides forward read-only access to JSON data by using the pull parsing programming model.
`javax.json.stream.JsonGenerator`	This class writes JSON to an output source as specified by the client application. It generates the name-value pairs for the JSON objects and values for the JSON arrays.

Streaming APIs read and write the content serially at runtime in accordance with client calls, which makes them suitable for handling a large amount of data.

 To refer to the complete list of the streaming APIs provided by JSR 353, visit `http://docs.oracle.com/javaee/7/api/javax/json/stream/package-summary.html`.

Using streaming APIs to parse JSON data

In this section, we will learn the use of streaming APIs for converting JSON data into appropriate Java classes.

This example illustrates the use of streaming APIs for converting a JSON array of the `employee` objects present in the `emp-array.json` file into an appropriate Java class representation.

The following code snippet illustrates how you can use `javax.json.stream.`
`JsonParser`, which follows the streaming parsing model, for reading the content
from the `emp-array.json` file:

1. The first step is to get the input stream for reading the `emp-array.json` file.
   Then, you can create a `JsonParser` instance with the input stream, as follows:

```
//Other imports are removed for brevity
import javax.json.stream.JsonParser;

//Read emp-array.json file that contains JSON array of
//employees
//This file is listed under the section:
//"A sample JSON file representing employee objects"
InputStream inputStream =
  getClass().getResourceAsStream("/emp-array.json");
JsonParser jsonParser = Json.createParser(inputStream);
```

2. Start parsing the content now. The following code snippet illustrates how
   the API is used for parsing the content with the pull parsing model:

```
// Returns true if there are more parsing states
while (jsonParser.hasNext()) {
//Returns the event for the next parsing state
  Event event = jsonParser.next();
//Start of a JSON object,
//position of the parser is after'{'
  if (event.equals(JsonParser.Event.START_OBJECT)) {
    employee = new Employee();
    employeeList.add(employee);
  } else if (event.equals(JsonParser.Event.KEY_NAME)) {
    String keyName = jsonParser.getString();
    switch (keyName) {
      case "firstName":
      jsonParser.next();
      employee.setFirstName(
      jsonParser.getString());
      break;
      case "lastName":
      jsonParser.next();
```

```
employee.setLastName(
jsonParser.getString());
break;
case "email":
jsonParser.next();
employee.setEmail(jsonParser.getString());
break;
case "employeeId":
jsonParser.next();
employee.setEmployeeId(jsonParser.getInt());
break;
case "hireDate":
jsonParser.next();
//Converts date string (from JSON) into
//java.util.Date object
SimpleDateFormat dateFormat =
  new SimpleDateFormat("yyyy-MM-dd");
Date hireDate=
  dateFormat.Parse
    (jsonObject.getString("hireDate"));
employee.setHireDate(hireDate);
break;
    }
  }

}
```

Remember that `JsonParser` parses JSON by using the pull parsing programming model. In this case, the client application code controls the progress of parsing. The client calls `next()` on `JsonParser` to advance the parser to the next state after processing each element. In response to the `next()` call from the client, the parser generates the following events on the basis of the type of the next token encountered: START_OBJECT, END_OBJECT, START_ARRAY, END_ARRAY, KEY_NAME, VALUE_STRING, VALUE_NUMBER, VALUE_TRUE, VALUE_FALSE, and VALUE_NULL.

To better understand this, consider the following JSON array as the input to the parser:

```
[{"country": "IN"}]
```

The parser generates the START_ARRAY event for the first call to the next() method and the START_OBJECT event with the second call to the next() method, and so on. The following diagram illustrates the events generated while parsing each token present in the JSON representation:

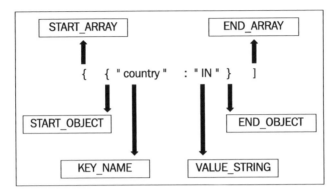

Using streaming APIs to generate JSON

You can use javax.json.stream.JsonGenerator to write JSON data to an output source as a stream of tokens. This approach does not keep the content in-memory throughout the process. Once a name-value pair is written to the stream, the content used for writing the name-value pair will be discarded from the memory.

JsonGenerator has support for writing both the JSON object and the JSON array. You can use the writeStartObject() method to generate the JSON object and then add the name-value pairs with the write() method. To finish the object representation, call writeEnd().

To generate the JSON arrays, call the writeStartArray() method and then add values with the write() method. To finish the array representation, call writeEnd(), which writes the end of the current context.

The following example illustrates the use of streaming APIs for converting an array of employee objects into a JSON string:

```
//Other imports are removed for brevity
import javax.json.stream.JsonGenerator;

//Get the employee list that needs to be converted to JSON
List<Employee> employees = getEmployeeList();
//Create file output stream for writing data to a File
OutputStream outputStream = new FileOutputStream(
  "emp-array.json");
```

```
//Generates JsonGenerator which converts data to JSON
JsonGenerator jsonGenerator = Json.createGenerator(outputStream);
// Writes the JSON 'start array' character : [
jsonGenerator.writeStartArray();
for(Employee employee : employees) {
  // Writes the JSON object for each Employee object
  jsonGenerator.writeStartObject()
  .write("employeeId", employee.getEmployeeId())
  .write("firstName", employee.getFirstName())
  .write("lastName", employee.getLastName())
  .write("email", employee.getEmail())
  .write("hireDate",
    employee.getHireDate().toString())
  .writeEnd();

}
// Writes the end of the current context(array).
jsonGenerator.writeEnd();
//Closes the output stream
//and releases any resources associated with it.
outputStream.close();
// Closes the generator and
//frees any resources associated with it.
jsonGenerator.close();
```

The use of the `JsonGenerator` class is very straightforward. Therefore, we are not going to discuss the methods in detail here.

With this, we are ending our discussion on JSR 353 - Java API for JSON Processing. In the next section, we will discuss Jackson, which is another popular framework available for processing JSON.

Using the Jackson API for processing JSON

Jackson is a multipurpose data processing Java library. The primary capability of this tool is the support for processing JSON. It also has additional modules for processing the data encoded in other popular formats such as Apache Avro (a data serialization system), **Concise Binary Object Representation (CBOR)**—a binary JSON format, Smile (a binary JSON format), XML, **comma-separated values (CSV)**, and YAML. In this section, we will learn how to use Jackson APIs for processing JSON.

Jackson provides the following three alternative methods for processing JSON:

- **Tree model APIs**: This method provides APIs for building a tree representation of a JSON document
- **Data binding API**: This method provides APIs for converting a JSON document into and from Java objects
- **Streaming API**: This method provides streaming APIs for reading and writing a JSON document

We will discuss the preceding three methods in detail in this section.

 To know the dependencies of Jackson2 APIs, visit `https://github.com/FasterXML/jackson-docs/wiki/Using-Jackson2-with-Maven`.

Processing JSON with Jackson tree model APIs

The Jackson tree model API provides an in-memory representation of the JSON data. A client can optionally modify the object model representation. Here is a list of the core classes that you may need to know while dealing with tree model APIs in Jackson:

Class	Description
`com.fasterxml.jackson.databind.ObjectMapper`	This mapper class provides the functionality for converting between Java objects and matching JSON representations.
`com.fasterxml.jackson.databind.JsonNode`	This class is the base class for all JSON nodes, which form the basis of the JSON tree model in Jackson.

Using Jackson tree model APIs to query and update data

You will use the `com.fasterxml.jackson.databind.ObjectMapper` class to convert the JSON data into a tree representation. This class has a variety of APIs to build a tree from the JSON data. The tree representation built from JSON is made up of `com.fasterxml.jackson.databind.JsonNode` instances. This is similar to the DOM nodes in an XML DOM tree. You can also navigate through `JsonNode` to identify specific elements present in the tree hierarchy. The following example illustrates the use of Jackson tree model APIs.

This example generates a tree hierarchy for the JSON array of `employee` objects and then queries the generated tree for the `employee` nodes with the null `email` value. This example updates all the null `email` values with the system-generated e-mail addresses for later processing.

The `readTree(InputStream in)` instance defined on the `com.fasterxml.jackson.databind.ObjectMapper` class helps you to deserialize the JSON content as a tree (expressed using a set of `JsonNode` instances). To query `JsonNode` for a specific field name, you can call `path(String fieldName)` on the underlying `JsonNode` instance. The following code snippet will help you understand the use of these APIs:

```
//Other imports are removed for brevity
import com.fasterxml.jackson.databind.JsonNode;
import com.fasterxml.jackson.databind.ObjectMapper;
import com.fasterxml.jackson.databind.node.ObjectNode;

// Read in the JSON employee array form emp-array.json file
InputStream inputStream =
  getClass().getResourceAsStream("/emp-array.json");
//Create ObjectMapper instance
//ObjectMapper provides functionality for creating tree
//structure for JSON content
ObjectMapper objectMapper = new ObjectMapper();

//Read JSON content in to tree
JsonNode rootNode = objectMapper.readTree(inputStream);

//Check if the json content is in array form
if (rootNode.isArray()) {
//Iterate over each element in the array
  for (JsonNode objNode : rootNode) {
    //Find out the email node by traversing tree
    JsonNode emailNode = objNode.path("email");
```

```
      //if email is null, then update with
      //a system generated email
      if(emailNode.textValue() == null ){
        String generatedEmail=getSystemGeneratedEmail();
        ((ObjectNode)objNode).put("email", generatedEmail );
      }
    }
  }
}
//Write the modified tree to a json file
objectMapper.writeValue(new File("emp-modified-array.json"),
  rootNode);
if(inputStream != null)
  inputStream.close();
```

The tree model API discussed in this section produces a generalized tree representation for the JSON content. To learn how to generate a more specific object representation for JSON, refer to the next section.

Processing JSON with Jackson data binding APIs

Jackson data binding is used to convert the JSON representation into and from **Plain Old Java Object (POJO)** by using property accessors or annotations. With this API, you can either generate generic collection classes or more specific Java objects, such as the Employee object, for representing JSON data. Let's take a quick look at these two variants available for representing JSON data.

Simple Jackson data binding with generalized objects

Sometimes, you may need to deal with highly dynamic JSON content where you may not be able to map data to a specific Java object as the structure of the data changes dynamically. In such a scenario, you can use the simple binding APIs offered by the Jackson framework. You will use the Java maps, lists, strings, numbers, Booleans, and nulls for representing dynamic JSON data.

The following code snippet converts a JSON string into a map object. The com.fasterxml.jackson.core.type.TypeReference class is used for passing a generic type definition, which defines a type to bind to, as follows:

```
String jsonString =
  "{\" firstName\":\"John\",\"lastName\":\"Chen\"}";
ObjectMapper objectMapper = new ObjectMapper();
```

```
//properties will store name and value pairs read from jsonString
Map<String, String> properties = objectMapper.readValue(
   jsonString, new TypeReference<Map<String, String>>() { });
```

Full Jackson data binding with specialized objects

If the JSON data format, which a client receives, is well structured, you can directly map the content to a concrete Java class. A full data binding solution fits such a scenario. For instance, you can create an `Employee` class for representing the `employee` data presented in the JSON format as long as the JSON content structure does not change. The following example uses the data binding offering from Jackson to convert the JSON content from the `emp.json` file into an `Employee` object. This example calls `readValue(InputStream src, Class<T> valueType)` on `ObjectMapper` to get the Java representation of the JSON content:

```
// emp.json file has following contents:
//{"employeeId":100,"firstName":"John","lastName":"Chen"}
ObjectMapper objectMapper = new ObjectMapper();
Employee employee = objectMapper.readValue(new File("emp.json"),
   Employee.class);
```

The next example demonstrates how you can create a Java collection containing the `Employee` objects from a JSON array of employees. Here, we need to construct a Java collection type, indicating the type of elements in the collection. To create a collection type, you can call the `constructCollectionType()` method on the `com.fasterxml.jackson.databind.type.TypeFactory` instance returned by `ObjectMapper`:

```
ObjectMapper objectMapper = new ObjectMapper();
CollectionType collectionType =
   objectMapper.getTypeFactory().constructCollectionType
   (List.class, Employee.class);
//"emp-array.json" file contains JSON array of employee data
List<Employee> emp = objectMapper.readValue(new File
   ("emp-array.json"), collectionType);
```

To convert a Java object into the JSON representation, you can call the `writeValue(OutputStream out, Object value)` method on `ObjectMapper`. The `writeValue()` method serializes any Java value to JSON and writes it to the output stream present in the method call. The following code snippet converts the `employee` object into the JSON structure and writes the content to the `emp.json` file:

```
//Get the employee object
Employee employee = getEmployeeEntity();
//Convert the object in to JSON and write to a file
objectMapper.writeValue(new File("emp.json"), employee);
```

How does Jackson map JSON object values to a Java class?

The default mapping mechanism used by Jackson is based on the bean naming properties. The binding layer copies the matching properties from the source to the destination. This implies that all names present in a JSON object need to match with the Java class properties for the default mapping mechanism to work. However, you can override the default mapping behavior by annotating a desired field (or by the `getter` and `setter` methods) with `@JsonProperty`. This annotation is used to override the default property name that is used during the serialization and deserialization processes. To learn more, visit `http://wiki.fasterxml.com/JacksonAnnotations`.

Processing JSON with Jackson streaming APIs

The Jackson framework supports the streaming API for reading and writing JSON content. You will use `org.codehaus.jackson.JsonParser` to read the JSON data and `org.codehaus.jackson.JsonGenerator` to write data. The following table lists important classes in the streaming model API:

Class	Description
`com.fasterxml.jackson.core.JsonParser`	This class is used for reading the JSON content.
`com.fasterxml.jackson.core.JsonGenerator`	This class is used for writing the JSON content.
`com.fasterxml.jackson.core.JsonFactory`	This is the main factory class of the Jackson package. It is used to generate `JsonParser` and `JsonWriter`.

Using Jackson streaming APIs to parse JSON data

The following example illustrates the Jackson streaming APIs for reading JSON data. This example uses streaming APIs to generate a Java model for the JSON array of `employee` objects. As in the earlier examples, the `emp-array.json` file is used as the input source. The steps are as follows:

1. Create the `com.fasterxml.jackson.core.JsonParser` instance by using `com.fasterxml.jackson.core.JsonFactory`. The `JsonParser` class reads the JSON content from the file input stream.

2. The next step is to start parsing the JSON content read from the input source. The client may call the `nextToken()` method to forward stream enough to determine the type of the next token. Based on the token type, the client can take appropriate action. In the following sample code, the client checks for the start of the object (`JsonToken.START_OBJECT`) in order to copy the current JSON object to a new `Employee` instance. We use `ObjectMapper` to copy the content of the current JSON object to the `Employee` class:

```
//Step 1: Finds a resource with a given name.
InputStream inputStream = getClass().getResourceAsStream(
  "/emp-array.json");
//Creates Streaming parser
JsonParser jsonParser = new
  JsonFactory().createParser(inputStream);

//Step 2: Start parsing the contents
//We will use data binding feature from ObjectMapper
//for populating employee object
ObjectMapper objectMapper = new ObjectMapper();
//Continue the parsing till stream is opened or
//no more token is available
while (!jsonParser.isClosed()) {
  JsonToken jsonToken = jsonParser.nextToken();
  // if it is the last token then break the loop
  if (jsonToken == null) {
    break;
  }
  //If this is start of the object, then create
  //Employee instance and add it to the result list
  if (jsonToken.equals(JsonToken.START_OBJECT)) {
    //Use the objectMapper to copy the current
    // JSON object to Employee object
    employee = objectMapper.readValue(jsonParser,
      Employee.class);
    //Add the newly copied instance to the list
    employeeList.add(employee);

  }

}
//Close the stream after the use to release the resources
if (inputStream != null) {
  inputStream.close();
}
```

```
if (jsonParser != null) {
  jsonParser.close();
}
```

 To learn all the possible token types returned by `JsonParser` in the Jackson framework, refer to `http://fasterxml. github.io/jackson-core/javadoc/2.5/com/ fasterxml/jackson/core/JsonToken.html`.

Using Jackson streaming APIs to generate JSON

The following example illustrates Jackson streaming APIs for writing JSON data. This example reads a list of `Employee` objects, converts them into the JSON representations, and then writes to the `OutputStream` object. The steps are as follows:

1. The following code snippet generates `com.fasterxml.jackson.core. JsonGenerator` by using `com.fasterxml.jackson.core.JsonFactory`:

```
OutputStream outputStream = new
  FileOutputStream("emp-array.json");
JsonGenerator jsonGenerator = new
  JsonFactory().createGenerator(outputStream,
    JsonEncoding.UTF8);
```

2. The next step is to build the JSON representation for the list of employees. The `writeStartArray()` method writes the starting marker for the JSON array ([). Now, write the marker for the object ({) by calling `writeStartObject()`. This is followed by the name-value pairs for the object by calling an appropriate write method. To write the end marker for the object (}), call `writeEndObject()`. Finally, to finish writing an array, call `writeEndArray()`:

```
jsonGenerator.writeStartArray();
List<Employee> employees = getEmployeesList();
for (Employee employee : employees) {
  jsonGenerator.writeStartObject();
  jsonGenerator.writeNumberField("employeeId",
    employee.getEmployeeId());
  jsonGenerator.writeStringField("firstName",
    employee.getFirstName());
  jsonGenerator.writeStringField("lastName",
    employee.getLastName());
  jsonGenerator.writeEndObject();

}
```

```
//JsonGenerator class writes the JSON content to the
//specified OutputStream.

jsonGenerator.writeEndArray();
```

3. Close the stream object after use:

```
//Close the streams to release associated resources
jsonGenerator.close();
outputStream.close();
```

With this topic, we are ending the discussion on Jackson. In this section, we discussed the various categories of APIs for processing JSON. In-depth coverage of the Jackson API is beyond the scope of this book. More details on Jackson are available at `https://github.com/FasterXML/Jackson`.

The link that answers some of the generic queries that you may have about Jackson is `http://wiki.fasterxml.com/JacksonFAQ`.

In the next section, we will discuss Gson, yet another framework for processing JSON. This is the last JSON processing framework on our discussion list.

Using the Gson API for processing JSON

Gson is an open source Java library that can be used for converting Java objects into JSON representations and vice versa. The Gson library was originally developed by Google for its internal use and later open sourced under the terms of Apache License 2.0.

To find out the dependencies of Gson APIs, refer to `https://sites.google.com/site/gson/gson-user-guide/using-gson-with-maven2`.

Processing JSON with object model APIs in Gson

The main class in the Gson library that you will use for building an object model from the JSON data is the `com.google.gson.Gson` class. Here is a list of the core `Gson` classes from the object model API category:

Class	Description
`com.google.gson.GsonBuilder`	This class is useful when you need to construct a `Gson` instance, overriding the default configurations such as custom date format, pretty printing, and custom sterilization.
`com.google.gson.Gson`	This class is the main class for using Gson. This class does the conversion from JSON into a Java object and the other way round.
`com.google.gson.reflect.TypeToken<T>`	This class is used for getting a generic type for a class. The resulting type can be used for serializing and deserializing JSON data.

Generating the object model from the JSON representation

Gson offers simpler APIs to convert the JSON representation into Java objects. To do this, you can call the `fromJson(Reader json, Class<T> classOfT)` method on the `com.google.gson.Gson` object. The following example will help you understand the end-to-end use of Gson APIs for deserializing the JSON content to Java objects:

1. The first step is to create a `Gson` instance. The `Gson` class offers all the necessary methods for serializing and deserializing JSON data. You can simply create an instance by calling `new Gson()`. However, in this example, we use `com.google.gson.GsonBuilder` to create a `Gson` instance. This is because `GsonBuilder` lets you override the default configuration for a `Gson` instance. We use this feature to override the default date format used for serializing and deserializing the date fields present in the JSON content. The following code snippet creates a `Gson` instance:

   ```
   //Other imports are removed for brevity
   import com.google.gson.Gson;
   import com.google.gson.GsonBuilder;
   ```

```
// Get GsonBuilder object
GsonBuilder gsonBuilder = new GsonBuilder();
//Set date format for converting date presented in
//form (in JSON data)  to java.util.Date
gsonBuilder.setDateFormat("yyyy-MM-dd");
//Get gson object
Gson gson = gsonBuilder.create();
```

2. The next step is to convert the JSON content into an appropriate Java class. You can do this by invoking `fromJson(Reader json, Class<T> classOfT)` on the `Gson` instance. The following sample code converts the JSON representation of the `employee` object into the `employee` Java object:

```
//Read the json input file with current class's class
//loader
// emp.json contains JSON employee object
   InputStream inputStream = getClass().getResourceAsStream("/emp.
json");
BufferedReader reader = new BufferedReader(
   new InputStreamReader(inputStream));
//Converts JSON string to Employee object
Employee employee = gson.fromJson(reader, Employee.class);
```

Generating the parameterized Java collection from the JSON representation

The previous example demonstrated the Gson APIs for converting a JSON representation of a single `employee` object into a Java object. This section discusses how to convert a JSON object array into a Java collection. You can do this by calling the `fromJson(JsonReader reader, Type typeOfT)` method on the `Gson` instance. Let's take an example to better understand this API. The steps are as follows:

1. The `emp-array.json` file used in this example contains a JSON array of the `employee` objects.

2. This example converts the JSON array read from the input file into the `List<Employee>` collection object, which is a parameterized collection type (generic type). We use `com.google.gson.reflect.TypeToken<T>` to define the collection type that holds the `Employee` objects.

3. To deserialize the JSON data read from the file into the `List<Employee>` object, call `fromJson(Reader json, Type typeOfT)` on the `Gson` object with the file input stream reader and the desired `TypeToken` object as the parameter.

The following code snippet illustrates these steps:

```
//Step 1: Read emp-array.json
InputStream inputStream =
getClass().getResourceAsStream(("/emp-array.json");
BufferedReader reader = new BufferedReader(new
  InputStreamReader(inputStream));
// Step 2: Define TypeToken
// Define a  parameterized collection type to hold the List
// of Employees returned by Gson::fromJSon method call.
Type listType = new TypeToken<ArrayList<Employee>>(){}
  .getType();
//Step 3: Convert JSON array to List<Employee>
//Generates list of employees by calling Gson::fromJson()
Gson gson = new Gson();
List<Employee> employees = gson.fromJson(reader, listType);
```

How does Gson map a JSON object to a Java class?

The default mapping mechanism used by Gson is based on the bean properties. The binding layer copies the matching properties from the source to the destination. This implies that all the names present in a JSON object need to match the Java class properties for the default mapping mechanism to work. However, you can override the default mapping behavior by annotating the desired attribute with @SerializedName. This annotation indicates that the annotated member should be serialized to JSON with the provided name value as its field name.

Generating the JSON representation from the object model

Gson has simplified APIs to convert the object model into the JSON content. Depending upon the type of the object model, you can use either of the following APIs to get the JSON representation:

- To convert a Java object into JSON, you can call the toJson(Object src) method. Here is an example:

```
// Get Employee object that needs
//to be converted into JSON
Employee emp=getEmployee();
Gson gson = new Gson();
// create JSON String from Object
String jsonEmp = gson.toJson(emp);
```

- To convert a parameterized collection into a JSON string, you can use `toJson(Object src, Type typeOfSrc)`. Here is an example:

```
//Get Employee list that needs to be converted into JSON
List<Employee>  employees= getEmployeeList();
Gson gson = new Gson();
//Specify collection type that you want
//to convert into JSON
Type typeOfSource = new
  TypeToken<List<Employee>>(){}.getType();
// create JSON String from Object
String jsonEmps = gson.toJson(employees, typeOfSource);
```

Processing JSON with Gson streaming APIs

In addition to the object model APIs, the Gson library supports the streaming APIs to read and write the JSON representations. The streaming APIs in Gson follow the pull parser model. Here is a list of the important streaming API classes in Gson:

Class	Description
`com.google.gson.stream.JsonReader`	This class reads the JSON-encoded value as a stream of tokens. Tokens are read in the same order as they appear in the JSON document.
`com.google.gson.stream.JsonWriter`	This class writes a JSON-encoded value to the stream, one token at a time.

Reading JSON data with Gson streaming APIs

The following example demonstrates the use of Gson streaming APIs for reading JSON data.

This example converts the JSON array of `employee` objects present in the `emp-array.json` file into a list of `Employee` objects. The steps are as follows:

1. Gson provides `com.google.gson.stream.JsonReader` to read the JSON-encoded value as a stream of tokens. You can create a `JsonReader` instance by supplying the `InputStreamReader` instance as input.

2. As the next step, start parsing the contents. The tokens returned by `JsonReader` are traversed in the same order as they appear in the JSON document. As this example uses an array of the JSON objects as input, the parser starts off by calling `beginArray()`. This call consumes the array's opening bracket. The client then calls `beginObject()` to consume the object's opening brace. This is followed by a series of API calls to read the name and value pairs representing the object. After reading the entire object, the client calls `endObject()` to consume the next token from the JSON stream and asserts that it is the end of the current object. Once all the objects are read, the client invokes `endArray()` to consume the next token from the JSON stream and asserts that it is the end of the current array.

The following code snippet implements the two preceding steps:

```
//Step 1: Read emp-array.json file containing JSON
// array of employees
InputStream inputStream =
  getClass().getResourceAsStream("/emp-array.json");
InputStreamReader inputStreamReader = new
  InputStreamReader(inputStream);

//Step 2: Start parsing the contents
List<Employee> employeeList = new ArrayList<Employee>();
JsonReader reader = new JsonReader(inputStreamReader);
reader.beginArray();
while (reader.hasNext()) {
  // The method readEmployee(...) is listed below
  Employee employee = readEmployee(reader);
  employeeList.add(employee);
}
reader.endArray();
reader.close();
```

Here is the definition of the `readEmployee(JsonReader reader)` method used in the preceding code snippet:

```
// This method is referred in the above code snippet to create
// Employee object
private Employee readEmployee(JsonReader reader) throws
  IOException {
  Employee employee = new Employee();

  reader.beginObject();
```

```
  while (reader.hasNext()) {
    String keyName = reader.nextName();
    switch (keyName) {
      case "firstName":
        employee.setFirstName(reader.nextString());
      break;
      case "lastName":
        employee.setLastName(reader.nextString());
      break;
      case "email":
        employee.setEmail(reader.nextString());
      break;
      case "employeeId":
        employee.setEmployeeId(reader.nextInt());
      break;
    }
  }
  reader.endObject();
  return employee;
}
```

Writing JSON data with Gson streaming APIs

You can use `com.google.gson.stream.JsonWriter` to write the JSON-encoded value to the stream. The following example demonstrates the use of Gson streaming APIs for writing JSON data. This example writes the JSON array representation of `employee` objects to the `emp-array.json` file. The steps are as follows:

1. To write the JSON content, build the `JsonWriter` object, which takes the implementation of `java.io.Writer` as the input.

2. Once the `JsonWriter` instance is created, start writing the JSON content. As this example writes an array of the `employee` objects, we start by invoking the `beginArray()` method. This call begins encoding a new array. Then, call `beginObject()` to start encoding a new object. This is followed by the encoding of the name and the value. To finish the encoding of the current object, call `endObject()`, and to finish the encoding of the current array, call `endArray()`:

```
//Step 1: Build JsonWriter to read the JSON contents
OutputStream outputStream = new FileOutputStream(
  "emp-array.json");
BufferedWriter bufferedWriter= new BufferedWriter(
```

```
                 new OutputStreamWriter(outputStream));
                 //Creates JsonWriter object
                 JsonWriter writer = new JsonWriter(bufferedWriter);

                 //Step 2: Start writing JSON contents

                 //Starts with writing array
                 writer.beginArray();
                 List<Employee> employees = getEmployeesList();
                 for (Employee employee : employees) {
                   //start encoding the object
                   writer.beginObject();
                   //Write name:value pair to the object
                   writer.name("employeeId").value
                     (employee.getEmployeeId());
                   writer.name("firstName").value(employee.getFirstName());
                   writer.name("lastName").value(employee.getLastName());
                   writer.name("email").value(employee.getEmail());
                   //Finish encoding of the object
                   writer.endObject();
                 }
                 //Finish encoding of the array
                 writer.endArray();
                 writer.flush();
                 //close writer
                 writer.close();
```

 In-depth coverage of the Gson API is beyond the scope of this book. To learn more about Gson, visit `https://code.google.com/p/google-gson/`. The Gson API documentation is available at `http://google-gson.googlecode.com/svn/trunk/gson/docs/javadocs/index.html`.

With this, we have finished our discussion on the three popular JSON processing frameworks that are available today. We may revisit some of these tools and frameworks with more complex use cases later in this book.

Summary

In this chapter, you were introduced to the various processing models for the JSON content and some of the popular Java-based JSON processing frameworks available today. This chapter is essential for understanding how the JSON-based request and response messages are bound to the Java model while building REST APIs later in the book.

This chapter is not meant for recommending any specific JSON framework for your application, but to help you understand the popular frameworks available today for processing JSON and what they have to offer.

In the next chapter, we will build our first REST service by using JAX-RS APIs.

3
Introducing the JAX-RS API

In the previous chapters, we covered the basics of RESTful web services and looked at Java APIs for JSON processing. By now, you have a good understanding of the RESTful architectural style and the main components that form a REST API. It is time for us to put all learning into practice. In this chapter, we will build simple RESTful web services using **JAX-RS APIs**. This chapter covers the following topics:

- Overview of JAX-RS annotations
- Understanding data binding in JAX-RS
- Building your first RESTful web service with JAX-RS
- Client APIs for accessing RESTful web services

An overview of JAX-RS

There are many tools and frameworks available in the market today for building RESTful web services. You can use tools of your choice as long as the REST implementation meets the RESTful architectural constraints discussed in the first chapter. There are some recent developments with respect to the standardization of various framework APIs by providing unified interfaces for a variety of implementations. Let's take a quick look at this.

As you may know, Java EE is the industry standard for developing portable, robust, scalable, and secure server-side Java applications. The Java EE 6 release took the first step towards standardizing RESTful web service APIs by introducing a Java API for RESTful web services (JAX-RS). JAX-RS is an integral part of the Java EE platform, which ensures portability of your REST API code across all Java EE-compliant application servers. The first release of JAX-RS was based on JSR 311. The latest version is JAX-RS 2 (based on JSR 339), which was released as part of the Java EE 7 platform. There are multiple JAX-RS implementations available today by various vendors. Some of the popular JAX-RS implementations are as follows:

- **Jersey RESTful web service framework**: This framework is an open source framework for developing RESTful web services in Java. It serves as a JAX-RS reference implementation. You can learn more about this project at `https://jersey.java.net`.

- **Apache CXF**: This framework is an open source web services framework. CXF supports both JAX-WS and JAX-RS web services. To learn more about CXF, refer to `http://cxf.apache.org`.

- **RESTEasy**: This framework is an open source project from JBoss, which provides various modules to help you build a RESTful web service. To learn more about RESTEasy, refer to `http://resteasy.jboss.org`.

- **Restlet**: This framework is a lightweight, open source RESTful web service framework. It has good support for building both scalable RESTful web service APIs and lightweight REST clients, which suits mobile platforms well. You can learn more about Restlet at `http://restlet.com`.

We will be using the Jersey implementation of JAX-RS for running the examples discussed in this book (unless otherwise specified). Remember that you are not locked down to any specific vendor here, the RESTful web service APIs that you build using JAX-RS will run on any JAX-RS implementation as long as you do not use any vendor-specific APIs in the code.

JAX-RS annotations

The main goal of the JAX-RS specification is to make the RESTful web service development easier than it has been in the past. As JAX-RS is a part of the Java EE platform, your code becomes portable across all Java EE-compliant servers. In this section, we will learn how to use the JAX-RS annotations for building RESTful web services.

Specifying the dependency of the JAX-RS API

To use JAX-RS APIs in your project, you need to add the `javax.ws.rs-api` JAR file to the class path. If the consuming project uses Maven for building the source, the dependency entry for the `javax.ws.rs-api` JAR file in the **Project Object Model (POM)** file may look like the following:

```
<dependency>
    <groupId>javax.ws.rs</groupId>
    <artifactId>javax.ws.rs-api</artifactId>
    <version>2.0.1</version><!-- set the tight version -->
    <scope>provided</scope><!-- compile time dependency -->
</dependency>
```

Using JAX-RS annotations to build RESTful web services

Java annotations provide the metadata for your Java class, which can be used during compilation, during deployment, or at runtime in order to perform designated tasks. The use of annotations allows us to create RESTful web services as easily as we develop a POJO class. Here, we leave the interception of the HTTP requests and representation negotiations to the framework and concentrate on the business rules necessary to solve the problem at hand.

 If you are not familiar with Java annotations, go through the tutorial available at `http://docs.oracle.com/javase/tutorial/java/annotations/`.

We will take a quick look at some of the very frequently used JAX-RS annotations in this section. We will see more annotations as we proceed further in this chapter.

Annotations for defining a RESTful resource

REST resources are the fundamental elements of any RESTful web service. A REST resource can be defined as an object that is of a specific type with the associated data and is optionally associated to other resources. It also exposes a set of standard operations corresponding to the HTTP method types such as the HEAD, GET, POST, PUT, and DELETE methods.

@Path

The `@javax.ws.rs.Path` annotation indicates the URI path to which a resource class or a class method will respond. The value that you specify for the `@Path` annotation is relative to the URI of the server where the REST resource is hosted. This annotation can be applied at both the class and the method levels.

 A `@Path` annotation value is not required to have leading or trailing slashes (/), as you may see in some examples. The JAX-RS runtime will parse the URI path templates in the same way even if they have leading or trailing slashes.

Specifying the @Path annotation on a resource class

The following code snippet illustrates how you can make a POJO class respond to a URI path template containing the `/departments` path fragment:

```
import javax.ws.rs.Path;

@Path("departments")
public class DepartmentService {
  //Rest of the code goes here
}
```

The `/department` path fragment that you see in this example is relative to the base path in the URI. The base path typically takes the following URI pattern: `http://host:port/<context-root>/<application-path>`. We will learn how to set an application path for a JAX-RS application in the *Specifying application path* section, which comes later in this chapter.

Specifying the @Path annotation on a resource class method

The following code snippet shows how you can specify `@Path` on a method in a REST resource class. Note that for an annotated method, the base URI is the effective URI of the containing class. For instance, you will use the URI of the following form to invoke the `getTotalDepartments()` method defined in the `DepartmentService` class: `/departments/count`, where `departments` is the `@Path` annotation set on the class.

```
import javax.ws.rs.GET;
import javax.ws.rs.Path;
import javax.ws.rs.Produces;
@Path("departments")
public class DepartmentService {
    @GET
    @Path("count")
```

```
        @Produces("text/plain")
        public Integer getTotalDepartments() {
            return findTotalRecordCount();
        }
    //Rest of the code goes here
}
```

Specifying variables in the URI path template

It is very common that a client wants to retrieve data for a specific object by passing the desired parameter to the server. JAX-RS allows you to do this via the URI path variables as discussed here.

The URI path template allows you to define variables that appear as placeholders in the URI. These variables would be replaced at runtime with the values set by the client.

The following example illustrates the use of the path variable to request for a specific department resource. The URI path template looks like /departments/{id}. At runtime, the client can pass an appropriate value for the id parameter to get the desired resource from the server. For instance, the URI path of the /departments/10 format returns the IT department details to the caller.

The following code snippet illustrates how you can pass the department ID as a path variable for deleting a specific department record. The path URI looks like /departments/10.

```
import javax.ws.rs.Path;
import javax.ws.rs.DELETE;

@Path("departments")
public class DepartmentService {

    @DELETE
    @Path("{id}")
    public void removeDepartment(@PathParam("id")
    short id) {
        removeDepartmentEntity(id);
    }
    //Other methods removed for brevity
}
```

In the preceding code snippet, the @PathParam annotation is used for copying the value of the path variable to the method parameter. We will discuss this in detail in the *Annotations for accessing request parameters* section.

Restricting values for path variables with regular expressions

JAX-RS lets you use regular expressions in the URI path template for restricting the values set for the path variables at runtime by the client. By default, the JAX-RS runtime ensures that all the URI variables match the following regular expression: [^/]+?. The default regular expression allows the path variable to take any character except the forward slash (/). What if you want to override this default regular expression imposed on the path variable values? Good news is that JAX-RS lets you specify your own regular expression for the path variables. For example, you can set the regular expression as given in the following code snippet in order to ensure that the department name variable present in the URI path consists only of lowercase and uppercase alphanumeric characters:

```
@DELETE
@Path("{name: [a-zA-Z][a-zA-Z_0-9]}")
public void removeDepartmentByName(@PathParam("name")
  String deptName) {
    //Method implementation goes here
}
```

If the path variable does not match the regular expression set of the resource class or method, the system reports the status back to the caller with an appropriate HTTP status code, such as 404 Not Found, which tells the caller that the requested resource could not be found at this moment.

Annotations for specifying request-response media types

The Content-Type header field in HTTP describes the body's content type present in the request and response messages. The content types are represented using the standard Internet media types. A RESTful web service makes use of this header field to indicate the type of content in the request or response message body. We discussed the Content-Type header fields in the *Representing content types using HTTP header fields* section in *Chapter 1, Introducing the REST Architectural Style*.

JAX-RS allows you to specify which Internet media types of representations a resource can produce or consume by using the @javax.ws.rs.Produces and @javax.ws.rs.Consumes annotations, respectively. We will learn these two annotations with examples in this section.

@Produces

The `@javax.ws.rs.Produces` annotation is used for defining the Internet media type(s) that a REST resource class method can return to the client. You can define this either at the class level (which will get defaulted for all methods) or the method level. The method-level annotations override the class-level annotations. The possible Internet media types that a REST API can produce are as follows:

- `application/atom+xml`
- `application/json`
- `application/octet-stream`
- `application/svg+xml`
- `application/xhtml+xml`
- `application/xml`
- `text/html`
- `text/plain`
- `text/xml`

The following example uses the `@Produces` annotation at the class level in order to set the default response media type as JSON for all resource methods in this class. At runtime, the binding provider will convert the Java representation of the return value to the JSON format. This is discussed in the *Understanding data binding rules in JAX-RS* section, which comes later in this chapter.

```
import javax.ws.rs.Path;
import javax.ws.rs.Produces;
import javax.ws.rs.core.MediaType;

@Path("departments")
@Produces(MediaType.APPLICATION_JSON)
public class DepartmentService{
  //Class implementation goes here...
}
```

@Consumes

The `@javax.ws.rs.Consumes` annotation defines the Internet media type(s) that the resource class methods can accept. You can define the `@Consumes` annotation either at the class level (which will get defaulted for all methods) or the method level. The method-level annotations override the class-level annotations. The possible Internet media types that a REST API can consume are as follows:

- `application/atom+xml`
- `application/json`

- application/octet-stream

- application/svg+xml

- application/xhtml+xml

- application/xml

- text/html

- text/plain

- text/xml

- multipart/form-data

- application/x-www-form-urlencoded

The following example illustrates how you can use the @Consumes attribute to designate a method in a class to consume a payload presented in the JSON media type. The binding provider will copy the JSON representation of an input message to the Department parameter of the createDepartment() method.

```
import javax.ws.rs.Consumes;
import javax.ws.rs.core.MediaType;
import javax.ws.rs.POST;

@POST
@Consumes(MediaType.APPLICATION_JSON)
public void createDepartment(Department entity) {
  //Method implementation goes here…
}
```

> The javax.ws.rs.core.MediaType class defines constants for all media types supported in JAX-RS. To learn more about the MediaType class, visit the API documentation available at http://docs.oracle.com/javaee/7/api/javax/ws/rs/core/MediaType.html.

Annotations for processing HTTP request methods

In general, RESTful web services communicate over HTTP with the standard HTTP verbs (also known as method types) such as GET, PUT, POST, DELETE, HEAD, and OPTIONS. In this section, we will see annotations provided by JAX-RS for enabling a POJO class to process the standard HTTP method types. If you need a quick brush-up on the HTTP method types used by a RESTful system, refer to the *Understanding the HTTP request methods* section in *Chapter 1, Introducing the REST Architectural Style.*

@GET

A RESTful system uses the HTTP GET method type for retrieving the resources referenced in the URI path. The @javax.ws.rs.GET annotation designates a method of a resource class to respond to the HTTP GET requests.

The following code snippet illustrates the use of the @GET annotation to make a method respond to the HTTP GET request type. In this example, the REST URI for accessing the findAllDepartments() method may look like /departments. The complete URI path may take the following URI pattern: http:// host:port/<context-root>/<application-path>/departments.

```
//imports removed for brevity
@Path("departments")
public class DepartmentService {
  @GET
  @Produces(MediaType.APPLICATION_JSON)
  public List<Department> findAllDepartments() {
    //Find all departments from the data store
    List<Department> departments = findAllDepartmentsFromDB();
    return departments;
  }
  //Other methods removed for brevity
}
```

@PUT

The HTTP PUT method is used for updating or creating the resource pointed by the URI. The @javax.ws.rs.PUT annotation designates a method of a resource class to respond to the HTTP PUT requests. The PUT request generally has a message body carrying the payload. The value of the payload could be any valid Internet media type such as the JSON object, XML structure, plain text, HTML content, or binary stream. When a request reaches a server, the framework intercepts the request and directs it to the appropriate method that matches the URI path and the HTTP method type. The request payload will be mapped to the method parameter as appropriate by the framework.

The following code snippet shows how you can use the @PUT annotation to designate the editDepartment() method to respond to the HTTP PUT request. The payload present in the message body will be converted and copied to the department parameter by the framework:

```
@PUT
@Path("{id}")
@Consumes(MediaType.APPLICATION_JSON)
public void editDepartment(@PathParam("id") Short id,
  Department department) {
```

```
    //Updates department entity to data store
    updateDepartmentEntity(id, department);
}
```

@POST

The HTTP `POST` method posts data to the server. Typically, this method type is used for creating a resource. The `@javax.ws.rs.POST` annotation designates a method of a resource class to respond to the HTTP `POST` requests.

The following code snippet shows how you can use the `@POST` annotation to designate the `createDepartment()` method to respond to the HTTP `POST` request. The payload present in the message body will be converted and copied to the `department` parameter by the framework:

```
@POST
public void createDepartment(Department department) {
    //Create department entity in data store
    createDepartmentEntity(department);
}
```

@DELETE

The HTTP `DELETE` method deletes the resource pointed by the URI. The `@javax.ws.rs.DELETE` annotation designates a method of a resource class to respond to the HTTP `DELETE` requests.

The following code snippet shows how you can use the `@DELETE` annotation to designate the `removeDepartment()` method to respond to the HTTP `DELETE` request. The department ID is passed as the path variable in this example.

```
@DELETE
@Path("{id}")
public void removeDepartment(@PathParam("id") Short id) {
    //remove department entity from data store
    removeDepartmentEntity(id);
}
```

@HEAD

The `@javax.ws.rs.HEAD` annotation designates a method to respond to the HTTP `HEAD` requests. The `HEAD` method is the same as the `GET` request, but it only transfers the status line along with the header section (without the response body) to the client. This method is useful for retrieving the metadata present in the response headers, without having to retrieve the message body from the server. You can use this method to check whether a URI pointing to a resource is active or to check the content size by using the `Content-Length` response header field, and so on.

The JAX-RS runtime will offer the default implementations for the HEAD method type if the REST resource is missing explicit implementation. The default implementation provided by runtime for the HEAD method will call the method designated for the GET request type, ignoring the response entity retuned by the method.

@OPTIONS

The @javax.ws.rs.OPTIONS annotation designates a method to respond to the HTTP OPTIONS requests. This method is useful for obtaining a list of HTTP methods allowed on a resource.

The JAX-RS runtime will offer a default implementation for the OPTIONS method type, if the REST resource is missing an explicit implementation. The default implementation offered by the runtime sets the Allow response header to all the HTTP method types supported by the resource.

> The JAX-RS annotations that we discussed in this section are the very commonly used APIs for building a typical RESTful web service application. If you want to try out a simple JAX-RS application at this moment, you can jump to the *Building your first RESTful web service with JAX-RS* section. Later, you can come back and finish reading the rest of the topics discussed in this chapter.

Annotations for accessing request parameters

In addition to the parameters mentioned in the previous section, JAX-RS offers annotations to pull information out of a request. You can use this offering to extract the following parameters from a request: a query, URI path, form, cookie, header, and matrix. Mostly, these parameters are used in conjunction with the GET, POST, PUT, and DELETE methods.

@PathParam

A URI path template, in general, has a URI part pointing to the resource. It can also take the path variables embedded in the syntax; this facility is used by clients to pass parameters to the REST APIs as appropriate. The @javax.ws.rs.PathParam annotation injects (or binds) the value of the matching path parameter present in the URI path template into a class field, a resource class bean property (the getter method for accessing the attribute), or a method parameter. Typically, this annotation is used in conjunction with the HTTP method type annotations such as @GET, @POST, @PUT, and @DELETE.

The following example illustrates the use of the @PathParam annotation to read the value of the path parameter, id, into the deptId method parameter. The URI path template for this example looks like /departments/{id}:

```
//Other imports removed for brevity
javax.ws.rs.PathParam

@Path("departments")
public class DepartmentService {
   @DELETE
   @Path("{id}")
   public void removeDepartment(@PathParam("id") Short deptId) {
      removeDepartmentEntity(deptId);
   }
   //Other methods removed for brevity
}
```

The REST API call to remove the department resource identified by id=10 looks like DELETE /departments/10 HTTP/1.1.

We can also use multiple variables in a URI path template. For example, we can have the URI path template embedding the path variables to query a list of departments from a specific city and country, which may look like /departments/{country}/ {city}. The following code snippet illustrates the use of @PathParam to extract variable values from the preceding URI path template:

```
@Produces(MediaType.APPLICATION_JSON)
@Path("{country}/{city}")
public List<Department> findAllDepartments(
  @PathParam("country")
String countyCode,    @PathParam("city") String cityCode) {
  //Find all departments from the data store for a country
  //and city
  List<Department> departments =
    findAllMatchingDepartmentEntities(countyCode,
      cityCode );
   return departments;
}
```

@QueryParam

The @javax.ws.rs.QueryParam annotation injects the value(s) of a HTTP query parameter into a class field, a resource class bean property (the getter method for accessing the attribute), or a method parameter.

The following example illustrates the use of @QueryParam to extract the value of the desired query parameter present in the URI. This example extracts the value of the query parameter, name, from the request URI and copies the value into the deptName method parameter. The URI that accesses the IT department resource looks like /departments?name=IT:

```
@GET
@Produces(MediaType.APPLICATION_JSON)
public List<Department>
  findAllDepartmentsByName(@QueryParam("name") String deptName) {
    List<Department> depts= findAllMatchingDepartmentEntities
        (deptName);
  return depts;
}
```

@MatrixParam

Matrix parameters are another way of defining parameters in the URI path template. The matrix parameters take the form of name-value pairs in the URI path, where each pair is preceded by semicolon (;). For instance, the URI path that uses a matrix parameter to list all departments in Bangalore city looks like /departments;city=Bangalore.

The @javax.ws.rs.MatrixParam annotation injects the matrix parameter value into a class field, a resource class bean property (the getter method for accessing the attribute), or a method parameter.

The following code snippet demonstrates the use of the @MatrixParam annotation to extract the matrix parameters present in the request. The URI path used in this example looks like /departments;name=IT;city=Bangalore.

```
@GET
@Produces(MediaType.APPLICATION_JSON)
@Path("matrix")
public List<Department>
  findAllDepartmentsByNameWithMatrix(@MatrixParam("name") String
    deptName, @MatrixParam("city") String locationCode) {
  List<Department> depts=findAllDepartmentsFromDB(deptName,
    city);
  return depts;
}
```

You can use `PathParam`, `QueryParam`, and `MatrixParam` to pass the desired search parameters to the REST APIs. Now, you may ask, when to use what?

Although there are no strict rules here, a very common practice followed by many is to use `PathParam` to drill down to the entity class hierarchy. For example, you may use the URI of the following form to identify an employee working in a specific department: `/departments/{dept}/employees/{id}`.

`QueryParam` can be used for specifying attributes to locate the instance of a class. For example, you may use URI with `QueryParam` to identify employees who have joined on January 1, 2015, which may look like `/employees?doj=2015-01-01`.

The `MatrixParam` annotation is not used frequently. This is useful when you need to make a complex REST style query to multiple levels of resources and subresources. `MatrixParam` is applicable to a particular path element, while the query parameter is applicable to the entire request.

@HeaderParam

The HTTP header fields provide necessary information about the request and response contents in HTTP. For example, the header field, `Content-Length: 348`, for an HTTP request says that the size of the request body content is 348 octets (8-bit bytes). The `@javax.ws.rs.HeaderParam` annotation injects the header values present in the request into a class field, a resource class bean property (the getter method for accessing the attribute), or a method parameter.

The following example extracts the `referer` header parameter and logs it for audit purposes. The `referer` header field in HTTP contains the address of the previous web page from which a request to the currently processed page originated:

```
@POST
public void createDepartment(@HeaderParam("Referer")
String referer,  Department entity) {
  logSource(referer);
  createDepartmentInDB(department);
}
```

Remember that HTTP provides a very wide selection of headers
that cover most of the header parameters that you are looking
for. Although you can use custom HTTP headers to pass some
application-specific data to the server, try using standard headers
whenever possible. Further, avoid using a custom header for
holding properties specific to a resource, or the state of the
resource, or parameters directly affecting the resource. For such
scenarios, you can consider the other approaches discussed in this
section, namely `PathParam`, `QueryParam`, or `MatrixParam`.

@CookieParam

The `@javax.ws.rs.CookieParam` annotation injects the matching cookie parameters
present in the HTTP headers into a class field, a resource class bean property (the
getter method for accessing the attribute), or a method parameter.

The following code snippet uses the `Default-Dept` cookie parameter present in the
request to return the default department details:

```
@GET
@Path("cook")
@Produces(MediaType.APPLICATION_JSON)
public Department getDefaultDepartment(@CookieParam("Default-Dept")
  short departmentId) {
  Department dept=findDepartmentById(departmentId);
  return dept;
}
```

@FormParam

The `@javax.ws.rs.FormParam` annotation injects the matching HTML form
parameters present in the request body into a class field, a resource class bean
property (the getter method for accessing the attribute), or a method parameter.
The request body carrying the form elements must have the content type specified
as `application/x-www-form-urlencoded`.

Consider the following HTML form that contains the data capture form for a
department entity. This form allows the user to enter the department entity details:

```
<!DOCTYPE html>
<html>
  <head>
  <title>Create Department</title>
  </head>
  <body>
    <form method="POST" action="/resources/departments">
```

```
Department Id:
<input type="text" name="departmentId">
<br>
Department Name:
  <input type="text" name="departmentName">
  <br>
  <input type="submit" value="Add Department" />
</form>
</body>
</html>
```

Upon clicking on the `submit` button on the HTML form, the department details that you entered will be posted to the REST URI, `/resources/departments`. The following code snippet shows the use of the `@FormParam` annotation for extracting the HTML form fields and copying them to the resource class method parameter:

```
@Path("departments")
public class DepartmentService {

  @POST
  //Specifies content type as
  //"application/x-www-form-urlencoded"
  @Consumes(MediaType.APPLICATION_FORM_URLENCODED)
  public void createDepartment(@FormParam("departmentId") short
    departmentId,
      @FormParam("departmentName") String departmentName) {
      createDepartmentEntity(departmentId, departmentName);
  }
}
```

@DefaultValue

The `@javax.ws.rs.DefaultValue` annotation specifies a default value for the request parameters accessed using one of the following annotations: `PathParam`, `QueryParam`, `MatrixParam`, `CookieParam`, `FormParam`, or `HeaderParam`. The default value is used if no matching parameter value is found for the variables annotated using one of the preceding annotations.

The following REST resource method will make use of the default value set for the `from` and `to` method parameters if the corresponding query parameters are found missing in the URI path:

```
@GET
@Produces(MediaType.APPLICATION_JSON)
public List<Department> findAllDepartmentsInRange
  (@DefaultValue("0")  @QueryParam("from") Integer from,
```

```
        @DefaultValue("100")   @QueryParam("to") Integer to) {
        findAllDepartmentEntitiesInRange(from, to);
}
```

@Context

The JAX-RS runtime offers different context objects, which can be used for accessing information associated with the resource class, operating environment, and so on. You may find various context objects that hold information associated with the URI path, request, HTTP header, security, and so on. Some of these context objects also provide the utility methods for dealing with the request and response content. JAX-RS allows you to reference the desired context objects in the code via dependency injection. JAX-RS provides the @javax.ws.rs.Context annotation that injects the matching context object into the target field. You can specify the @Context annotation on a class field, a resource class bean property (the getter method for accessing the attribute), or a method parameter.

The following example illustrates the use of the @Context annotation to inject the javax.ws.rs.core.UriInfo context object into a method variable. The UriInfo instance provides access to the application and request URI information. This example uses UriInfo to read the query parameter present in the request URI path template, /departments/name=IT:

```
@GET
@Produces(MediaType.APPLICATION_JSON)
public List<Department> findAllDepartmentsByName(
  @Context UriInfo  uriInfo){
  String deptName =
    uriInfo.getPathParameters().getFirst("name");
  List<Department> depts= findAllMatchingDepartmentEntities
    (deptName);
  return depts;
}
```

Here is a list of the commonly used classes and interfaces, which can be injected using the @Context annotation:

- javax.ws.rs.core.Application: This class defines the components of a JAX-RS application and supplies additional metadata

- javax.ws.rs.core.UriInfo: This interface provides access to the application and request URI information

- javax.ws.rs.core.Request: This interface provides a method for request processing such as reading the method type and precondition evaluation

- `javax.ws.rs.core.HttpHeaders`: This interface provides access to the HTTP header information

- `javax.ws.rs.core.SecurityContext`: This interface provides access to security-related information

- `javax.ws.rs.ext.Providers`: This interface offers the runtime lookup of a provider instance such as `MessageBodyReader`, `MessageBodyWriter`, `ExceptionMapper`, and `ContextResolver`

- `javax.ws.rs.ext.ContextResolver<T>`: This interface supplies the requested context to the resource classes and other providers

- `javax.servlet.http.HttpServletRequest`: This interface provides the client request information for a servlet

- `javax.servlet.http.HttpServletResponse`: This interface is used for sending a response to a client

- `javax.servlet.ServletContext`: This interface provides methods for a servlet to communicate with its servlet container

- `javax.servlet.ServletConfig`: This interface carries the servlet configuration parameters

@BeanParam

The `@javax.ws.rs.BeanParam` annotation allows you to inject all matching request parameters into a single bean object. The `@BeanParam` annotation can be set on a class field, a resource class bean property (the getter method for accessing the attribute), or a method parameter. The bean class can have fields or properties annotated with one of the request parameter annotations, namely `@PathParam`, `@QueryParam`, `@MatrixParam`, `@HeaderParam`, `@CookieParam`, or `@FormParam`. Apart from the request parameter annotations, the bean can have the `@Context` annotation if there is a need.

Consider the example that we discussed for `@FormParam`. The `createDepartment()` method that we used in that example has two parameters annotated with `@FormParam`:

```
public void createDepartment(
  @FormParam("departmentId") short departmentId,
  @FormParam("departmentName") String departmentName)
```

Let's see how we can use `@BeanParam` for the preceding method to give a more logical, meaningful signature by grouping all the related fields into an aggregator class, thereby avoiding too many parameters in the method signature.

The `DepartmentBean` class that we use for this example is as follows:

```
public class DepartmentBean {

  @FormParam("departmentId")
    private short departmentId;

  @FormParam("departmentName")
    private String departmentName;

  //getter and setter for the above fields
  //are not shown here to save space
}
```

The following code snippet demonstrates the use of the `@BeanParam` annotation to inject the `DepartmentBean` instance that contains all the `FormParam` values extracted from the request message body:

```
@POST
public void createDepartment(@BeanParam DepartmentBean deptBean)
{
  createDepartmentEntity(deptBean.getDepartmentId(),
    deptBean.getDepartmentName());
}
```

@Encoded

By default, the JAX-RS runtime decodes all request parameters before injecting the extracted values into the target variables annotated with one of the following annotations: `@FormParam`, `@PathParam`, `@MatrixParam`, or `@QueryParam`. You can use `@javax.ws.rs.Encoded` to disable the automatic decoding of the parameter values. With the `@Encoded` annotation, the value of parameters will be provided in the encoded form itself. This annotation can be used on a class, method, or parameters. If you set this annotation on a method, it will disable decoding for all parameters defined for this method. You can use this annotation on a class to disable decoding for all parameters of all methods. In the following example, the value of the path parameter called `name` is injected into the method parameter in the URL encoded form (without decoding). The method implementation should take care of the decoding of the values in such cases:

```
@GET
@Produces(MediaType.APPLICATION_JSON)
public List<Department>
  findAllDepartmentsByName(@QueryParam("name") String deptName) {
  //Method body is removed for brevity
}
```

URL encoding converts a string into a valid URL format, which may contain alphabetic characters, numerals, and some special characters supported in the URL string. To learn about the URL specification, visit `http://www.w3.org/Addressing/URL/url-spec.html`.

Returning additional metadata with responses

We discussed a few examples in the previous section for retrieving resources via the HTTP GET request. The resource class implementations that we used in these examples were simply returning the plain Java constructs in response to the method call. What if you want to return extra metadata, such as the `Cache-Control` header or the status code, along with the result (resource representation)?

JAX-RS allows you to return additional metadata via the `javax.ws.rs.core.Response` class that wraps the entity and additional metadata such as the HTTP headers, HTTP cookie, and status code. You can create a `Response` instance by using `javax.ws.rs.core.Response.ResponseBuilder` as a factory. The following example demonstrates the use of the `Response` class to return the response content along with the additional HTTP header fields:

```java
//Other imports removed for brevity
import javax.ws.rs.core.CacheControl;
import javax.ws.rs.core.Response;
import javax.ws.rs.core.Response.ResponseBuilder;

@GET
@Produces(MediaType.APPLICATION_JSON)
public Response findAllDepartmentsByName(@QueryParam("name")
  String deptName) {
  List<Department> depts= findAllMatchingDepartmentEntities
    (deptName);
  //Sets cache control directive to the response
  CacheControl cacheControl = new CacheControl();
  //Cache the result for a day
  cacheControl.setMaxAge(86400);
  return Response.ok().
    cacheControl(cacheControl).entity(depts).build();
}
```

Understanding data binding rules in JAX-RS

While injecting variable values from the URI path and the query parameter into the resource class or mapping the request-response entity body with the Java types, the JAX-RS runtime follows certain rules for the Java types present in the resource class. We will discuss this topic in this section.

Mapping the path variable with Java types

At runtime, the framework automatically detects and copies the parameter values present in the inbound request into the appropriate Java types on the basis of the following rules:

JAX-RS allows you to use `@QueryParam` and `@PathParam` on the following Java types:

- All primitive types such as `short`, `int`, `float`, `double`, and `Boolean`, except `char`.

- All the wrapper classes of primitive types, such as `short`, `integer`, `BigDecimal`, and `Boolean`, except `char`.

- All classes with a constructor that accepts a single string type argument. In this case, you can define your own class with a single string type constructor and use it as a method parameter or member variable with an appropriate annotation for reading the parameter value.

- Any class with the static method named `valueOf(String)` that accepts a single string argument.

- If the parameters contain more than one value for the same name, you can have `java.util.List<T>`, `java.util.Set<T>`, or `java.util.SortedSet<T>` as the Java variable type at the receiving end, where `T` represents the types that satisfy the first two criteria that we defined.

It would be interesting to see how the framework initializes the Java class types when there are no matching request parameters found. The following outcomes will occur if there is no matching value found in the request URI for a Java variable type and `@DefaultValue` is not defined:

- All primitive Java types follow the default value rules set for the primitive types in Java, which are listed at `http://docs.oracle.com/javase/tutorial/java/nutsandbolts/datatypes.html`

- All Java objects will be set to null

- `List`, `set`, or `SortedSet` will have a corresponding empty collection instance

Now, let's see how the mapping is done between the request-response body content and Java types.

Mapping the request and response entity body with Java types

JAX-RS uses `javax.ws.rs.ext.MessageBodyReader` for mapping the HTTP request entity body to an appropriate Java type. On the other hand, `javax.ws.rs.ext.MessageBodyWriter` is used for mapping the Java type returned by a resource class method to the appropriate HTTP response entity body representation, such as JSON, XML, and text. The `MessageBodyReader` and `MessageBodyWriter` implementations will raise `javax.ws.rs.WebApplicationException` if they do not know how to convert the input data.

JAX-RS offers the default content handlers (entity providers) for all common data types. Here is a list of the Java types supported by JAX-RS by default:

- JAX-RS supports mapping between the following Java data types and request-response entity bodies for all media forms: `byte[]`, `java.lang.String`, `java.io.InputStream`, `java.io.Reader`, `java.io.File`, `javax.activation.DataSource`, and `javax.xml.transform.Source`

- JAX-RS supports the `javax.ws.rs.core.MultivaluedMap<K,V>` type for reading or writing the form content, whose media type is `application/x-www-form-urlencoded`

- JAX-RS supports the `javax.xml.bind.JAXBElement` type for reading or writing contents represented using the XML media types (`text/xml`, `application/xml`, and `application/*+xml`)

- JAX-RS supports the `java.lang.Boolean`, `java.lang.Character`, and `java.lang.Number` types for reading and writing the Boolean strings (`true` or `false`), characters, and numerical content presented in the `text/plain` media type

Using JAXB to manage the mapping of the request and response entity body to Java objects

If you want more control on the marshalling and unmarshalling of objects, such as skipping some fields or renaming field names, you can use the **Java Architecture for XML Binding (JAXB)** annotations to indicate this to the runtime. Let's take a quick look at this feature.

JAXB offers annotations that map XML to the Java class and vice versa, letting you work on the Java objects. The default entity provider used by JAX-RS runtime makes use of JAXB annotation to map Java objects to XML or JSON representations. Our discussions in this section are focused on using the JAXB annotation for managing the serialization of Java objects.

Here is a brief description of the commonly used JAXB annotations to control the serialization of Java objects:

- `@javax.xml.bind.annotation.XmlRootElement`: When a top-level class is annotated with the `@XmlRootElement` annotation, the JAX-RS runtime takes care of the serialization of all its instances at runtime.

- `@javax.xml.bind.annotation.XmlAccessorType`: This annotation controls whether the fields or JavaBean properties are serialized by default. It takes the following values:

  - `XmlAccessType.FIELD`: Every non-static, non-transient field will be copied in the XML or JSON representation

  - `XmlAccessType.NONE`: No fields are copied

  - `XmlAccessType.PROPERTY`: Every getter/setter pair will be copied in the XML or JSON representation

  - `XmlAccessType.PUBLIC_MEMBER`: Every public field and the public getter/setter pair will be copied in the XML or JSON representation

- `@javax.xml.bind.XmlElement`: This value maps a JavaBean property to an XML or JSON element derived from the property name

- `@javax.xml.bind.XmlTransient`: This value prevents the mapping of a JavaBean property/type to JSON

Consider the following `Department` object with the JAXB annotation to manage the serialization of contents:

```
//Other imports removed for brevity
import javax.xml.bind.annotation.XmlAccessType;
import javax.xml.bind.annotation.XmlAccessorType;
import javax.xml.bind.annotation.XmlElement;
import javax.xml.bind.annotation.XmlRootElement;
import javax.xml.bind.annotation.XmlTransient;

@XmlRootElement(name="department")
@XmlAccessorType(XmlAccessType.FIELD)
public class Department implements Serializable {
  @XmlElement(name="departmentId")
```

```
    private Short id;
    private String departmentName;
    @XmlTransient
    public List<Employee> employees;
    //Rest of the code removed for brevity
}
```

Let's see how the JAX-RS runtime makes use of the JAXB annotations while serializing results returned by a resource method into the JSON representation:

1. The following resource class method returns the `Department` object in response to a `GET` request, for example, `GET /departments/10 HTTP/1:1`:

    ```
    @GET
    @Path("{id}")
    @Produces(MediaType.APPLICATION_JSON)
    public Department find(@PathParam("id") Short id) {
        return findDepartmentEntity(id);
    }
    ```

2. The JAX-RS runtime deploys entity providers that implement `javax.ws.rs.ext.MessageBodyWriter` to serialize Java objects into an appropriate output stream representation such as JSON or XML. The `MessageBodyWriter` implementation scans through the JAXB annotations defined on the `Department` class and converts values to the JSON data as appropriate.

The sample JSON output produced by the preceding resource class method will look like the following code:

```
{"departmentId":30,
  "departmentName":"HR"}
```

Note that the `List<Employee> employees` field that you see in the `Department` class is not present in the JSON output data because this field is marked as `@XmlTransient` in the class definition. Further, `@XmlElement(name="departmentId")` for the id field causes the provider to rename id to `departmentId` in the JSON representation.

You now have enough information of all the commonly used JAX-RS annotations that you will need for a RESTful web service. Let's move on and build a simple RESTful web service by using JAX-RS to get a real feel of the topics that we have discussed so far in this chapter.

EclipseLink MOXy is the default entity provider used by the Jersey framework for converting the message body content to and from the Java types. The JAX-RS framework allows you to override the default entity provider with the implementation of your choice. The provider that you choose should implement the `javax.ws.rs.ext.MessageBodyReader` interface for converting a stream into a Java type and the `javax.ws.rs.ext.MessageBodyWriter` interface for converting the Java types into a stream. For example, the Jackson framework, discussed in *Chapter 2, Java APIs for JSON Processing*, implements all the necessary contracts set by JAX-RS for binding Java types with the message body content. Your JAX-RS application can automatically discover and register the Jackson entity provider if it is found in the class path. To learn more about various binding providers for Jersey, visit `https://jersey.java.net/documentation/latest/media.html`.

Building your first RESTful web service with JAX-RS

In the earlier sections, we discussed the commonly used annotations and APIs in JAX-RS that one may need to be aware of while building REST APIs with JAX-RS. It is now time for us to put all these theories into practice. In this section, we will build a simple yet complete end-to-end RESTful web service by using JAX-RS.

Setting up the environment

This example uses the following software and tools:

- Java SE Development Kit 8 or newer
- NetBeans IDE 8.0.2 (with Java EE bundle) or newer
- Glassfish Server 4.1 or newer
- Maven 3.2.3 or newer
- Oracle Database Express Edition 11g Release 2 or newer with HR sample database schema
- Oracle Database JDBC Driver (`ojdbc7.jar` or newer)

Detailed instructions for procuring and setting up all the
required tools for running the examples used in this book
are discussed in the *Appendix, Useful Features and Techniques*.

Make sure that your machine has all tools ready before starting with the tutorial.
In this tutorial, we will build a RESTful web service by using the JAX-RS APIs. We
will use Maven as a build tool for our sample application as it does a great job in the
dependency management department for the application and provides a standard
structure for the source code. NetBeans has great support for building Maven-based
applications, and this is one of the reasons for us to choose NetBeans as the IDE for
this exercise.

Once the development environment is set up, you are ready to launch NetBeans IDE
for application development.

Building a simple RESTful web service application using NetBeans IDE

To create a JAX-RS application, perform the following steps:

1. Launch NetBeans IDE.
2. In the main toolbar, navigate to **File | New Project**.
3. On the **New Project** dialog screen, navigate to **Maven | Web Application** for
    building the RESTful web service. Proceed to the next screen by clicking on
    the **Next** button.
4. In the **Name and Location** screen, enter **Project Name**, **Project Location**
    (for storing the source), **Group Id**, **Version** (for the Maven project), and
    Package (for the Java source files) as follows:
    -   **Project Name**: `rest-chapter3-service`
    -   **Group Id**: `com.packtpub`
    -   **Package**: `com.packtpub.rest.ch3.service`

Refer to the following screenshot for the values used for this example:

If you are not familiar with Maven, enter the same values as you see in the preceding screenshot to save time and avoid getting the focus diverted. Otherwise, there is nothing preventing you from having your own values for any of the fields that you see in the wizard. After setting all values, click on **Next** to continue to the **Settings** screen in the wizard.

5. On the **Settings** screen, select **GlassFish Server** that you have installed along with NetBeans IDE as **Server** for running your JAX-RS application, and then click on **Java EE 7 Web** as the Java EE version for the application that you build.

6. The server list on this screen may appear empty if you have not configured any server for the IDE yet. To add a new server reference, perform the following steps:

    1. Click on the **Add** button. In the **Add Server Instance** wizard, choose GlassFish as the server and click on **Next** to continue the wizard.

    2. Set **Server Location** to the folder where you installed GlassFish. Select **Local Domain** and click on **Next** to continue the wizard.

3. On the **Domain Name** screen, enter `domain1` in the **Domain** field (which is the default one) and `localhost` in the **Host** field. Click on **Finish** to complete the server creation.

4. Now, IDE will take you back to the **Setting** screen once again where you can choose GlassFish (that you have added in the previous step) as the server and Java EE 7 Web as the Java EE version.

7. You can now click on the **Finish** button to finish the project configuration wizard. NetBeans will now set up a Maven-based web project for you as shown in the following screenshot:

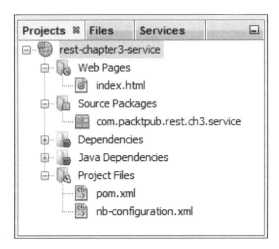

8. The next step is to build a simple RESTful web service implementation by using a POJO class to get a feel of the JAX-RS APIs.

   To build a POJO class, you can right-click on the project and navigate to **New** | **Java Class** in the menu. In the **New Java Class** editor, enter `DepartmentService` in the **Class Name** field and enter `com.packtpub.rest.ch3.service` in the **Package** field. This class will contain the service implementation for this example.

9. We will add `@Path("departments")` to this class so that `DepartmentService` becomes a REST resource class and responds to the REST API calls with the URI path fragment `\departments`. Let's add a simple `helloWorld()` method to this class and add `@Path("hello")` to this method. Add the `@GET` annotation to designate this method to respond to the HTTP GET methods. The `DepartmentService` class now looks like the following:

```
package com.packtpub.rest.ch3.service;
import javax.ws.rs.GET;
```

```
import javax.ws.rs.Path;
import javax.ws.rs.Produces;
import javax.ws.rs.core.MediaType;

@Path("departments")
public class DepartmentService{
  @GET
  @Path("hello")
  @Produces(MediaType.APPLICATION_JSON)
  public String helloWorld(){
    return "Hello world";
  }
}
```

10. To configure resources, add a REST configurations class, which extends
    `javax.ws.rs.core.Application`. This class defines the components
    of a JAX-RS application and supplies additional metadata, if any. The
    configuration class looks like the following:

```
package com.packtpub.rest.ch3.jaxrs.service;

import java.util.Set;
import javax.ws.rs.core.Application;

@javax.ws.rs.ApplicationPath("webresources")
public class RestAppConfig extends Application {
// Get a set of root resource and provider classes.
  @Override
  public Set<Class<?>> getClasses() {
    Set<Class<?>> resources =
      new java.util.HashSet<>();
    resources.add(com.packtpub.rest.ch3.service.
      DepartmentService.class);
    return resources;
  }
}
```

Specifying application path

The `@javax.ws.rs.ApplicationPath` annotation
that you see in the preceding code snippet identifies the
application path that serves as the base URI for all the
resources defined in this application.

Alternatively, you can define the application path in `web.xml`. However, to keep things simple, we will not use `web.xml` for configuring resources in this example.

To learn more about configuring JAX-RS applications, refer to the *Packaging and deploying JAX-RS applications* section, in the *Appendix*, *Useful Features and Techniques*, of this book. With this step, we have finished building a very simple JAX-RS RESTful web service.

11. To deploy and run the RESTful web service application, you can right-click on the `rest-chapter3-service` project and click on **Run**. This will build and deploy the application to the GlassFish server integrated with NetBeans IDE.

12. To test the desired REST API, right-click on the appropriate HTTP methods, as shown in the following screenshot, and select **Test Resource Uri**. This action will open up the default browser with the response content returned by the REST call. The URI for accessing the `helloWorld` RESTful web API will look like `http://localhost:8080/rest-chapter3-service/webresources/departments/hello`.

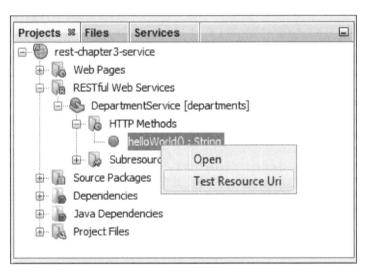

Adding CRUD operations on the REST resource class

In the previous section, we built a very basic RESTful web API by using JAX-RS. In this section, we will enhance this example by introducing more realistic real-life use cases. We will add a department model class to the application and then, introduce the REST APIs to perform the CRUD operations on the `department` object.

We will use the `DEPARTMENT` table from the HR database schema as the data source for this example. This example uses **Java Persistence API (JPA)** for mapping the database table with the Java objects. JPA is a specification for the persistence of the Java objects to any relational data store. If you are not familiar with JPA, read the official documentation available at `https://docs.oracle.com/javaee/7/tutorial/persistence-intro.htm`.

 The Oracle Database XE database comes with a sample database schema user named `HR`. We will use this schema for building most of the examples in this book. To learn more about the HR sample schema in Oracle XE, visit `https://docs.oracle.com/cd/E17781_01/admin.112/e18585/toc.htm`.

Here are the detailed steps for building a model for the project:

1. Open the `rest-chapter3-service` project that we built in the previous section in NetBeans IDE (if it is not opened).

2. Add a `department` JPA entity class to the project. To do this, right-click on the `rest-chapter3-service` project opened in the **Projects** pane, and then, navigate to **New | Entity Classes from Database** from the menu.

3. On the **Database Table** screen, you can choose a data source to which your application wants to connect. We will use the HR schema for this example. If you have not yet created the data source for connecting to the HR database schema, perform the following steps:

    1. To connect to the HR database schema, click on the **Data Source** drop-down list and select the **New Data Source** option.

    2. In the **Create Data Source** dialog, enter the **JNDI** field (for example, `HRDS`), and then, select **New Database Connection** from the **Database Connection** drop-down list. You will see a **New Connection** wizard window now. In the **Locate Driver** screen, click on the **Oracle Thin** driver, and then, add the path to the folder where you have downloaded `ojdbc7.jar`. Click on **Next** to continue with the wizard.

3. On the **Customize Connection** screen, enter the connection details to connect to your local Oracle XE instance (or any Oracle database, which has the HR schema). This is shown in the following screenshot. The parameter that you enter on this screen depends on your Oracle database settings. Click on the **Finish** button to create the connection. Once the connection is created, the wizard will take you back to the **Database Tables** screen.

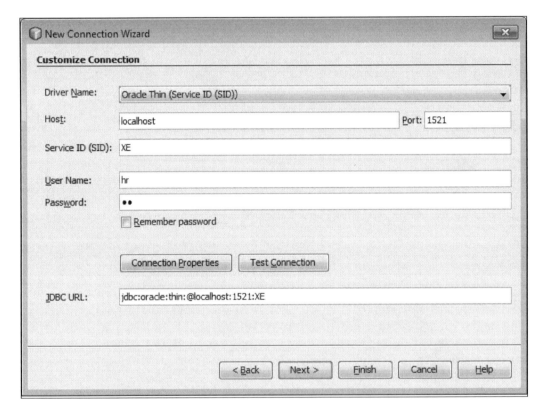

4. On the **Database Tables** screen, choose the data source that you have created for connecting to the HR database schema (for example, HRDS). Uncheck the **Include Related Tables** checkbox as we want to generate the model only for the DEPARTMENTS table for this project. Select the DEPARTMENTS table and shuttle it to the right. Click on **Next** to generate the entity class for the selected table.

4. On the **Entity Classes** creation screen, change the package to com.packtpub. rest.ch3.model and leave all other default values as is; then, click on **Next** to continue.

5. On the **Mapping Options** screen, check **Generate Fields for Unresolved Relationships** and click on **Finish** to generate the entity class and standard JPA configuration files such as the `persistence.xml` file. IDE now has `Departments.java` and `persistence.xml`:

    ° `Departments.java`: This file is a JPA entity class mapped to the `DEPARTMENTS` table.

    ° `persistence.xml`: This file is a standard configuration file in JPA. It is located in the `META-INF` folder of the project source.

6. In this part of the tutorial, we will convert the `DepartmentService` POJO class that we created in the first part to a stateless session bean by annotating it with the `@javax.ejb.Stateless` annotation. A stateless session bean (being an Enterprise JavaBean) offers declarative security, container-managed transactions, and instance-pooling capabilities. Next, add a method that returns a list of departments queried from the `DEPARTMENTS` table by using JPA. With the introduction of the JPA entity in the `DepartmentService` class, we will need the `javax.persistence.EntityManager` instance to manage the entities. You can use the `@PersistenceContext` annotation to inject the `EntityManager` instance into the stateless session bean. As the last step in this exercise, you should define methods that use the standard JPA APIs to perform the CRUD operations on the `Departments` entity and expose them as the REST APIs. The implementation of `DepartmentService` now looks like the following:

```
package com.packtpub.rest.ch3.service;

import com.packtpub.rest.ch3.model.Departments;
import java.util.List;
import javax.ejb.Stateless;
import javax.persistence.EntityManager;
import javax.persistence.PersistenceContext;
import javax.ws.rs.GET;
import javax.ws.rs.Path;
import javax.ws.rs.Produces;
import javax.ws.rs.core.MediaType;

@Path("departments")
@Stateless
public class DepartmentService {
//Inject EntityManager instance
  @PersistenceContext(unitName =
    "com.packtpub_rest-chapter3-service_war_1.0-
      SNAPSHOTPU")
  private EntityManager entityManager;
  //Method that responds to HTTP GET request
```

```
//Returns list of departments
@GET
@Produces(MediaType.APPLICATION_JSON)
public List<Departments> findAllDepartments() {
  //Find all departments from the data store
  javax.persistence.criteria.CriteriaQuery cq =
    entityManager.getCriteriaBuilder()
      .createQuery();
  cq.select(cq.from(Departments.class));
  List<Departments> departments =
    entityManager.createQuery(cq).getResultList();
  return departments;
}

//Method that responds to HTTP POST request
//Creates a new department object
@POST
@Consumes(MediaType.APPLICATION_JSON)
public void createDepartment(Departments entity) {
  entityManager.persist(entity);
}

//Method that responds to HTTP PUT request
//Modifies the department identified by 'id' path param
@PUT
  @Path("{id}")
@Consumes(MediaType.APPLICATION_JSON)
public void editDepartment(@PathParam("id") Short id,
  Departments entity) {
  entityManager.merge(entity);
}

//Method that responds to HTTP DELETE request
//Removes the department identified by 'id' path param
@DELETE
@Path("{id}")
public void removeDepartment(@PathParam("id") Short id)
{

  Departments entity =
    entityManager.find(Departments.class,
      id);
  entityManager.remove(entityManager.merge(entity));

}

}
```

Wow… congratulations! You are done with the implementation.

To deploy and run the web application, you can right-click on the `rest-chapter3-service` project and click on **Run**. This will build and deploy the application to the integrated GlassFish server.

 The source code for the preceding example is available on the Packt website. You can download the example from the Packt website link mentioned at the beginning of this book, in the *Preface* section.

To test the REST API, you can either build a Java client or use one of the many ready-made REST client testing tools available today in the industry. **Postman**—a REST client—is one of the popular API testing tools, which come as a Google Chrome extension. You can learn more about this tool at `https://www.getpostman.com/`.

The following screenshot demonstrates how you can use the Postman REST client for testing the POST operation on the /departments resource. Similarly, you can use Postman to test the other HTTP methods, such as PUT, DELETE, and GET, on the /departments resource.

The following table will help you to quickly identify the REST URI path for accessing each REST API used in this example. The REST URI paths shown in this table are subject to change on the basis of the actual server name and port used:

HTTP method	Sample URI	REST resource
GET	`http://localhost:8080/rest-chapter3-service/webresources/departments`	`DepartmentService::findAllDepartments()`
POST	`http://localhost:8080/rest-chapter3-service/webresources/departments`	`DepartmentService::createDepartment(Departments)`
PUT	`http://localhost:8080/rest-chapter3-service/webresources/departments/300`	`DepartmentService:: editDepartment(Departments)`
DELETE	`http://localhost:8080/rest-chapter3-service/webresources/departments/30`	`DepartmentService :: removeDepartment(Short)`

We will look at the JAX-RS client APIs for building the REST API client in the next section.

Client APIs for accessing RESTful web services

There are many frameworks available for building a Java client for accessing REST. The JAX-RS specification standardizes the client APIs and provides fluent APIs for interaction with the RESTful web service.

> Fluent APIs allow you to chain method calls to perform the desired operation, which improves the readability of the code. The return value of the called method gives a context for the next call and is terminated through the return of a void. You can learn more about the fluent APIs at `https://en.wikipedia.org/wiki/Fluent_interface`.

Specifying a dependency of the JAX-RS client API

To use the client part of the JAX-RS specification, the client application needs to depend only on the client part of the JAX-RS libraries. If you use the Jersey implementation, the dependency entry in `pom.xml` may look like the following:

```
<dependency>
    <groupId>org.glassfish.jersey.core</groupId>
    <artifactId>jersey-client</artifactId>
    <version>2.17</version><!--sets the correct version -->
</dependency>
```

This is the minimum dependency that the application needs to have for using the Jersey implementation of the JAX-RS client APIs. You need to add additional modules for availing specific runtime features. For instance, to enable the automatic conversion of the response content type (for example, JSON) to a desired Java class at runtime, you need to add a dependency to the `jersey-media-moxy` JAR file as shown here:

```
<dependency>
    <groupId>org.glassfish.jersey.media</groupId>
    <artifactId>jersey-media-moxy</artifactId>
    <version>2.17</version>
</dependency>
```

Calling REST APIs using the JAX-RS client

The JAX-RS client API encapsulates the uniform interface constraint, which is a key constraint of the REST architectural style, and offers many convenient APIs for accessing the web resources. We will start by looking at the JAX-RS client API for reading a simple RESTful web service.

You will use the `javax.ws.rs.client.ClientBuilder` factory class as the entry point to the client API. The `javax.ws.rs.client.Client` instance returned by `ClientBuilder` exposes a set of high-level APIs for accessing the web resources.

Let's now apply our learnings and see how we can access the REST resource identified by the following URI: `http://localhost:8080/rest-chapter3-service/webresources/departments`.

The preceding URI has the following two parts:

- **Base URI**: `http://localhost:8080/rest-chapter3-service/webresources`

- **URI path fragments that identifies REST resource**: `/departments`

We will build `WebTarget` pointing to the base URI as follows:

```
import javax.ws.rs.client.Client;
import javax.ws.rs.client.ClientBuilder;
import javax.ws.rs.client.WebTarget;

Client client = javax.ws.rs.client.ClientBuilder.newClient();
String BASE_URI =
  "http://localhost:8080/rest-chapter3-service/webresources";
//Builds a web resource target pointing to BASE_URI
WebTarget  webTarget = client.target(BASE_URI);
```

You can append `/departments` to the base web target instance in order to complete the URI for the REST API, which returns the JSON representation of the `department` objects. You do this by calling `path(String path)` on the `WebTarget` instance as follows:

```
webTarget.path("departments");
```

This call creates a new `WebTarget` instance by appending the input path to the URI of the current target instance.

Once you have a `WebTarget` instance pointing to a valid REST resource, you can start building a request to the targeted REST API by calling the `request()` method. In the request method, you can specify the desired media types for the response, such as `text/html`, `text/plain`, `text/xml`, and `application/json`.

A resource class method implementation can return resources in different representations such as JSON, XML, and plain text. The client can indicate the content types that are acceptable for response via the HTTP `Accept` request header. The process of agreeing on what content format is used for sending messages between the client and the server is known as **Content Negotiation**.

To learn about the HTTP request headers, refer to `http://www.w3.org/Protocols/rfc2616/rfc2616-sec14.html`.

The `request()` method returns the `javax.ws.rs.client.Invocation.Builder` object, which can be used for building the appropriate innovation handlers. The last step in this process is to invoke the request and get a response.

The following code snippet illustrates all the steps that we discussed so far for calling the REST APIs:

```
Client client = javax.ws.rs.client.ClientBuilder.newClient();
String BASE_URI =
  "http://localhost:8080/rest-chapter3-service/webresources";
WebTarget  webTarget = client.target(BASE_URI);
//Append departments URI path to Base URI
WebTarget resource = webTarget.path("departments");

// Build appropriate request type by specifying the content
// type for the response
Builder builder=resource.
  request(javax.ws.rs.core.MediaType.APPLICATION_JSON);
//Build a GET request invocation
Invocation invocation=builder.buildGet();
//Invoke the request and receive the response in
// specified format type.
GenericType responseType=new GenericType<List<Department>>() { };
List<Department> depts = invocation.invoke(responseType);
```

While calling the `invoke(Class<T> responseType)` method on the `Invocation` object, you can specify the desired response Java type as the input. The runtime will automatically convert the response message content into the desired Java type.

Simplified client APIs for accessing REST APIs

Apart from the preceding approach, you can use a simplified version of the client API available on the `Invocation.Builder` object, such as `head()`, `get()`, `post()`, `update()`, `put()`, or `delete()`, to invoke the appropriate REST API. The following code snippet invokes the HTTP GET method on the `department` resource API in a more simplified way:

```
// Obtain a client reference
Client client = javax.ws.rs.client.ClientBuilder.newClient();
// Bind the target to the REST service
String BASE_URI =
  "http://localhost:8080/rest-chapter3-service/webresources";
WebTarget  resource = client.target(BASE_URI).path("departments");
GenericType responseType=new GenericType<List<Department>>() { };
```

```
// Invoke GET  method on the resource
List<Department> depts =
  resource.request(javax.ws.rs.core.MediaType.APPLICATION_JSON).
    get(responseType);
```

The following code snippet illustrates how you can invoke the PUT method on a REST resource. This example updates the Department resource and posts the modified content to the RESTful web API:

```
departments/{id}. }
//Get the modified department object
Department department = getModifiedDepartment();
String id = department.getDepartmentId();
Client client = javax.ws.rs.client.ClientBuilder.newClient();
String BASE_URI =
  "http://localhost:8080/rest-chapter3-service/webresources";
WebTarget resource = client.target(BASE_URI).path("departments")
  .path(java.text.MessageFormat.format("{0}", new Object[]{id}));
Builder builder =
  resource.request(javax.ws.rs.core.MediaType.APPLICATION_JSON);
//Invoke PUT method on resource to update the contents on server
builder.put( javax.ws.rs.client.Entity.entity(department,
  javax.ws.rs.core.MediaType.APPLICATION_JSON));
```

 NetBeans IDE has a good support for building the RESTful web service client by using the JAX-RS client APIs. To avail this offering, navigate to **File** | **New** | **Web Services** | **RESTful Java Client**, and then, follow the steps in the wizard.

Summary

With the use of annotations, the JAX-RS API provides a simple development model for RESTful web service programming. In this chapter, we covered the frequently used features of the JAX-RS framework and developed a non-trivial RESTful web service to get a feel of the offerings.

In next chapter, we will discuss the advanced features of JAX-RS, such as asynchronous REST APIs, advanced topics on filters and interceptors, validations and error handling, custom message body providers, and custom media types. Take a deep breath and be prepared for a deep dive.

4
Advanced Features in the JAX-RS API

In the previous chapter, we introduced you to JAX-RS APIs for building RESTful web services. This chapter is in continuation of what we discussed in the previous chapter. This chapter will take you further into the JAX-RS APIs, and some complex use cases and their solutions.

The following topics are covered in this chapter:

- Understanding subresources and subresource locators in JAX-RS
- Exception handling in JAX-RS
- Introducing validations in JAX-RS applications
- Supporting custom request-response message formats
- Asynchronous RESTful web services
- Asynchronous RESTful web service client
- Managing the HTTP cache in a RESTful web service
- Understanding filters and interceptors in JAX-RS
- Understanding the JAX-RS resource lifecycle

Discussions on the JAX-RS framework would not be complete without covering the advanced features offered by the framework for building subresources, validations, exception handling, and extensions for handling various message types. Take a deep breath and get ready for a deep dive into the JAX-RS API.

Understanding subresources and subresource locators in JAX-RS

While discussing the JAX-RS APIs in the previous chapter, we covered the resource class and the resource class methods in RESTful web APIs. If you need a quick brush-up on this topic, refer to the *Annotations for defining a RESTful resource* section in *Chapter 3, Introducing the JAX-RS API*. In this section, you will get introduced to two new concepts, namely **subresources** and **subresource** locators in REST. You will find them very useful while designing well-structured RESTful web APIs.

Subresources in JAX-RS

In the previous chapter, we discussed about the @Path annotation that identifies the URI path that a resource class or class method will serve requests for. A class annotated with the @Path annotation (at the class level) is called the **root resource** class. You can also use the @Path annotation on the methods of the root resource classes. If a resource method with the @Path annotation is annotated with the request method designator(s) such as @GET, @POST, @PUT, or @DELETE, it is known as a subresource method.

The concept of subresources is to have a root resource class that resolves a generic URI path and to have the @Path annotated methods in the class to further resolve the request. This helps you to keep the REST resource class implementation more structured and readable.

Let's consider a simple example to understand this topic better. Look at the following code snippet:

```
//imports are omitted for brevity
@Path("hr")
public class HRService {

    @GET
    @Path("departments")
    @Produces(MediaType.APPLICATION_JSON)
    public List<Department> findAllDepartmnets () {

        List<Department> departments =
            findAllDepartmentEntities();
        return departments;
    }

    @GET
```

```
@Path("departments/{id}")
@Produces(MediaType.APPLICATION_JSON)
public Department findDepartment(@PathParam("id") Short id) {

    Department department = findDepartmentEntity(id);
    return department;
}
}
```

When a client calls the HTTP GET method with the following URI: `hr/departments`, the JAX-RS runtime on the server resolves the `hr` portion of the URI first. In this example, the `hr` path fragment resolves to the `HRService` class. Next, it identifies a subresource that matches the remaining part of the URI for the given HTTP request type. This part is resolved to the `findAllDepartmnets()` method. However, if the request URI is `hr/departments/10`, the URI path will be resolved to the `findDepartment()` subresource method.

Subresource locators in JAX-RS

Having discussed subresources, we will now see a subresource locator.

It is perfectly legal to use the `@Path` annotations on methods in a REST resource class without any resource method designators such as `@GET`, `@POST`, `@PUT`, or `@DELETE`. The objects returned by these methods will be used for resolving the incoming HTTP request further. These methods are called as the subresource locators. These locators are useful when requests need to be further resolved dynamically by other objects. This gives you more flexibility in the implementation.

In the following example, `DepartmentResource` is the root resource and the `findManagerForDepartment()` method is a subresource locator method. The `findManagerForDepartment()` method has only the `@Path` annotation in the code snippet. The `EmployeeResource` object returned by this method further resolves the HTTP request:

```
// Imports are omitted for brevity
@Path("departments")
public class DepartmentResource {

    //Sub-resource locator method
    @Path("{id}/manager")
    public EmployeeResource
        findManagerForDepartment(@PathParam("id")
        Short deptId) {
        //Find the department for id
```

```
            Department department = findDepartmentEntity(deptId);
            //Create the instance of Employee object
            //This instance will be used for further resolving request
            EmployeeResource employeeResource = new
                EmployeeResource(department.getManagerId());
            return employeeResource;
        }
    //Other methods are omitted for brevity
    }


    /**
      *This class that defines the subresource used in
      *DepartmentResource
    */
    //imports are omitted for brevity
    public class EmployeeResource{
        Short employeeId;
        public EmployeeResource(Short employeeId){
            this.employeeId=employeeId;
        }
        //Resolves GET request to findEmployee() method
        @GET
        @Produces(MediaType.APPLICATION_JSON)
        public Employee findEmployee(){
            Employee employee = findEmployeeEntity(employeeId);
            return employee;
        }
        //Other methods are omitted for brevity


    }
```

In this example, let's see what happens on the server when client calls the HTTP GET method with the following URI: departments/10/manager.

The JAX-RS runtime on the server resolves the URI part of the HTTP request to the findManagerForDepartment() method defined on the DepartmentResource class. Runtime further resolves the request on the EmployeeResource object returned by the findManagerForDepartment() method and identifies findEmployee() that matches the HTTP request type. The HTTP request will be then dispatched to the findEmployee() method defined on the EmployeeResource instance. In real-life scenarios, a subresource locator method can return different implementations of the subresource class on the basis of various conditions. This makes the implementation more flexible and dynamic.

In the preceding example, you are managing the lifecycle of the subresource by creating an instance of `EmployeeResource` in the code and returning it from the `findManagerForDepartment()` method. You can ask the JAX-RS runtime to manage the subcomponent instance by returning the class instead of an instance as given in the following code:

```
@Path("{id}/manager")
public Class<EmployeeResource>
    findManagerForDepartment(@PathParam("id") Short deptId) {
    return EmployeeResource.class;
}
```

In this case, runtime will manage the initialization of the subresource instance (`EmployeeResource`), including all dependency injections via **Context and Dependency Injection (CDI)**, if any. If you are not familiar with CDI, go through the tutorial available at `http://docs.oracle.com/javaee/7/tutorial/partcdi.htm`.

Exception handling in JAX-RS

Exceptions in Java are a way to tell the client that an abnormal condition has occurred while executing specific statements in the code. In this section, you will see how a REST resource method handles exceptions.

Reporting errors using ResponseBuilder

The `javax.ws.rs.core.Response.ResponseBuilder` class provides easy-to-use utility methods for creating the `javax.ws.rs.core.Response` instance by using a builder pattern. The `Response` instance can hold metadata, such as the HTTP status code, along with the entity body. The REST resource method can return the `Response` object to report back the status of the REST API call to the caller.

For example, the following resource method returns `HTTP 404 Not Found` (represented by the following Enum constant: `Response.Status.NOT_FOUND`) if the `department` entity object is not found in the data store:

```
@DELETE
@Path("departments/{id}")
public Response remove(@PathParam("id") Short id) {
    Department department = entityManager.find(Department.class,
        id);
    if(department == null){
        //Department to be removed is not found in data store
        return Response.status(Response.Status.NOT_FOUND).entity
            ("Entity not found for : " + id).build();
```

```
        }
        entityManager.remove(entityManager.merge(department));
        return  Response.status(Response.Status.OK).build();
    }
```

Although the approach of using the `Response` object for reporting errors back to the caller works for basic use cases, it may not really scale up in real life. With this approach, every resource method in a class should have the `Response` object as the return type. Further, developers may need to catch all exceptions in the resource method and convert them to the `Response` object programmatically. This may eventually result in repetitive coding, silly coding errors, and maintenance issues. JAX-RS addresses this issue by allowing you to directly throw exceptions from the REST resource methods to report errors back to the caller. This model is explained in the next two sections.

Reporting errors using WebApplicationException

The JAX-RS framework provides `javax.ws.rs.WebApplicationException` that you can throw from the JAX-RS resource methods or provider implementations to report exceptions back to the caller. Later, in the request processing cycle, the default exception mapper class deployed by the JAX-RS runtime will intercept the exception thrown by the method and will generate an appropriate HTTP response object. `WebApplicationException` can be created by wrapping the response content, error text, or HTTP status code. As `WebApplicationException` is extended from `RuntimeException`, the methods that throw this exception do not need to have the `throws` clause for `WebApplicationException` in the method signature. When a method throws `WebApplicationException`, the server stops the execution of the request and sends the response created from `WebApplicationException` back to the client. Here is an example:

```
@DELETE
@Path("departments/{id}")
public void removeDepartment(@PathParam("id") Short id) {
    //Read department from data store for id
    Department department = findDepartmentEntity(id);
    //throw exception if department to be deleted is not found
    if(department == null){
        throw new
            WebApplicationException(Response.Status.NOT_FOUND);
    }
    removeDepartmentEntity(department);
}
```

The preceding example throws WebApplicationException with the following HTTP status: 404 Not Found, if the department is not found in the data store. You can use different HTTP status codes, depending upon the use case. The javax. ws.rs.core.Response.Status class holds the commonly used status codes defined by HTTP. We discussed the HTTP status codes and their meaning in the *HTTP status codes* section in *Chapter 1, Introducing the REST Architectural Style*.

There are many exceptions available in JAX-RS, subclassed from javax.ws.rs. WebApplicationException. You can use the most appropriate one in your use case. Some of the exceptions extended from WebApplicationException are as follows: BadRequestException, ForbiddenException, NotAcceptableException, NotAllowedException, NotAuthorizedException, NotFoundException, NotSupportedException, RedirectionException, InternalServerErrorException, and ServiceUnavailableException.

 Refer to the API documentation to learn more about the child exceptions derived from WebApplicationException available at http://docs.oracle.com/javaee/7/api/ javax/ws/rs/WebApplicationException.html.

You can also extend WebApplicationException to hold more meaningful error messages for your application as shown in the following code:

```
import javax.ws.rs.WebApplicationException;
import javax.ws.rs.core.MediaType;
import javax.ws.rs.core.Response;

public class DepartmentNotFoundWebAppException extends
    WebApplicationException {

    /**
     * Generates a HTTP 404 (Not Found) exception.
     */
    public DepartmentNotFoundWebAppException() {
        super(Response.Status.NOT_FOUND);
    }

    /**
     * Generates a HTTP 404 (Not Found) exception.
     * @param message
     */
    public DepartmentNotFoundWebAppException(String message) {
        super(Response.status(Status.NOT_FOUND).
        entity(message).type(MediaType.TEXT_PLAIN).build());
    }
}
```

WebApplicationException is subclassed from RuntimeException. This fits well for handling unexpected exceptions that may occur in the REST API implementation. However, for a typical business application, there may be many modules and certain modules may be reused in a non-REST context as well. So, you cannot live with WebApplicationException (which is automatically handled by the JAX-RS runtime) for all scenarios. The next section discusses the usage of the checked business exception in the JAX-RS application.

Reporting errors using application exceptions

It is recommended to use a checked application exception for recoverable error scenarios. In this section, we will see how a checked exception can be used in a RESTful web API implementation.

Here is a checked business exception definition for use in the JAX-RS resource method:

```
//Business exception class
public class DeprtmentNotFoundBusinessException extends Exception{

    public DeprtmentNotFoundBusinessException(String message) {
        super(message);
    }

    public DeprtmentNotFoundBusinessException(String message,
        Throwable cause) {
        super(message, cause);
    }

    //Rest of the implementation code go here
}
```

The following code snippet uses DeprtmentNotFoundBusinessException for reporting the DepartmentNotFound error to the caller:

```
@DELETE
@Path("departments/{id}")
public void remove(@PathParam("id") Short id) throws
    DeprtmentNotFoundBusinessException {
    //Read department from data store for id
    Department department = findDepartmentEntity(id);
```

```
    // throw exception if department to be deleted is not found
    if(department == null){
        throw new DeprtmentNotFoundBusinessException
            ("Department is missing in store");

    }
    removeDepartmentEntity(department);
}
```

The preceding implementation is simple and easy to follow. However, you may want to perform an additional step to map exceptions to the HTTP response body content. Note that the JAX-RS runtime, by default, does not know how to generate the right response content for the custom application exception thrown by a method. All the unhandled exceptions are handled by the underlying servlet container, which may wrap or swallow your application exception. The solution is to use the exception mapper feature offered by JAX-RS. JAX-RS allows you to deploy a custom exception mapper implementation, which will map the business exception to the appropriate response message. The next section discusses this topic in detail.

Mapping exceptions to a response message using ExceptionMapper

You can use the `javax.ws.rs.ext.ExceptionMapper` class to map the checked or unchecked exceptions to the appropriate HTTP response content. Annotate the custom exception mapper class with `@javax.ws.rs.ext.Provider` for registering it with JAX-RS runtime. At runtime, when an exception is thrown by a method, the JAX-RS runtime will scan through all registered exception mappers to find the best match for handling the exception. If there is no exact match found, runtime considers a mapper class that matches with the parent class of the checked exception class. After identifying the exception mapper class for handling an exception, the framework invokes the `toResponse()` method on the exception mapper instance to generate the appropriate HTTP response content for the exception.

Here is an example for the `ExceptionMapper` class, which creates the HTTP response for `DepartmentNotFoundBusinessException`:

```
import javax.ws.rs.core.Response;
import javax.ws.rs.ext.ExceptionMapper;
import javax.ws.rs.ext.Provider;

@Provider
public class DepartmentNotFoundExceptionMapper implements
```

```
ExceptionMapper<DeprtmentNotFoundBusinessException> {

    // Map an exception to a Response
    @Override
    public Response toResponse(DeprtmentNotFoundBusinessException
        exception) {
        return Response.status(
            Response.Status.NOT_FOUND).
        entity(exception.getMessage()).build();
    }

}
```

When runtime fails to find an exception mapper for the custom exceptions, the exception will be propagated to the underlying container, which will eventually result in `javax.servlet.ServletException`, sending the `HTTP 500` status back to the client.

Introducing validations in JAX-RS applications

Validation is the process of ensuring the completeness and sanity of business data before posting to the underlying data source. Validating the client input is very important for any REST API that you build. In this section, we will see the offering in JAX-RS for validating the client input.

The JAX-RS 2.0 release allows you to validate the resource class and methods via Java **Bean Validation**. This framework is a Java specification, which lets you specify the validation rules on the objects or hierarchy of objects via the built-in annotations; it also lets you write the reusable validation rules for handling various use cases. Bean Validation is integrated into the Java EE platform, allowing developers to easily define and enforce the validation rules across various components that come as a part of Java EE. The following list of the Java EE components supports Bean Validation: `JAX-RS`, `JAXB`, `JPA`, `EJB`, `JSF`, and `CDI`.

The latest release of Bean Validation is Version 1.1, which is based on JSR 349. You can learn more about JSR 349 at `https://www.jcp.org/en/jsr/detail?id=349`.

A brief introduction to Bean Validation

The Bean Validation framework allows you to specify the validation rules in the form of annotations on a field, method, or a Java class. You can either use built-in constraints offered by Bean Validation or build custom constraints by using the extension mechanisms offered by the framework. The following table summarizes the built-in constraints offered by Bean Validation, which are applicable to all data types:

Validation constraints	Supported Java types	Details of the imposed constraints
@NotNull	Applicable to all Java types	The annotated variable must not be `null`.
@Null	Applicable to all Java types	The annotated variable must be `null`.

The following table summarizes the built-in constraints offered by Bean Validation, which are applicable to the Boolean data types:

Validation constraints	Supported Java types	Details of the imposed constraints
@AssertFalse	• `java.lang.Boolean` • `Boolean`	The annotated variable must be `false`.
@AssertTrue	• `java.lang.Boolean` • `Boolean`	The annotated variable must be `true`.

The following table summarizes the built-in constraints offered by Bean Validation, which are applicable to the number data types:

Validation constraints	Supported Java types	Details of the imposed constraints
@DecimalMax	• `java.math.BigDecimal` • `java.math.BigInteger` • `java.lang.String` • `byte, short, int, long,` and their wrapper types	The annotated variable must not exceed the maximum specified limit.
@DecimalMin	• `java.math.BigDecimal` • `java.math.BigInteger` • `java.lang.String` • `byte, short, int, long,` and their wrapper types	The annotated variable must be higher than or equal to the minimum specified value.

Validation constraints	Supported Java types	Details of the imposed constraints
@Digits	• `java.math.BigDecimal` • `java.math.BigInteger` • `java.lang.String` • `byte, short, int, long,` and their wrapper types	The annotated variable must be a number within the acceptable range.
@Max	• `java.math.BigDecimal` • `java.math.BigInteger` • `byte, short, int, long,` and their wrapper types	The annotated variable must be a number with a value less than or equal to the specified maximum value.
@Min	• `java.math.BigDecimal` • `java.math.BigInteger` • `byte, short, int, long,` and their wrapper types	The annotated variable must be a number with a value larger than or equal to the specified minimum value.

The following table summarizes the built-in constraints offered by Bean Validation, which are applicable to the date data types:

Validation constraints	Supported Java types	Details of the imposed constraints
@Future	• `java.util.Date` • `java.util.Calendar`	The annotated variable must be a date in the future.
@Past	• `java.util.Date` • `java.util.Calendar`	The annotated variable must be a date in the past.

The following table summarizes the built-in constraints offered by Bean Validation, which are applicable to the string data types:

Validation constraints	Supported Java types	Details of the imposed constraints
@Pattern	`java.lang.String`	The annotated string must match the regular expression specified.

The following table summarizes the built-in constraints offered by Bean Validation, which are applicable to the collection and string data types:

Validation constraints	Supported Java types	Details of the imposed constraints
@Size	<ul><li>`java.lang.String` (string length is evaluated)</li><li>`jav.util.Collection` (collection size is evaluated)</li><li>`java.util.Map` (map size is evaluated)</li><li>`java.lang.Array` (array length is evaluated)</li></ul>	The annotated string or collection size must be between the specified boundaries (included).

The following code snippet illustrates the use of built-in validation constraints provided by Bean Validation for validating an input to a JAX-RS method call. This example validates the input parameter for a positive number:

```
@GET
@Path("departments/{id}")
@Produces(MediaType.APPLICATION_JSON)
public Department findDepartment(@PathParam("id")
    @Min(value = 0, message = "Department Id must be a
    positive value")
    Short id, @Context Request request) {

    Department department = findDepartmentEntity(id);
    return department;
}
```

Building custom validation constraints

In the previous section, we had a quick look at the built-in validation constraints offered by the Bean Validation framework. There may be cases where you may want to build your own validation constraints. The Bean Validation framework supports that as well.

The core contracts that you should implement for a custom validation constraint are as follows:

- Annotation for the custom validation constraint.
- Implementation of the `javax.validation.ConstraintValidatorContext` interface. This class contains your custom validation logic.
- Definition of a default error message.

Let's build a custom validation constraint for checking whether a department with the same name already exists for a given location. This constraint avoids the duplicate department entities.

The first step is to build an annotation for the custom constraint that you are going to construct. The Bean Validation framework specification demands the following attribute definitions in a constraint annotation:

- `message`: This attribute returns the default key for reading the validation error messages.
- `groups`: This attribute specifies the validation groups to which this constraint belongs to. This is default to an empty array of the `Class<?>` type.
- `payload`: This attribute can be used by clients for assigning custom payload objects to a constraint. This attribute is not used here.

Let's define an annotation for the custom validation constraint, `ValidDepartmentValidator`, which we are going to build next:

```
//Other import statements are omitted for brevity
import java.lang.annotation.ElementType;
import java.lang.annotation.Retention;
import java.lang.annotation.Target;
import java.lang.annotation.RetentionPolicy;
import javax.validation.Constraint;
import javax.validation.Payload;

//@Constraint links a constraint annotation with
//its constraint validation implementations.
@Constraint(validatedBy = {ValidDepartmentValidator.class})
@Target({ElementType.FIELD, ElementType.PARAMETER})
@Retention(value = RetentionPolicy.RUNTIME)
public @interface ValidDepartment {

    //The message key for validation error message
    //fails the validation.
    String message() default
```

```
    "{com.packtpub.rest.validation.deptrule}";
    Class<?>[] groups() default {};
    Class<? extends Payload>[] payload() default {};
}
```

As the next step, we need to provide the implementation for the custom validation constraint called ValidDepartmentValidator. Here is the code snippet:

```
//Other import statements are omitted for brevity
import javax.validation.ConstraintValidator;
import javax.validation.ConstraintValidatorContext;

//Defines the logic to validate the constraint 'ValidDepartment'
//for the object type 'Department'
public class ValidDepartmentValidator implements
    ConstraintValidator<ValidDepartment, Department> {

    @Override
    public void initialize(ValidDepartment constraintAnnotation) {
    }

    @Override
    public boolean isValid(Department department,
        ConstraintValidatorContext context) {
        //Implementation of isDeptExistsForLoc() is not shown here
        //to save space. This method return true if the given
        // department id is found in the database
        if(isDeptExistsForLoc(department.getDepartmentId(),
            department.getDepartmentName(),
            department.getLocationId())) {
            return false;

        }

        return true;
    }
    //Rest of the code goes here

}
```

The last step is to define the error message in a resource bundle in order to localize the validation error messages. This file should be added to the root folder with the following name: ValidationMessages.properties. The file contents may look like the following code:

```
com.packtpub.rest.validation.deptrule= Department already exists
```

This feature lets you localize the validation error messages. For example, `ValidationMessages_fr.properties` contains messages for the French locale. The custom validation constraint for checking a duplicate department entity is ready for use now!

You can apply this constraint on the method parameters or class fields, as shown in the following code snippet:

```
@POST
@Path("departments")
@Consumes(MediaType.APPLICATION_JSON)
public void create(@ValidDepartment Department entity) {
    createDepartmentEntity(entity);
}
```

> To learn more about Bean Validation, visit the following link: `http://beanvalidation.org/`. The official tutorial for Bean Validation is available at `http://docs.oracle.com/javaee/7/tutorial/partbeanvalidation.htm`.

What happens when Bean Validation fails in a JAX-RS application?

The framework throws `javax.validation.ValidationException` or its subclass exceptions, such as `javax.validation.ConstraintViolationException`, when the Bean Validation rules that you set on the model class fails at runtime. The JAX-RS runtime will report the validation error back to the client with a `500` (internal server error) HTTP status code. You can override the default validation exception handling by providing a custom `javax.ws.rs.ext.ExceptionMapper` class. We discussed about `ExceptionMapper` a while ago in the *Mapping exceptions to a response message using ExceptionMapper* section.

Supporting custom request-response message formats

The JAX-RS framework uses entity provider components for the marshalling and unmarshalling of the message body content (entity) present in the response and request objects, respectively. It is the entity provider component that maps an entity with the associated Java types.

The following table lists the default entity mappings provided by the JAX-RS runtime via a set of built-in entity providers. When you use one of the Internet media types present in the following table for representing the request or response entity body, the framework takes care of the conversion and reconversion of the entity body to the associated Java type:

Data types	Internet media type
`byte[]`	`*/*`
`java.lang.String`	`*/*`
`java.io.Reader`	`*/*`
`java.io.File`	`*/*`
`javax.activation.DataSource`	`*/*`
`javax.ws.rs.core.StreamingOutput`	`*/*`
`All primitive types`	`text/plain`
`java.lang.Boolean`	`text/plain`
`java.lang.Character`	`text/plain`
`java.lang.Number`	`text/plain`
`javax.xml.transform.Source`	`text/xml`, `application/xml`, and `application/*+xml`
`javax.xml.bind.JAXBElement`	`text/xml`, `application/xml`, and `application/*+xml`
Application supplied JAXB annotated objects (types annotated with `@XmlRootElement` or `@XmlType`)	`text/xml`, `application/xml`, and `application/*+xml`
`javax.ws.rs.core.MultivaluedMap<String, String>`	`application/x-www-form-urlencoded`

What if you want to build your own media type for representing the message content? Or what if you want to customize the marshalling and unmarshalling process for specific media types?

JAX-RS has a solution for both these use cases. The JAX-RS extension API allows you to handle the request or response message bodies via custom entity providers. You can have custom entity providers configured for an application for serializing the Java type into the appropriate media type. They can also be used for deserializing the message body content present in a request to the appropriate Java types. In this section, we will learn how to use the JAX-RS provider APIs for building custom message handlers.

The JAX-RS providers are application components that offer a way for extending and customizing the runtime behavior. There are mainly three categories of providers: entity provider, context provider, and exception provider. Each JAX-RS provider class must be annotated with the `@javax.ws.rs.ext.Provider` annotation. During deployment, the server scans through the deployment units for the `@Provider` annotations and automatically registers all the identified provider components. You do not need to do any extra configurations or API calls for integrating the provider components.

The JAX-RS extension API offers the following two contracts (interfaces) for managing the marshalling and unmarshalling of the entity body present in the request and response messages:

- `javax.ws.rs.ext.MessageBodyWriter<T>`: This interface provides the contract for the conversion of a Java type to the output stream. The class that implements this interface converts the message payload represented in Java into the one on the Internet media type representation format that is sent over the wire to the client.

- `javax.ws.rs.ext.MessageBodyReader<T>`: This interface provides the contract for the conversion of the input stream to a Java type. The provider class that implements this interface reads the message body representation from the input stream and converts the incoming message body into an appropriate Java type.

Building a custom entity provider

Let's have some fun now! In this section, we will build a custom entity provider for handling the request and response message content represented using the `application/csv` media type. Note that JAX-RS, by default, does not support the CSV media type. The custom entity providers, which we will build in a short while, leverage the runtime extension mechanism offered by JAX-RS via the `MessageBodyWriter` and `MessageBodyReader` interfaces.

Marshalling Java objects to the CSV representation with MessageBodyWriter

The JAX-RS framework uses `MessageBodyWriter` to serialize the Java representation of resources returned by the REST web API into an appropriate format, which is sent back to the client. The JAX-RS runtime natively supports the serialization of the commonly used Java types, such as `java.lang.String`, `java.io.InputStream`, and Java custom objects annotated with JAXB binding annotations. You can provide your own implementation of `MessageBodyWriter` if you find that the default implementation provided by JAX-RS is not meeting your use case requirements.

A `javax.ws.rs.ext.MessageBodyWriter<T>` provider should implement the following methods:

- `isWriteable()`: This method checks whether this `MessageBodyWriter` implementation supports converting the Java type present in the method argument to the designated Internet media type. This method is invoked when the framework tries to find a `MessageBodyWriter` implementation for serializing the Java objects returned by a resource method to the designated Internet media type.

- `getSize()`: JAX-RS 2.0 deprecated this method, and the value returned by the method is ignored by the JAX-RS runtime. You can return `-1` from this method.

- `writeTo()`: This method writes a Java type object to an HTTP message.

Keep a note of the following points when building a `MessageBodyWriter` implementation:

- A `MessageBodyWriter` provider implementation may be annotated with `@Produces` to restrict the media types for which it will be considered suitable

- A `MessageBodyWriter` provider implementation must be either programmatically registered in the JAX-RS runtime or must be annotated with `@Provider annotation`

 The API documentation for `MessageBodyWriter` is available at `https://docs.oracle.com/javaee/7/api/javax/ws/rs/ext/MessageBodyWriter.html`.

The following example shows how you can build a custom `MessageBodyWriter` implementation that converts a list of the `Department` Java objects into the CSV format:

```java
//Other imports omitted for brevity
import javax.ws.rs.Produces;
import javax.ws.rs.WebApplicationException;
import javax.ws.rs.core.MediaType;
import javax.ws.rs.core.MultivaluedMap;
import javax.ws.rs.ext.MessageBodyWriter;
import javax.ws.rs.ext.Provider;
import org.supercsv.io.CsvBeanWriter;
import org.supercsv.io.ICsvBeanWriter;
import org.supercsv.prefs.CsvPreference;


@Provider
@Produces("application/csv")
public class CSVMessageBodyWriter implements MessageBodyWriter<List<D
epartment>> {

    /**
     * Ascertain if MessageBodyWriter supports
     * a particular type.
     */
    @Override
    public boolean isWriteable(Class<?> type, Type genericType,
        Annotation[] annotations, MediaType mediaType) {
        //Is this MessageBodyWriter implementation capable
        //of serializing the object type returned by
        //the current REST API call?
        return (List.class.isAssignableFrom(type));
    }

    /**
     *Deprecated by JAX-RS 2.0 and ignored by Jersey runtime
     */
    @Override
    public long getSize(List<Department> t, Class<?> type, Type
        genericType, Annotation[] annotations,
            MediaType mediaType) {
        return 0;
    }

    /**
```

```
    * Converts Java to desired media type and Writes it
    * to an HTTP response
    */
   @Override
   public void writeTo(List<Department> dataList, Class<?> type,
       Type genericType, Annotation[] annotations, MediaType
          mediaType, MultivaluedMap<String, Object> httpHeaders,
             OutputStream entityStream) throws IOException,
                WebApplicationException {
      // This class uses CsvBeanWriter for converting
      // Java to CSV. It is an open source framework
      // that writes a CSV file by mapping each field
      // on the bean to a column in the CSV file
      //(using the supplied name mapping).
      ICsvBeanWriter writer = new CsvBeanWriter(
         new PrintWriter(entityStream),
            CsvPreference.STANDARD_PREFERENCE);
      //No data then return
      if (dataList == null || dataList.size() == 0) {
         return;
      }
      //Columns headers in CSV
      String[] nameMapping ={"departmentId","departmentName",
      "managerId","locationId"} ;

      //CsvBeanWriter writes the header with the property names
      writer.writeHeader(nameMapping);
      for (Object p : dataList) {
         //Write each row
         writer.write(p, nameMapping);
      }
      writer.close();
   }
}
```

The following RESTful web service call illustrates a sample output (in the CSV format) generated by the CSVMessageBodyWriter implementation:

```
GET /api/hr/departments HTTP/1.1
Host: localhost:8080
Accept: application/csv

departmentId,departmentName,locationId,managerId
1001,"Finance",1700,101
1002,"Office Administration",1500,205
```

Marshalling CSV representation to Java objects with MessageBodyReader

In the previous section, we discussed how the entity provider supported the marshalling of the Java object to media types. In this section, we will see the entity provider doing the reverse process, unmarshalling of the input stream to the Java types.

The JAX-RS framework uses `MessageBodyReader` to deserialize the message body into the Java type. The JAX-RS runtimes natively supports the deserialization of input stream to the commonly used Java types. You can use the custom `MessageBodyReader` implementation to manage the deserialization of the input stream.

A `javax.ws.rs.ext.MessageBodyReader<T>` provider should implement the following methods and contracts:

- `isReadable()`: This method checks whether the `MessageBodyReader` interface can produce an instance of a particular Java type. This method is invoked when the framework tries to find a matching `MessageBodyReader` interface for reading the input stream into a Java type parameter present in the resource method.
- `readFrom()`: This method reads the input stream into the designated Java type.

Keep a note of the following points when building a `MessageBodyReader` interface:

- A `MessageBodyReader` implementation may be annotated with `@Consumes` to restrict the media types for which it will be considered suitable
- A `MessageBodyReader` provider implementation must be either programmatically registered in the JAX-RS runtime or must be annotated with the `@Provider` annotation

The following example illustrates a custom `MessageBodyReader` implementation, which converts the CSV representation of the department items present in the input stream to list the `Department` Java objects:

```
//Other imports are omitted for brevity
import javax.ws.rs.Consumes;
import javax.ws.rs.WebApplicationException;
import javax.ws.rs.core.MediaType;
import javax.ws.rs.core.MultivaluedMap;
import javax.ws.rs.ext.MessageBodyReader;
import javax.ws.rs.ext.Provider;
```

```
import org.supercsv.cellprocessor.ift.CellProcessor;
import org.supercsv.io.CsvBeanReader;
import org.supercsv.io.ICsvBeanReader;
import org.supercsv.prefs.CsvPreference;

@Provider
@Consumes("application/csv")
public class CSVMessageBodyReader implements MessageBodyReader<List<D
epartment>> {

    /**
     * Ascertain if the MessageBodyReader can produce
     * an instance of a particular type.
     */
    @Override
    public boolean isReadable(Class<?> type, Type genericType,
        Annotation[] annotations, MediaType mediaType) {
        return Collection.class.isAssignableFrom(type);
    }

    /**
     * Read a type from InputStream.
     */
    @Override
    public List readFrom(Class<List<Department>> type, Type
        genericType, Annotation[] annotations,
        MediaType mediaType,
        MultivaluedMap<String, String> httpHeaders,
        InputStream entityStream)
        throws IOException, WebApplicationException {

        ArrayList list = new ArrayList();
        //Following code uses Super CSV lib for reading CSV data
        //Define the type for each column in CSV
        final CellProcessor[] processors = new CellProcessor[]{
            new NotNull(new ParseShort()), // departmentId
            new NotNull(), // departmentName
            new NotNull(new ParseShort()), // locationId
            new Optional(new ParseInt()) //managerId
        };
        //Reads CSV input stream
        ICsvBeanReader beanReader = new CsvBeanReader(new
            InputStreamReader(entityStream),
            CsvPreference.STANDARD_PREFERENCE);
        //Start building object from CVS
        String[] header = beanReader.getHeader(false);
        Object obj = null;
```

```
        while ((obj = beanReader.read(Department.class,
    header, processors)) != null) {
            list.add(obj);
            logger.log(Level.INFO, obj.toString());
        }

        return list;
    }
}
```

The following RESTful web service call illustrates how a JAX-RS application can use CSVMessageBodyReader for taking input in the CSV format:

```
POST /api/hr/departments HTTP/1.1
Host: localhost:8080
Content-Type: application/csv

departmentId,departmentName,locationId,managerId
1001,"Finance",1700,101
1002,"Office Administration",1500,205
```

> You can download this example from the Packt website link mentioned at the beginning of this book, in the *Preface* section. See the CSVMessageBodyReader.java and CSVMessageBodyWriter.java files in the <rest-chapter4-service> project.

Asynchronous RESTful web services

All the discussions on the RESTful web services that we have had so far were based on the synchronous request and response model. When a client invokes a RESTful web API synchronously, the server keeps the request handling thread engaged till its request is processed. In this case, the entire request is processed in a single thread on the server. This model works if the request processing is finished quickly. The problem starts when a request takes more time to finish. In such a case, the thread used by the container to handle the long running request will remain busy till the processing is over. This may adversely affect the scalability of the application when the load (concurrent requests) increases because the server will not have enough threads in the pool to handle the incoming requests. The asynchronous processing feature in JAX-RS solves this by processing the long running requests asynchronously, thereby releasing the thread that is handling the current request back to the container. This essentially increases the throughput of the server.

The following example demonstrates how to use the asynchronous REST API in JAX-RS. This example exposes the `findAllDepartments()` resource class method as an asynchronous REST API. You can do this by injecting `javax.ws.rs.container.AsyncResponse` as a parameter to the desired resource method, as shown in the following code snippet:

```
@GET
@Path("departments")
@Produces(MediaType.APPLICATION_JSON)
public void findAllDepartments(@Suspended AsyncResponse asyncResponse)
```

The `@Suspended` annotation used for injecting `AsyncResponse` tells the JAX-RS runtime that this method is expected to be executed in the asynchronous mode and the client connection should not be automatically closed by the runtime when the method returns. The asynchronous REST resource method can use the injected `AsyncResponse` instance to send the response back to the client by using another thread. The `AsyncResponse` instance that is injected to methods is bound to the running request and can be used to asynchronously provide the request processing result. The core operations available on this instance are as follows:

- `cancel()`: This method cancels the request processing and passes the message to the suspended thread, which was handling the current client request.

- `resume()`: This method resumes the request processing and passes the message to the suspended thread that was handling the current client request.

- `register()`:This method is used for registering call backs such as `CompletionCallback`, which is executed when the request finishes or fails, and `ConnectionCallback`, which is executed when a connection to a client is closed or lost.

- `setTimeout()`: This method is used for specifying the timeout value for the asynchronous process. Upon timeout, runtime will throw `javax.ws.rs.ServiceUnavailableException`, which will be translated into the `503 Service Unavailable` HTTP status code and sent back to the caller. You can even plug in a custom timeout handler implementation (which implements `javax.ws.rs.container.TimeoutHandler`) by invoking the `setTimeoutHandler(TimeoutHandler)` method on the `AsyncResponse` object.

The following code snippet illustrates a complete asynchronous method implementation for your reference. This method reads the department's records from the database in a different thread. Upon successful retrieval of records, the result is set on the AsyncResponse instance and resumes the suspended request processing. The resumed request is processed in a new thread as a normal request. The framework executes all configured filters, interceptors, and exception mappers before sending the response back to the client:

```
//Other imports are omitted for brevity
import javax.ws.rs.container.AsyncResponse;
import javax.ws.rs.container.Suspended;
import javax.ws.rs.container.TimeoutHandler;

@Stateless
@Path("hr/asynch")
public class HRAsynchService {
    private final ExecutorService executorService =
        Executors.newCachedThreadPool();

    @GET
    @Path("departments")
    @Produces(MediaType.APPLICATION_JSON)
    public void findAllDepartments(@Suspended final
        AsyncResponse asyncResponse) {
        //Set time out for the request
        asyncResponse.setTimeout(10, TimeUnit.SECONDS);
        Runnable longRunningDeptQuery = new Runnable(){
            EntityManagerFactory emf =
                Persistence.
                    createEntityManagerFactory
                        ("HRPersistenceUnit");
            EntityManager entityManagerLocal =
                emf.createEntityManager();

            public void run() {
                CriteriaQuery cq =
                    entityManagerLocal.
                        getCriteriaBuilder().createQuery();
                cq.select(cq.from(Department.class));
                List<Department> depts =
                    entityManagerLocal.createQuery(cq).
                        getResultList();
                GenericEntity<List<Department>> entity
                    = new GenericEntity<List<Department>>(depts) {
                };
```

```
                  asyncResponse.
                     resume(Response.ok().entity(entity).build());
              }
          };
          executorService.execute(longRunningDeptQuery);
      }
  }
```

Asynchronous RESTful web service client

This section describes the usage of the asynchronous JAX-RS API on the client for calling the RESTful web APIs.

To invoke a REST API asynchronously on the client, you use `javax.ws.rs.client.AsyncInvoker`. The `AsyncInvoker` instance is obtained from the call of the `Invocation.Builder.async()` method, as shown in the following code:

```java
//Other imports are omitted for brevity
import javax.ws.rs.client.AsyncInvoker;
import javax.ws.rs.client.Client;
import javax.ws.rs.client.WebTarget;
import javax.ws.rs.core.GenericType;
import javax.ws.rs.core.Response;

String BASE_URI =
    "http://localhost:8080/hr-services/webresources";
Client client = ClientBuilder.newClient();
WebTarget webTarget =
    client.target(BASE_URI).path("hr").path("departments");
AsyncInvoker asyncInvoker =
    webTarget.request(APPLICATION_JSON).async();
Future<Response> responseFuture = asyncInvoker.get();
Response response = responseFuture.get();
List<Department> depts = response.readEntity(new
    GenericType<List<Department>>() { });
response.close();
client.close();
```

The JAX-RS client-side API allows you to listen to events generated during the asynchronous invocation of the REST APIs by registering the callback handlers. To do this, you may need to implement `javax.ws.rs.client.InvocationCallback` and pass this instance as parameter to the appropriate HTTP method call on the `AsyncInvoker` instance. The following code snippet illustrates how you can implement `InvocationCallback` for a GET method type. The `InvocationCallback::completed()` method is called upon the successful completion of a request. The `InvocationCallback::failed()` method is called upon the failure of a request:

```
//Other imports are omitted for brevity
import javax.ws.rs.client.InvocationCallback;

String BASE_URI =
    "http://localhost:8080/hr-services/webresources";

final Client client =
    javax.ws.rs.client.ClientBuilder.newClient();
WebTarget webTarget =
    client.target(BASE_URI).path("hr").path("departments");
AsyncInvoker asyncInvoker = webTarget.
    request(javax.ws.rs.core.MediaType.APPLICATION_JSON).async();
Future<List<Department>> entity = asyncInvoker.get(
    new InvocationCallback<List<Department>>() {
    @Override
    public void completed(List<Department> response) {
        //Call back on request completion
        //You can process the result here, if required
        client.close();
    }

    @Override
    public void failed(Throwable throwable) {
        //Call back on request failure
        //Handle the exception
        //log(...) method definition is not shown here
        log(throwable);
    }
});
```

Managing HTTP cache in a RESTful web service

Reading resources over the web is always a challenging process in terms of time and network latency. As a result, when you build a web application or web service, the ability to cache and reuse previously retrieved resources is a critical aspect of optimizing for performance. The HTTP/1.1 protocol specification provides a number of features to facilitate the caching of network resources.

In this section, we will discuss the native support in the HTTP protocol for managing the cache of the resources retrieved from the server. Similarly, we will see how the JAX-RS framework APIs embrace the HTTP caching features for managing the cache of the results returned by the RESTful web services.

Using the Expires header to control the validity of the HTTP cache

You can use the `Expires` HTTP header field to let all entities involved in the request-response chain know when a resource is expired. The `Expires` HTTP header was defined as part of the HTTP/1.0 specification. You can specify the date and time in the `Expires` header, after which the resource fetched from the server is considered stale.

The following code snippet shows how you can add the `Expires` HTTP header to the resource returned by the method:

```
@GET
@Path("departments/{id}/holidays")
@Produces(MediaType.APPLICATION_JSON)
public Response getHolidayListForCurrentYear(@PathParam("id")
    Short deptId) {
    //Reads the list of holidays
    List<Date> holidayList = getHolidayListForDepartment(deptId);
    //Build response
    Response.ResponseBuilder response = Response.ok(holidayList).
        type(MediaType.APPLICATION_JSON);
    //Set the expiry for response resource
    //This example sets validity as
    //Dec 31 of the current year
    int currentYear = getCurrentYear();
    Calendar expirationDate = new GregorianCalendar
        (currentYear,12, 31);
    response.expires(expirationDate.getTime());
    return response.build();
}
```

Here is the sample response header generated by the preceding method for the
`GET departments/10/holidays HTTP/1.1` request:

```
Server: GlassFish Server Open Source Edition 4.1
Expires: Sat, 31 Dec 2015 00:00:00 GMT
Content-Type: application/json
Date: Mon, 02 Mar 2015 05:24:58 GMT
Content-Length: 20
```

The `Expires` headers are good for the following factors:

- Making static resources returned by the server, such as images, cacheable.

- Controlling the caching of a resource retuned by servers that change only at specific intervals. For instance, a list of public holidays for an organization for a specific year, which does not usually change within a year.

Using Cache-Control directives to manage the HTTP cache

The `Cache-Control` header was defined as part of HTTP/1.1 and offers more options than the `Expires` HTTP header. This header is used for specifying the directives that must be obeyed by all caching mechanisms involved in the HTTP communication. These directives indicate who can do the caching of a resource returned by the server, how the caching is done, and for how long the resource can be cached.

> The `Expires` header is recommended for static resources such as images. The `Cache-Control` header is useful when you need more control over how caching is done.

Here is a list of the useful `Cache-Control` directives:

- `private`: This directive indicates only those clients who originally requested the resource (for example, browser) can do the caching and no other entity in the request-response chain (for example, proxy) is expected to do the caching.

- `public`: This marks a response as cacheable and caching can be done by any entity in the request-response chain.

- `no-cache`: This directive tells the client (for example, browser or proxies) that it should validate with the server before serving the resource from the cache. The validation can be done with the server by sending a request with the appropriate header fields such as `If-Modified-Since`, `If-Unmodified-Since`, `If-Match`, and `If-None-Match`.

- `no-store`: This directive indicates that a response can be cached (for example, in-memory), but should not be stored on a permanent storage (for example, a disk).

- `no-transform`: This directive tells that the resource should not be modified by any entity in the request-response chain. This directive is used for avoiding the loss of data while transforming a response from one format to another by intermediate entities.

- `max-age`: This value (measured in seconds) indicates how long the cached resource will be considered fresh. After this, the cached content needs to be validated with the server while serving the next request.

- `s-maxage`: This directive is similar to the `max-age` directive, except that it only applies to shared (for example, proxy) caches, not for the client who originated the request.

- `must-revalidate`: This directive tells all caches that they must follow the freshness information set by the server while generating the resource. Note that the HTTP protocol allows caches to serve stale resources under special conditions. By specifying the must-revalidate directive in the header of a response, you are telling all caches not to use any stale resource from the cache and validate the expired cache resources with the server before serving the request.

- `proxy-revalidate`: This directive is similar to the `must-revalidate` header item, except that it only applies to the proxy caches (not for the client that originally requested the resource).

 A detailed discussion of the `Cache-Control` directives in HTTP/1.1 is available at `http://www.w3.org/Protocols/rfc2616/rfc2616-sec14.html`.

JAX-RS allows you to specify the `Cache-Control` directives on the `javax.ws.rs.core.Response` object returned by your REST resource method via the `javax.ws.rs.core.CacheControl` class. The `CacheControl` class exposes methods for accessing all possible `Cache-Control` directives.

The following code snippet illustrates the use of the `CacheControl` class for specifying cache expiry directives on the response object (the `Department` object) returned by the resource class method:

```
//Other imports are omitted for brevity
import javax.ws.rs.core.CacheControl;
import javax.ws.rs.core.MediaType;
import javax.ws.rs.core.Response;
```

```
import javax.ws.rs.core.Response.ResponseBuilder;

@GET
@Path("departments/{id}")
@Produces(MediaType.APPLICATION_JSON)
public Response findDepartmentById(@PathParam("id") Short deptId)
    {

    Department department = findDepartmentEntityById(deptId);
    //Specifies max-age and private directive for the response
    CacheControl cc = new CacheControl();
    //Cache is valid for a day (86400 sec)
    cc.setMaxAge(86400);
    cc.setPrivate(true);

    ResponseBuilder builder = Response.ok(myBook);
    //set the CacheControl object and build Response
    builder.cacheControl(cc);
    return builder.build();
}
```

Here is the sample response header generated by the preceding method for the
GET departments/10 HTTP/1.1 request:

```
Server: GlassFish Server Open Source Edition 4.1
Cache-Control: private, no-transform, max-age=86400
Content-Type: application/json
Date: Mon, 02 Mar 2015 05:56:29 GMT
Content-Length: 82
```

Conditional request processing with the Last-Modified HTTP response header

The Last-Modified header field value in HTTP is often used for validating the cached response contents. The Last-Modified entity-header field indicates the date and time at which the entity present in the response body was last modified. A client can use the Last-Modified header field value in combination with the If-Modified-Since or If-Unmodified-Since request headers to perform conditional requests.

The following example illustrates the use of the Last-Modified HTTP header field in the JAX-RS application. The Last-Modified field contains the date when the resource was last changed. When a client requests the same resource next time, it sends the If-Modified-Since header field, with the value set to the date and the time at which the resource was last updated on the server. On the server, you can call javax.ws.rs.core.Request::evaluatePreconditions() to check whether the resource has been modified in between the requests. This method evaluates request preconditions on the basis of the passed-in value. If this method returns null, the resource is out of date and needs to be sent back in the response. Otherwise, this method returns the 304 Not Modified HTTP status code to the client. Here is the code snippet for this example:

```
//Other imports are removed for brevity
import javax.ws.rs.core.Request;
import javax.ws.rs.core.Context;
import javax.ws.rs.core.Response.ResponseBuilder;

@GET
@Path("departments/{id}")
@Produces(MediaType.APPLICATION_JSON)
public Response
    findDepartmentWithCacheValidationWithLastModifiedDate(
        @PathParam("id") Short id, @Context Request request) {

    //Reads the latest Department object from DB
    Department department = entityManager.find(Department.class,
        id);
    //Gets the last modified date
    Date latModifiedDate = department.getModifiedDate();
    //Evaluates request preconditions on the basis
    //of the passed-in value.
    //evaluatePreconditions() return null If-Modified-Since
    //check succeeds. This implies that resource is modified
    ResponseBuilder builder =
        request.evaluatePreconditions(latModifiedDate);

    //cached resource did change; send new one
    if (builder == null) {
        builder = Response.ok(department);
        builder.lastModified(latModifiedDate);

    }
    return builder.build();

}
```

To learn more about the `javax.ws.rs.core.Request::eva` `luatePreconditions()` method, read the API documentation available at `https://jax-rs-spec.java.net/nonav/2.0/` `apidocs/javax/ws/rs/core/Request.html`.

Conditional request processing with the ETag HTTP response header

Sometimes, you may find that the precision of the HTTP date object (precision in seconds) is not granular enough to decide the freshness of the cache. You can use **Entity Tags (ETag)** present in the HTTP response header field for such scenarios. ETag is part of HTTP/1.1 and provides a way of incorporating caching into HTTP. This tag can be used for comparing the validity of a cached object on the client side with the original object on the server.

When a server returns a response to a client, it attaches an opaque identifier in the ETag HTTP header present in the response. This identifier represents the state of the resource entity returned in response to the client's request. If the resource identified by the URI changes over time, a new identifier is assigned to ETag. When the client makes a request for a resource, it attaches the last received ETag header for the same resource (if any) as the value for the `If-None-Match` or `If-Match` HTTP header field in the request. The server uses this identifier for validating the cached representation of the resource. If the state of the requested resource has not been changed, the server responds with a `304 Not Modified` status code, which instructs the client to use a copy of the resource from its local cache.

At the bottom level, ETag is different from the `Client-Cache` and `Expires` HTTP headers discussed in the previous sections. The ETag header does not have any information that the client can use to determine whether or not to make a request for a specific resource again in the future. However, when the server reads the ETag header from the client request, it can determine whether to send the resource (HTTP status code: `200 OK`) or tell the client to just use the local copy (STTP status code: `304 Not Modified`). You can treat ETag as a checksum for a resource that semantically changes when the content changes.

To learn more about ETag, visit the following page: `http://` `tools.ietf.org/html/rfc7232#section-2.3`.

The following code snippet shows the use of the JAX-RS APIs for building and validating ETag on the server. In this example, the client uses the `If-None-Match` header field to attach ETag to the request:

```
@GET
@Path("departments/{id}")
@Produces(MediaType.APPLICATION_JSON)
public Response findDepartmentWithCacheValidationWithEtag(
    @PathParam("id") Short deptId, @Context Request request) {

        //Reads latest department object from server
        Department department = findDepartmentEntity(deptId);
        //Builds ETag for department resource
        EntityTag etag = new
            EntityTag(Integer.toString(department.hashCode()));

        //Checks whether client-cached resource has changed
        //by checking ETag value present in request with value
        //generated on server
        //If changed, sends new resource with new ETag
        ResponseBuilder builder =
            request.evaluatePreconditions(etag);
        if (builder == null) {
            builder = Response.ok(department);
            builder.tag(etag);
        }

    return builder.build();
}
```

Here is the sample response header generated by the preceding method for the GET departments/10 HTTP/1.1 request:

```
Server: GlassFish Server Open Source Edition 4.1
ETag: "03cb35ca667706c68c0aad4cb04c7a211"
Content-Type: application/json
Date: Mon, 02 Mar 2015 05:30:11 GMT
Content-Length: 82
```

Conditional data update in RESTFul web services

In the previous two sections, we learned how to leverage HTTP caching features to optimize read operations (the HTTP GET type) in RESTful web APIs. In this section, we will discuss how to leverage these features during the entity updates in these APIs (the HTTP POST or PUT request types). Conditional updates help you to avoid performing modifications on the stale representation of resources, thereby avoiding the overwriting of changes performed by other users of the system on the same resource. You can perform conditional updates by using either of the following approaches:

- **Comparing the last modified date of the resource**: When a client sends a modified resource to the server via the PUT or POST method, the request also carries the If-Modified-Since HTTP header field with the value set to the last modified date of the resource. The server can evaluate the If-Modified-Since header field to see whether it matches with the timestamp on the resource residing on the server.

- **Comparing Etag of the resource**: If the modified date is not precise enough to decide the freshness of the resource, you can use ETag. In this case, the PUT or POST request from the client carries the If-None-Match header field with the value set to that of the ETag header sent by the server when the resource was last retrieved. The server can evaluate the value of the If-None-Match header field present in the HTTP request header to see whether it matches with the current ETag of the resource on the server.

If the validation check fails for the preceding two cases, the server will return an error response code of 412 (precondition failed). The client can take an appropriate action on the basis of the status code received as part of the response. If all checks go through, the update succeeds on the server. The following code snippet illustrates how you can use the last modified date or the ETag header present in the request for performing the conditional updates on a resource:

```
@PUT
@Path("etag/departments/{id}")
@Consumes(MediaType.APPLICATION_JSON)
public Response edit(@PathParam("id") Short deptId,
    @Context Request request, Department entity) {

    //Reads latest Department object from DB and generates ETag
    Department detEntityInDB = finDepartmentEntity(deptId);
    //You can use a better algorithm for getting ETag in real life
    EntityTag etag = new
```

```
        EntityTag(Integer.toString(detEntityInDB.hashCode()));

    //A client may pass either ETag or last modified date
    //in the request.
    // evaluatePreconditions() returns null if the
    //preconditions are met or a ResponseBuilder is set with
    //the appropriate status if the preconditions are not met.
    Response.ResponseBuilder builder =
        request.evaluatePreconditions(
            detEntityInDB.getModifiedDate(), etag);
    // Client is not up to date (send back 412)
    if (builder != null) {
        return builder.status(
            Response.Status.PRECONDITION_FAILED).build();
    }
    updateDepartmentEntity(entity);

    EntityTag newEtag = new
        EntityTag(Integer.toString(entity.hashCode()));
    builder = Response.noContent();
    builder.lastModified(entity.getModifiedDate());
    builder.tag(newEtag);
    return builder.build();
}
```

 The ETag and Last-Modified entity tags in the HTTP header
can be used for reducing the network usage of the REST APIs
by introducing the conditional retrieval of the resources on the
server. You may also find it useful for the concurrency control for
the REST APIs by introducing conditional updates on the server.

Understanding filters and interceptors in JAX-RS

The default request-response model offered in the JAX-RS implementation fits
well for many common use cases. However, at times, you may look for extending
the default request-response model. For instance, you may need such extension
capabilities while adding support for the custom authentication, customized caching
of responses, encoding request content, and so on, without polluting the application
code. JAX-RS allows you to do this by adding your own interceptors and filters for
both the REST requests and responses, as appropriate.

Typically, filters are used for processing the request-response headers, whereas interceptors are concerned with the marshalling and unmarshalling of the HTTP message bodies. Filters and interceptors can be set on both the client and the server. Let's learn more about these offerings in this section.

Modifying request and response parameters with JAX-RS filters

The JAX-RS APIs offer distinct filters for both the client and the server. Let's take a quick look at the JAX-RS filter APIs in this section.

Implementing server-side request message filters

You can build a request filter for the server by implementing the `javax.ws.rs.container.ContainerRequestFilter` interface. This filter intercepts the REST API calls and runs before the request invokes the REST resource. You will find this useful for performing authorization checks, auditing requests, or manipulating the request header parameters before invoking the REST API implementation.

The `ContainerRequestFilters` implementation falls into two categories on the basis of the stage in the request processing cycle that the filters are executed at:

- **Postmatching**: These filters are executed after identifying the matching Java class resource method for processing the incoming HTTP request (the REST API call). The `ContainerRequestFilters` implementations, by default, are postmatching (unless you designate them as `@PreMatching`).

- **Prematching**: These filters are executed before identifying the matching resource class for a REST API call. Prematching `ContainerRequestFilters` are designated with the `@javax.ws.rs.container.PreMatching` annotation.

Postmatching server-side request message filters

These postmatching filters are applied only after a matching Java class resource method has been identified to process the incoming request. As these filters are executed after the resource matching process, it is no longer possible to modify the request in order to influence the resource matching process.

Here is an example for a postmatching server-side request filter. `AuthorizationRequestFilter` given in the following example ensures that only users with the `ADMIN` role can access the REST APIs used for configuring the system.

The configuration APIs are identified in this example by checking whether the request URI path has the /config/ part embedded in it:

```java
//Other imports are omitted for brevity
import java.io.IOException;
import javax.ws.rs.container.ContainerRequestContext;
import javax.ws.rs.container.ContainerRequestFilter;
import javax.ws.rs.core.Response;
import javax.ws.rs.core.SecurityContext;
import javax.ws.rs.core.UriInfo;
import javax.ws.rs.ext.Provider;

@Provider
public class AuthorizationRequestFilter implements
    ContainerRequestFilter {

    @Override
    public void filter(ContainerRequestContext requestContext)
        throws IOException {

        //Get the URI for current request
        UriInfo uriInfo = requestContext.getUriInfo();
        String uri = uriInfo.getRequestUri().toString();
        int index = uri.indexOf("/config/");
        boolean isSettingsService = (index != -1);
        if (isSettingsService) {
            SecurityContext securityContext
                    = requestContext.getSecurityContext();
            if (securityContext == null
                || !securityContext.isUserInRole("ADMIN")) {

                requestContext.abortWith(Response
                    .status(Response.Status.UNAUTHORIZED)
                    .entity("Unauthorized access.")
                    .build());
            }
        }
    }
}
```

The @javax.ws.rs.ext.Provider annotation on the implementation of a filter or an interceptor makes it discoverable by the JAX-RS runtime. You do not need to do any extra configurations for integrating the filters or interceptors.

Prematching server-side request message filters

You can designate ContainerRequestFilters as the prematching filter by annotating with the @javax.ws.rs.container.PreMatching annotation. The prematching filters are applied before the JAX-RS runtime identifies the matching Java class resource method. As this filter is executed before executing the resource matching process, you can use this type of filter to modify the HTTP request contents. Apparently, this can be used for influencing the request matching process, if required.

The following code snippet illustrates how you can use a prematching filter to modify the method type in the incoming HTTP request. This example modifies the method type from POST to PUT. As this is executed before identifying the Java resource method, the change in method type will influence the identification of the Java class resource method for executing the call:

```
import java.io.IOException;
import javax.ws.rs.container.ContainerRequestContext;
import javax.ws.rs.container.ContainerRequestFilter;
import javax.ws.rs.ext.Provider;
import javax.ws.rs.container.PreMatching;

@Provider
@PreMatching
public class JAXRSContainerPrematchingRequestFilter implements
    ContainerRequestFilter {
    @Override
    public void filter(ContainerRequestContext requestContext)
        throws IOException {
          //Modify the method type from POST to PUT
        if (requestContext.getMethod().equals("POST")) {
            requestContext.setMethod("PUT");
        }
    }
}
```

Implementing server-side response message filters

You can build a server-side response filter by implementing the `javax.ws.rs.container.ContainerResponseFilter` interface. This filter gets executed after the response is generated by the REST API. The response filters, in general, can be used to manipulate the response header parameters present in the response messages. The following example shows how you can use it to modify the response header.

When a REST web client is no longer on the same domain as the server that hosts the REST APIs, the REST response message header should have the **Cross Origin Resource Sharing (CORS)** header values set to the appropriate domain names, which are allowed to access the APIs. This example uses `ContainerResponseFilter` to modify the REST response headers to include the CORS header, thus making the REST APIs accessible from a different domain:

```
//Other imports are omitted for brevity
import javax.ws.rs.container.ContainerRequestContext;
import javax.ws.rs.container.ContainerResponseContext;
import javax.ws.rs.container.ContainerResponseFilter;
import javax.ws.rs.ext.Provider;
import java.io.IOException;

@Provider
public class CORSFilter implements ContainerResponseFilter {

    @Override
    public void filter(ContainerRequestContext requestContext,
        ContainerResponseContext cres) throws IOException {
      //Specify CORS headers: * represents allow all values
        cres.getHeaders().add("Access-Control-Allow-Origin", "*");
        cres.getHeaders().add("Access-Control-Allow-Headers",
            "*");
        cres.getHeaders().add("Access-Control-Allow-Credentials",
            "true");
        cres.getHeaders().add("Access-Control-Allow-Methods",
            "GET, POST, PUT, DELETE, OPTIONS, HEAD");
        cres.getHeaders().add("Access-Control-Max-Age",
            "1209600");
    }
}
```

Implementing client-side request message filters

JAX-RS lets you build a client-side request filter for the REST API calls by implementing the `javax.ws.rs.client.ClientRequestFilter` interface. This filter is used for intercepting the REST API calls on the client itself.

A very common use case scenario where you may find these filters useful is for checking the accuracy of specific request parameters on the client itself. Even you can abort the call and return the error response object from these filters if the request parameters values are not properly specified.

The following code snippet illustrates how you can use `ClientRequestFilter` to ensure that all the requests carry the `Client-Application` header field, which you may use on the server for tracking all clients:

```
//Other imports are omitted for brevity
import javax.ws.rs.HttpMethod;
import javax.ws.rs.client.ClientRequestContext;
import javax.ws.rs.client.ClientRequestFilter;

@Provider
public class JAXRSClientRequestFilter implements
    ClientRequestFilter {

    @Override
    public void filter(ClientRequestContext requestContext)
        throws IOException {
        if(requestContext.getHeaders()
          .get("Client-Application") == null) {
              requestContext.abortWith(
                  Response.status(Response.Status.BAD_REQUEST)
                    .entity(
                        "Client-Application header is
                            required.")
                            .build());
        }
    }
}
```

You can register the `ClientRequestFilter` interface to the client by calling the `register()` method on the `javax.ws.rs.client.Client` object. Note that the client object implements the `javax.ws.rs.core.Configurable` interface, and all the configurations that you see on `Client` are offered by the `Configurable` interface.

The following code snippet shows how you can add JAXRSClientRequestFilter to the JAX-RS client implementation:

```
import javax.ws.rs.client.Client;
import javax.ws.rs.client.ClientBuilder;

Client client = ClientBuilder.newClient();
client.register(JSXRSClientRequestFilter.class);
```

Implementing client-side response message filters

You can build a client-side response filter by implementing the javax.ws.rs.client.ClientResponseFilter interface. This filter is used for manipulating the response message returned by the REST APIs.

The following code snippet shows the use of JAXRSClientResponseFilter to check the response received from the server and then log the error (if any) for audit purposes:

```
//Other imports are omitted for brevity
import javax.ws.rs.client.ClientRequestContext;
import javax.ws.rs.client.ClientResponseContext;
import javax.ws.rs.client.ClientResponseFilter;

public class JAXRSClientResponseFilter implements
    ClientResponseFilter {

    @Override
    public void filter(ClientRequestContext reqContext,
        ClientResponseContext respContext) throws IOException {
        if (respContext.getStatus() == 200) {
            return;
        }else{
            logError(respContext);
        }
    }

    private void logError(ClientResponseContext respContext) {
        //Code for logging error goes here.
    }
}
```

You can register the `ClientResponseFilter` interface to the JAX RS client by calling the `register()` method on the `javax.ws.rs.client.Client` object. An example is given here:

```
import javax.ws.rs.client.Client;
import javax.ws.rs.client.ClientBuilder;

Client client = ClientBuilder.newClient();
client.register(JAXRSClientResponseFilter.class);
```

Modifying request and response message bodies with JAX-RS interceptors

JAX-RS provides the request and response interceptors to manipulate entities or message bodies by intercepting the input and output streams, respectively. In this section, we will learn the request and response interceptors offered by JAX-RS. You can use the interceptors on both the client and the server.

 Unlike JAX-RS filters, interceptors do not have separate contracts for the client and the server.

Implementing request message body interceptors

You use the `javax.ws.rs.ext.ReaderInterceptor` interface to intercept and manipulate the incoming message body.

The following example illustrates how you can implement `ReaderInterceptor` to intercept the incoming message in order to unzip the zipped body content:

```
//Other imports are omitted for brevity
import java.util.zip.GZIPInputStream;
import javax.ws.rs.WebApplicationException;
import javax.ws.rs.ext.Provider;
import javax.ws.rs.ext.ReaderInterceptor;
import javax.ws.rs.ext.ReaderInterceptorContext;

@Provider
public class JAXRSReaderInterceptor implements ReaderInterceptor {

    @Override
    public Object aroundReadFrom(ReaderInterceptorContext context)
        throws IOException, WebApplicationException {
        List<String> header = context.getHeaders()
            .get("Content-Encoding");
```

```
    // decompress gzip stream only
    if (header != null && header.contains("gzip")) {

        InputStream originalInputStream =
        context.getInputStream();
        context.setInputStream(new
        GZIPInputStream(originalInputStream));
    }
    return context.proceed();

  }
}
```

You will follow the same interface contract (`ReaderInterceptor`) for building the read interceptors for the client-side use as well. You can register the `ReaderInterceptor` interface to the JAX RS client by calling the `register()` method on the `javax.ws.rs.client.Client` object.

Implementing response message body interceptors

You may use the `javax.ws.rs.ext.JAXRSWriterInterceptor` interface to intercept and manipulate the outgoing message body. The following example illustrates the use of `WriterInterceptor` to compress the response body content:

```
//Other imports are omitted for brevity
import java.util.zip.GZIPOutputStream;
import javax.ws.rs.WebApplicationException;
import javax.ws.rs.core.MultivaluedMap;
import javax.ws.rs.ext.Provider;
import javax.ws.rs.ext.WriterInterceptor;
import javax.ws.rs.ext.WriterInterceptorContext;

@Provider
public class JAXRSWriterInterceptor implements WriterInterceptor {
    @Override
    public void aroundWriteTo(WriterInterceptorContext context)
        throws IOException,
        WebApplicationException {
        MultivaluedMap<String, Object> headers =
            context.getHeaders();
        headers.add("Content-Encoding", "gzip");
        OutputStream outputStream =
            context.getOutputStream();
        context.setOutputStream(new
            GZIPOutputStream(outputStream));
```

```
        context.proceed();
    }
}
```

You will use the same interface contract for building the write interceptors for client-side use as well. You can register the `WriterInterceptor` interface to the JAX RS client by calling the `register()` method on the `javax.ws.rs.client.Client` object.

Managing the order of execution for filters and interceptors

It is perfectly legal to have multiple filters or interceptors added for a REST client or server. In such a case, you might want to control the order in which they are executed at runtime. JAX-RS allows you to manage the order of execution by adding the `@javax.annotation.Priority` annotation on the filter or the interceptor class. The `Priority` values should be non-negative. You can use standard constants defined in the `javax.ws.rs.Priorities` class to set the priorities. An example is given here:

```
@Provider
@Priority(Priorities.HEADER_DECORATOR)
public class JAXRSReaderInterceptor implements ReaderInterceptor {
    //Interceptor implementation goes here
}
```

Interceptors and filters are sorted on the basis of their priority in an ascending manner. While processing a request, the request filter with the least priority will be executed first and followed by the next one in the sequence. While processing a response, filters are executed in the reverse order. In other words, the response filter with the highest priority will be executed first, followed by the next lowest one in the sequence.

Selectively applying filters and interceptors on REST resources by using @NameBinding

The `@javax.ws.rs.NameBinding` annotation is used for creating the name-binding annotation for filters and interceptors. Later developers can selectively apply the name-binding annotation on the desired REST resources classes or methods.

For example, consider the following name-binding annotation, `RequestLogger`:

```
@NameBinding
@Retention(RetentionPolicy.RUNTIME)
@Target({ElementType.METHOD,ElementType.TYPE})
public @interface RequestLogger {
}
```

You can use the preceding name-binding annotation, `RequestLogger`, to decorate the desired filters and interceptors as shown here:

```
//imports are removed for brevity
@RequestLogger
public class RequestLoggerFilter implements ContainerRequestFilter {
    @Override
    public void filter(ContainerRequestContext requestContext)
        throws IOException {
    //Method implementation is not shown in this
    //example for brevity
    }
}
```

Note that the preceding filter is not annotated with the `@Provider` annotation, and therefore, it will not be applied globally on all resources.

As the last step, you can apply the name-binding annotation to the resource class or method to which the name-bound JAX-RS provider(s) should be bound to. In the following code snippet, we apply the `@RequestLogger` name-binding annotation to the `findDepartment()` method. At runtime, the framework will identify all filters and interceptors decorated with `@RequestLogger` and will apply all of them to this method:

```
//imports are omitted for brevity
@Stateless
@Path("hr")
public class HRService {
    @GET
    @Path("departments/{id}")
    @Produces(MediaType.APPLICATION_JSON)
    @RequestLogger
    public Department findDepartment(@PathParam("id")  Short id) {

        findDepartmentsEntity(id);
        return department;
    }
}
```

The @NameBinding annotation really helps you to selectively apply JAX-RS providers to REST resources. However, you need to choose the resource methods to which the name-binding annotation should be applied while developing the API. What if you want to apply the filters or interceptors to the REST resources dynamically on the basis of some business conditions? JAX-RS offers the javax.ws.rs.container. DynamicFeature metaprovider for such use cases. Let's discuss this feature in the next section.

Dynamically applying filters and interceptors on REST resources using DynamicFeature

The javax.ws.rs.container.DynamicFeature contract is used by the JAX-RS runtime to register providers, such as interceptors and filters, to a particular resource class or method during application deployment.

The following code snippet shows how you can build the DynamicFeature provider. This example applies RequestLoggerFilter to resource methods annotated with @ RequestLogger.

```java
import javax.ws.rs.container.DynamicFeature;
import javax.ws.rs.container.ResourceInfo;
import javax.ws.rs.core.FeatureContext;
import javax.ws.rs.ext.Provider;

@Provider
public class DynamicFeatureRegister implements DynamicFeature {
    @Override
    public void configure(ResourceInfo resourceInfo,
        FeatureContext context) {
        //This simple example adds RequestLoggerFilter to methods
        //annotated with @ RequestLogger
        if (resourceInfo.getResourceMethod().isAnnotationPresent
            (RequestLogger.class)) {
            context.register(RequestLoggerFilter.class);
        }
    }
}
```

The DynamicFeature interface is executed at the deployment time for each resource method. You can register filters or interceptors on the desired resource class or method in the DynamicFeature implementation.

Understanding the JAX-RS resource lifecycle

Before winding up this chapter, let's take a quick look at the lifecycle of the JAX-RS components on the server when a client makes a RESTful web API call. This discussion would be a good summary of the topics that we learned so far on JAX-RS.

The following diagram depicts the sequence of actions taking place on the server when a client invokes the JAX-RS RESTful web service:

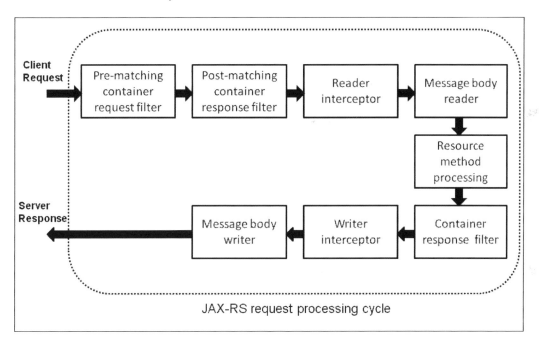

Here are the steps:

1. For an incoming REST API call, the container identifies the Java servlet configured for handling the REST API calls by parsing the URI and then delegates the request to the designated servlet.

2. The servlet initializes the JAX-RS runtime and kicks off the RESTful web service request processing cycle for the REST API call.

3. The JAX-RS runtime processes the filters and interceptors configured in the application in the following sequence:

   1. Runtime executes prematching filters (ContainerRequestFilter with the @Prematching annotation), which happens before resolving the resource method. The prematching filters are useful if you want to influence resource method resolution.

   2. The next step is to identify the resource method for serving the request. After the resolution of the resource method, postmatching filters are executed (filters without @Prematching). Postmatching filters are useful for performing an authentication check or for performing a basic sanity check on the request parameters.

   3. After executing all filters, the JAX-RS runtime invokes ReaderInterceptor. The reader interceptors are useful for manipulating the inbound request stream. A common use case may be to unzip the compressed stream before converting it into Java objects.

   4. The next phase in the cycle is to convert the inbound stream into the Java object representation. This is done by the matching the MessageBodyReader provider identified by the runtime.

4. After taking the incoming request through the configured filters, interceptors, and message body readers, the JAX-RS runtime invokes the resource class method identified for serving the request. If you have any Bean Validation annotation configured on the method parameters, it will get executed at this stage:

   1. If the validation fails and results in ConstraintViolationException, the runtime skips the execution of the method and identifies ExceptionMapper to handle the exception. The exception mapper generates the HTTP response content for the exception. The control flow proceeds to step 5.

   2. Upon successful validation, the resource method is executed.

   3. If the resource method throws some exception, the framework invokes the matching exception mapper to generate the HTTP response body for the exception and skips to step 5.

   4. Upon the successful execution of the method, the framework reads the response object returned by the method.

5. The runtime takes the response content through the following stages before sending it to the client:

   1. The runtime executes `ContainerResponseFilter`, which can be used for adding the desired response header such as cache parameters and content type.

   2. The runtime executes `WriterInterceptors` for the response content. The interceptor class can hold logic for manipulating the response before sending it to the client, such as zipping the response body.

   3. As the next step, the runtime invokes the appropriate `MessageBodyWriter`, which writes the Java type to an HTTP message to send it over HTTP. `MessageBodyWriter` can optionally amend or add the HTTP response headers. For instance, `200 OK` is added to the response header if the method execution went well and returned an object. If the method is void, `204 No Content` is set.

6. Once the response is ready, the container passes the response back to the client.

 Note that the default scope of the root resource classes is a request. This means that a new instance of a root resource class is created for serving the next request.

Summary

In this chapter, we explored the advanced offerings in the JAX-RS framework. In particular, we discussed subresources and subresource locators, validations, exception handling, JAX-RS entity providers, asynchronous RESTful web services and interceptors, and filters for JAX-RS applications. We concluded this chapter by discussing the lifecycle of all JAX-RS components that we have learnt so far.

In the next chapter, we will learn about the Jersey framework in detail.

5
Introducing the Jersey Framework Extensions

In the last two chapters, we discussed standard JAX-RS APIs for building RESTful Web APIs. JAX-RS is a specification for RESTful web services with Java, and not a product. We have been using Jersey for running the JAX-RS samples that we built in the previous chapters. As you may know, Jersey is one of the many reference implementations available in the market today for the JAX-RS specification. In reality, the Jersey framework is more than a just JAX-RS reference implementation. It offers additional features and utilities to further simplify RESTful services and client development.

In this chapter, we will discuss some of the very useful Jersey framework extension APIs which are not part of the JAX-RS standard.

We will cover the following topics in this chapter:

- Specifying dependencies for Jersey
- Programmatically configuring JAX-RS resources during deployment
- Modifying JAX-RS resources during deployment using ModelProcessor
- Building HATEOAS APIs
- Reading and writing large binary objects using Jersey APIs
- Generating chunked output using Jersey APIs
- Supporting Server Sent Event (SSE) in RESTful web services
- Understanding Jersey server-side configuration properties
- Monitoring RESTful web services using Jersey APIs

All the Jersey features that we discuss in this chapter are based on the latest Jersey release version (Jersey 2.17) available while writing this chapter.

 All the examples that you see in this chapter are downloadable from the Packt website link mentioned at the beginning of this book, in the *Preface* section.

Specifying dependencies for Jersey

Let us start our discussions on Jersey with a baby step. If you want to use any Jersey-specific feature in an application, then you will have to add a dependency to the appropriate Jersey libraries. For instance, to use a Jersey configuration class such as org.glassfish.jersey.server.ResourceConfig in your application, you need to depend on the jersey-container-servlet jar. If the consuming application uses Maven for building the source, then specifying a dependency to the jersey-container-servlet jar in the **Project Object Model (POM)** file may look like the following:

```
<dependency>
    <groupId>org.glassfish.jersey.containers</groupId>

  <!-- module -->
    <artifactId>jersey-container-servlet</artifactId>

  <!-2.17: latest release version -->
    <version>2.17</version>

    <!-- container(GlassFish) provides dependency
        for this example -->
    <scope>provided</scope>
</dependency>
```

 A list of the core Jersey modules and the features offered by each module is available at https://jersey.java.net/documentation/latest/modules-and-dependencies.html.

Programmatically configuring JAX-RS resources during deployment

The JAX-RS supports multiple ways to configure a RESTful web service application. A common approach is to subclass `javax.ws.rs.core.Application` and configure RESTful resources by overriding the appropriate methods. To learn more about configuring JAX-RS applications, refer to the *Packaging and deploying JAX-RS applications* section in *Appendix, Useful Features and Techniques*, of this book.

The Jersey framework provides more advanced configuration options for JAX-RS applications through the `org.glassfish.jersey.server.ResourceConfig` class. The `ResourceConfig` class is subclassed from `javax.ws.rs.core.Application`. We have used the `Application` class in the previous chapter for configuring a vanilla JAX-RS application. The `ResourceConfig` class offers many extra configuration features on top of the standard JAX-RS `Application` class. With the `ResourceConfig` class, you can define the JAX-RS resources via an array of class names; you can even specify package names where you have defined the JAX-RS component. During deployment, Jersey will automatically discover and register all the components found in the packages that you set.

What if you want to define a JAX-RS resource during deployment?

Apart from static resource class definitions, Jersey allows you to define and configure JAX-RS components during the deployment of the application. The following is an example that illustrates this idea.

In this example, we will build a REST API resource during deployment to return server information. We will expose this API only to selective customer deployments, managed via an application configuration parameter. The following code snippet illustrates how you can do this with Jersey APIs. While deploying the application, the `ApplicationConfig` class that you see in the code snippet will read the context parameter's `system.info.allow` entry from `web.xml`. If this flag is configured to return `true`, then `ApplicationConfig` will build a REST resource method during deployment to return system information for the REST API with the following path URI: `GET /server/info HTTP/1.1`:

```
//Other imports are omitted for brevity
import org.glassfish.jersey.process.Inflector;
import org.glassfish.jersey.server.ResourceConfig;
import org.glassfish.jersey.server.model.Resource;
import org.glassfish.jersey.server.model.ResourceMethod;
import org.glassfish.jersey.filter.LoggingFilter;
import org.glassfish.jersey.media.multipart.MultiPartFeature;
```

```
@Provider

@javax.ws.rs.ApplicationPath("webresources")
public class ApplicationConfig extends ResourceConfig {

    public ApplicationConfig(@Context ServletContext context) {

        // Package names that will be used
        //to scan for components.
        packages("com.packtpub.rest.ch5");

        //Read the context param
        String configSysInfoParam =
            context.getInitParameter("system.info.allow");
        boolean allowViewServerInfo =
            (configSysInfoParam == null) ?
             false : Boolean.valueOf(configSysInfoParam);

        //Register REST resource for returning server information
        //if param 'system.info.allow=true'
        if (allowViewServerInfo) {
            //Set URI path for the resource
            Resource.Builder resourceBuilder = Resource.builder();
            resourceBuilder.path("server/info");
            //Set HTTP request type for the resource
            ResourceMethod.Builder methodBuilder =
                resourceBuilder.addMethod("GET");
            //Provide implementation for the resource
            methodBuilder.produces(MediaType.APPLICATION_JSON)
                .handledBy(
                new Inflector<ContainerRequestContext, SystemInfo>() {
                    @Override
                    public SystemInfo apply(ContainerRequestContext
                    containerRequestContext) {
                     //Return object containing server details in
                     //response to REST request HTTP GET /server/info
                     //SystemInfo is not shown to save space
                            return SystemInfo.getInstance();
                    }
                });
```

```
                    //Finish building resource
                    Resource resource = resourceBuilder.build();
                    //Register the newly built
                    //resource with ResourceConfig
                    registerResources(resource);
              }
          }
      }
```

The sample response content generated by the newly added resource for the GET /
server/info HTTP/1.1 REST API call may look like the following:

```
{"hostName":"localhost","processor":"Intel",
"serverName":"GlassFish Server Open Source Edition
4.1","threads":334235}
```

Let us briefly discuss some of the core APIs used in this example. The org.glassfish.
jersey.server.model.Resource.Builder instance that you will obtain by calling
Resource.builder() has many useful builder methods for generating a complete
REST resource dynamically. Some of the important methods in Resource.Builder
that need your attention are as follows:

- Resource.Builder::path(String path): This method defines the path
  for the resource that you build. The client can use this URI path to invoke
  the resource.

- Resource.Builder::addMethod(String httpMethod): This method adds
  a new HTTP method model to the resource. The httpMethod parameter
  defines specific HTTP request types (such as GET, POST, and PUT) to which
  this method responds to. This call returns an instance of org.glassfish.
  jersey.server.model.ResourceMethod.Builder, which can later be used
  for building the body for the method.

  You can dynamically implement the method for handling the REST call by
  invoking handledBy(Class<? extends Inflector> inflectorClass)
  on ResourceMethod.Builder.

- ResourceConfig::registerResources(Resource... resources):
  This method registers newly created resource models in ResourceConfig.

A quick look at the static resource configurations

In the earlier `ApplicationConfig` class, you will also notice a call to the `Resource Config::packages(String... packages)` method with an array of package(s) as the parameter. This tells the runtime to scan the input packages for discovering the JAX-RS components (which include REST resources and provider components) used in the application. You can also use the `ResourceConfig::register()` method to register an individual JAX-RS component as appropriate.

> To learn more about the APIs exposed in the `ResourceConfig` class, visit the API documentation at `https://jersey.java.net/apidocs/latest/jersey/org/glassfish/jersey/server/ResourceConfig.html`.

Modifying JAX-RS resources during deployment using ModelProcessor

Sometimes, you may want to modify the existing JAX-RS resources during deployment to meet the specific business conditions set by customers. For instance, consider a scenario where you want to add additional APIs to return the JSON schema, which describes the content structure for all the REST resources that your application exposes. Further, there may be scenarios where you may want to change the entire resource method implementation itself to meet the requirements of some of the customers. In this section, we will learn how to address such use case requirements with the Jersey framework.

The Jersey framework allows you to modify or enhance JAX-RS resources during deployment by registering your own JAX-RS resource model processor providers. Let us take a closer look at this feature.

What is Jersey ModelProcessor and how does it work?

When you deploy a JAX-RS application into a Jersey-based container, the Jersey runtime generates the `org.glassfish.jersey.server.mode.ResourceModel` instance to store all the root REST resources registered in the application. Jersey allows you to enhance the generated resource model via the `org.glassfish.jersey.server.model.ModelProcessor` providers.

You can build your own model processor providers by implementing the `ModelProcessor` interface. This implementation can have the logic to enhance the current resource model by adding additional methods or resources. For instance, you can build a model processor to inject support for the `HTTP OPTION` method on every REST resource during deployment.

A brief look at the ModelProcessor interface

The `ModelProcessor` interface has the following methods:

- `processResourceModel(ResourceModel, Configuration)`: This method is invoked during deployment, right after parsing all the registered root resources. The `ResourceModel` parameter to this method comprises all the registered root resources. This method can have the logic to modify the REST resources before publishing them for use.

- `processSubResource(ResourceModel, Configuration)`: This method is meant for processing the subresource model. Remember that when a request is handled by a subresource, the subresource class instance that handles requests will be resolved only during runtime. Therefore, the `processSubResource()` method is invoked only at runtime (not during deployment) when the framework can resolve the subresource class type. The `ResourceModel` parameter for this method contains only one subresource model that was returned by the subresource locator.

[If you need a quick brush up on subresources, refer to the *Understanding subresources and subresource locators in JAX-RS* section, in *Chapter 4, Advanced Features in the JAX-RS API*.]

Let us see an example to understand how to use model processor APIs provided by Jersey to add additional HTTP methods to all registered top-level JAX-RS resources. This example uses a custom model processor implementation to add an additional `HTTP GET` method on all the registered resources to return the latest version of the resource for the following request path: `GET /<resource>/version HTTP/1.1`.

```
//Other imports are omitted for brevity
import org.glassfish.jersey.process.Inflector;
import org.glassfish.jersey.server.model.ModelProcessor;
import org.glassfish.jersey.server.model.Resource;
import org.glassfish.jersey.server.model.ResourceModel;

@Provider
public class VersionsModelProcessor implements ModelProcessor {
```

```
@Override
public ResourceModel processResourceModel(ResourceModel
    resourceModel, Configuration configuration) {

    // Get the resource model and enhance each resource in it
    // by adding support for a new REST API that returns
    // latest version info
    ResourceModel.Builder newResourceModelBuilder = new
        ResourceModel.Builder(false);
    for (final Resource resource :
            resourceModel.getResources()){
        // For each resource, create a new builder
        final Resource.Builder resourceBuilder =
            Resource.builder(resource);
        // Add a new child resource to the resource and
        // designate a GET method to handle:
        // HTTP GET '/version'
        resourceBuilder.addChildResource("version")
            .addMethod(HttpMethod.GET)
            .handledBy(
                new Inflector<ContainerRequestContext,
                    String>(){

                    @Override
                    public String apply(
                        ContainerRequestContext cr) {
        //return a latest version of this resource
                        return "version : 1.0" ;
                    }
                }).produces(MediaType.TEXT_PLAIN)
                    .extended(true);
        // extended(true) means: not part of core RESTful API

        // Add enhanced resource to the builder
        newResourceModelBuilder.addResource
            (resourceBuilder.build());
    }

    final ResourceModel newResourceModel =
        newResourceModelBuilder.build();
    //return new model
    return newResourceModel;

}

@Override

public ResourceModel processSubResource(ResourceModel
```

```
        subResourceModel, Configuration configuration) {
            // For this demo, do not do anything on subResourceModel
        // return it as is. In real life, you may want to handle
            // subResourceModel as well
            return subResourceModel;
    }

}
```

The preceding model processor example modifies all the registered resources during deployment by adding a child resource to each root resource. The child resource added via the model processor is configured to respond to the `version` query from the client. For example, a RESTful web API call to read the version of the department resource, `GET /departments/version HTTP/1.1`, will now return the following result: `version : 1.0`.

In the last two sections, we were talking about runtime configurations and resource enhancement APIs offered by the Jersey framework for a RESTful application. The next section is a bit of different in nature. In the coming section, we will learn about using hypermedia links in the REST resource representation.

Building Hypermedia as the Engine of Application State (HATEOAS) APIs

HATEOAS is a constraint of the REST application architecture that keeps the RESTful style architecture unique from most other network application architectures. This architectural style lets you use hypermedia links in the response contents so that the client can dynamically navigate to the appropriate resource by traversing the hypermedia links. This is conceptually the same as a web user navigating through web pages by clicking the appropriate hyperlinks in order to achieve a final goal. We have briefly covered this topic in *Chapter 1, Introducing the REST Architectural Style*, under the *Hypermedia as the Engine of Application State* section. In this section, we will learn how to build HATEOAS APIs using JAX-RS as well as Jersey APIs.

Before we get into the details of the JAX-RS and Jersey offerings, let us take a step back to understand how HATEOAS APIs are implemented in typical RESTful web services. The following is the response returned by a RESTful web API that follows the HATEOAS principle for the `GET /departments HTTP/1.1` request:

```
{"departmentId":10,
"departmentName":"Administration",
"locationId":1700,
"managerId":200,
"links":[{"href":"10/employees","rel":"employees"}]}
```

In the preceding example, the response returned by the server contains hypermedia links to employee resources (`10/employees`), which can be traversed by the client to read employees belonging to the department. One of the core benefits of applying the hypermedia constraint in RESTful web APIs is that the client's state is driven by the server and not the other way around. In other words, hypermedia links returned from the server drive the application's state. When you build a HATEOAS-compliant API, you must include all possible links in the API responses.

Please be warned that there is no universally accepted format for representing links between two resources in JSON. Various API vendors or enterprises use different formats depending upon the API guidelines that they follow. In the last example, we saw that hypermedia links were present in the response body content. This is not the only place to keep links for accessing the next set of resources. You can even place links in the HTTP header portion in the response content as follows:

```
HTTP/1.1 200 OK
...
Link: <10/employees>; rel="employees"
```

Choosing where to place links is based on the REST API guidelines that you follow for your application. We will discuss this topic in detail in *Chapter 8, RESTful API Design Guidelines*. As in the case of the placement of links, there are many guidelines for formatting links. Let us take a quick look at a couple of popular formats in the next section.

Formats for specifying JSON REST API hypermedia links

The following are the two popular formats for specifying JSON REST API hypermedia links:

- **RFC 5988 (web linking)**: RFC 5988 puts forward a framework for building links that defines the relation between resources on the web. Note that although this specification defines the properties for the links, it does not define how the links as a whole should be represented in the HTTP message. The syntax set for links in HTTP headers in this specification may supplement JSON resources as well. Each link in RFC 5988 contains the following properties:
    - **Target URI**: Each link should contain a target **Internationalized Resource Identifiers (IRIs)**. This is represented by the `href` attribute. In case you are not familiar with IRI, it is the same as URI in terms of function. However, IRI extends upon URI by using the **Universal Character Set (UCS)**, whereas URI is limited to ASCII characters.

- ◦ **Link relation type**: The link relation type describes how the current context (source) is related to the target resource. This is represented by the `rel` attribute.

- ◦ **Attributes for target IRI**: The attributes for a link include `hreflang`, `media`, `title`, `title*`, and `type`, and any extension link parameters.

 You can learn more about RFC 5988 web linking at `http://tools.ietf.org/html/rfc5988`.

- • **JSON Hypermedia API Language (HAL)**: JSON HAL is a promising proposal that sets the conventions for expressing hypermedia controls, such as links, with JSON. HAL also lets you embed resources within a resource. It is in the draft stage at the time of writing this book. Each link in HAL may contain the following properties:

  - ◦ **Target URI**: It indicates the target resource URI. This is represented by the `href` attribute.

  - ◦ **Link relation**: The link relation type describes how the current context is related to the target resource. This is represented by the `rel` attribute.

  - ◦ **Type**: This indicates the expected resource media type. This is represented by the `type` attribute.

  A resource object (JSON object) in HAL has two reserved properties:

  - ◦ `_links`: This contains links to other resources.

  - ◦ `_embedded`: This contains embedded resources.

 To learn more about HAL, visit `http://tools.ietf.org/html/draft-kelly-json-hal-06`.

Apart from the earlier mentioned formats, there are many other formats defining standards for links in JSON, such as JSON Schema (`http://tools.ietf.org/html/draft-zyp-json-schema-04`), Home Documents (`http://tools.ietf.org/html/draft-nottingham-json-home-03`), JavaScript Object Notation for Linked Data (`http://json-ld.org`), and Collection+JSON (`http://amundsen.com/media-types/collection/`). There is no right or wrong in choosing a hypermedia link format for your application. You should pick up a format that meets most of your use case requirements and stick to it. The link APIs offered by both JAX-RS and Jersey are flexible enough to meet the requirements of many of the common formats.

Programmatically building entity body links using JAX-RS APIs

Before getting into the declarative offerings from the Jersey framework to build HATEOAS APIs, let us see what is there in the JAX-RS API specification for solving this use case. JAX-RS 2.0 has the basic API support for representing hypermedia links with resources.

Let us take an example to understand the APIs provided by JAX-RS for building resource links. Consider the following REST resource class method, which returns a list of department resources:

```
//Rest of the code is omitted for brevity
@GET
@Path("departments")
@Produces(MediaType.APPLICATION_JSON)
public List<Department> findAllDeprtments(){
  //Finds all departments from database
  List<Department> departments = findAllDepartmentEntities();
  return departments;
}
```

Let us see how to add hypermedia links for accessing employee resources in each department resource representation returned by the above method. This link can be traversed by a client to read employees for a department. To add a link, you use the `javax.ws.rs.core.Link` API. The entity provider components that come with the JAX-RS implementation will automatically convert the links to the appropriate media type representation at runtime:

```
//Other imports are omitted for brevity
import javax.ws.rs.core.Link;
import javax.xml.bind.annotation.adapters.XmlAdapter;
@XmlRootElement
public class Department {

    private Short departmentId;
    private String departmentName;
    private Integer managerId;
    private Short locationId;

    Link employeesLink;

    @XmlElement(name = "link")
    @XmlJavaTypeAdapter(XmlAdapter.class)
```

```
    public Link getEmployeesLink() {
        employeesLink = Link.fromUri("{id}/employees")
                .rel("employees").build(departmentId);
        return employeesLink;
    }
  //Rest of the getters and setters are omitted for brevity


}
```

Here is a quick overview of the APIs used in this example:

- In the preceding code snippet, the `Link.fromUri()` method call creates a new hypermedia link builder object, which is an instance of `javax.ws.rs. core.Link.Builder`. This `Builder` instance is used for building hypermedia links.

- The `rel()` method on the `Builder` instance lets you set the name for the `link` field present in the resource. This example sets the link relation as `employees`.

- You can also set attributes on a link object such as a media type, title, or parameter by calling the respective methods, such as `type()`, `title()`, or `param()`, defined on the `Builder` instance.

- The final `build()` method results in building the hypermedia link with the supplied values. In this example, the `build()` method will replace the `param {id}` template present in the URI with the supplied `departmentId` parameter.

> To know the full list of APIs, refer to the API documentation available at `http://docs.oracle.com/javaee/7/api/ javax/ws/rs/core/Link.Builder.html`.

Here is the sample JSON representation generated for the `Department` resource that we discussed in this example:

```
[{"departmentId":300,"departmentName":"Administration",
"link":{"href":"300/employees","rel":"employees"},
"locationId":1700,"managerId":200} ...]
```

Programmatically building header links using JAX-RS APIs

JAX-RS APIs allow you to add links to the HTTP header content as well. In the following code snippet, a link to the access manager for a department resource is added to the HTTP response header:

```java
//Rest of the code is omitted for brevity
@GET
@Path("{id}")
@Produces(MediaType.APPLICATION_JSON)
public Response find(@PathParam("id") Short id) {

  Department deptEntity = findDepartmentEntity(id);
   //Add links to header
  return
     Response.ok()
        .links(getLinks(deptEntity.getManagerId()))
        .entity(deptEntity).build();

}
//Get the link object representing URI for manager
private Link[] getLinks(int departmentId) {
  Link managerLink = Link.fromUri("{id}/employees")
      .rel("employees").build(departmentId);
  return new Link[]{managerLink};
}
```

The following is the sample response generated by the above resource method implementation for the GET /departments/60 HTTP/1.1 request:

```
Server: GlassFish Server
Link: <60/employees>; rel="employees"
Content-Type: application/json
Date: Sun, 29 Mar 2015 11:12:26 GMT
Content-Length: 124
{
departmentId: 60
departmentName: "IT"
locationId: 1400
managerId: 103
}
```

Declaratively building links using Jersey annotations

In the previous section, we have seen offerings in JAX-RS APIs for programmatically building hypermedia links for the REST resources. Jersey simplifies this task further with its annotation-driven API model. In this session, we will take a quick look at Jersey annotations for building HATEOAS APIs.

Specifying the dependency to use Jersey declarative linking

The first step to use Jersey declarative linking features is to add a dependency to the `jersey-declarative-linking` jar. If you use Maven for building a source, then the dependency to `jersey-declarative-linking` in `pom.xml` will look like the following:

```
<dependency>
      <groupId>org.glassfish.jersey.ext</groupId>
      <artifactId>jersey-declarative-linking</artifactId>
      <!-- Choose the right version -->
      <version>2.17</version>
</dependency>
```

Enable Jersey declarative linking feature for the application

Once you have the appropriate dependency set up, the next step is to enable the declarative linking feature by registering the `org.glassfish.jersey.linking.DeclarativeLinkingFeature` class with the application. You can do this via the `org.glassfish.jersey.server.ResourceConfig` class as shown in the following code snippet:

```
//Other imports are omitted for brevity
import org.glassfish.jersey.server.ResourceConfig;
import org.glassfish.jersey.linking.DeclarativeLinkingFeature;
@Provider
@javax.ws.rs.ApplicationPath("webresources")
public class ApplicationConfig extends ResourceConfig {
  public ApplicationConfig(@Context ServletContext context) {
    // Register a class of JAX-RS component
    register(DeclarativeLinkingFeature.class);
    //Package that needs to be scanned for other resource
    packages("com.packtpub.rest.ch5.service");
  }
}
```

Declaratively adding links to resource representation

We are now ready with all the necessary measures for using the Jersey declarative hyperlink feature. Let us get started on using the Jersey annotation in a recourse class to declaratively generate links in the resource representation generated at runtime.

Take a look at the following `Department` resource class. This class is almost the same as the one that we discussed a while ago in the *Programmatically building entity body links using JAX-RS APIs* section. One difference that you may find in the `Department` resource class used in this section is the presence of the `@org.glassfish.jersey.linking.InjectLink` annotation. This is used for generating hypermedia links in the resource representation and can be used on fields of type `String` or URI. The following code snippet uses `InjectLink` for generating hypermedia links for accessing employee resources:

```
//Other imports are removed for brevity
import org.glassfish.jersey.linking.Binding;
import org.glassfish.jersey.linking.InjectLink;
import org.glassfish.jersey.linking.InjectLink.Style;
import javax.xml.bind.annotation.adapters.XmlAdapter;
@XmlRootElement
public class Department {

    private Short departmentId;
    private String departmentName;
    private Integer managerId;
    private Short locationId;

    @InjectLink(
            value = "{id}/employees",
            style = Style.RELATIVE_PATH,
            bindings = @Binding(name = "id",
            value = "${instance.departmentId}"),
            rel = "employees"
    )
    @XmlJavaTypeAdapter(XmlAdapter.class)
    @XmlElement(name = "link")
    Link link;
    //getters and setters for the properties are omitted for brevity
}
```

The entity providers offered by Jersey will take care of generating the appropriate representation for the preceding class when returned in response to a REST API call at runtime. For instance, when the preceding resource class is used with the `public List<Department> findAllDeprtments()` methods that we discussed in the *Programmatically building entity body links using JAX-RS APIs* section, the runtime will generate the appropriate hypermedia links as shown here (without you doing any extra coding, except using appropriate hyperlink annotations):

```
[{"link":{"href":"300/employees","rel":"employees"},"departmentId":300
,"departmentName":"Administration","locationId":1700,"managerId":200},
...]
```

Let us take a look at the `@InjectLink` annotation to understand the usage better.

```
@InjectLink(
                value = "{id}/employees",
                style = Style.RELATIVE_PATH,
                bindings = {@Binding(name = "id",
                value = "${instance.departmentId}")},
                rel = "employees"
)
@XmlJavaTypeAdapter(XmlAdapter.class)
@XmlElement(name = "link")
Link link;

private Short departmentId;
```

Here is a quick summary of the important elements that you can use in the `@InjectLink` annotation:

- `value`: The `value` element specifies a URI template that will be used to build the injected URI. The URI template may contain parameters referring to properties in the current object and **Expression Language (EL)** expressions. For instance, the `${instance.departmentId}` EL expression refers to `departmentId` in the current object. The EL expression that you use here can refer to three types of implicit objects:
    - **Instance**: This represents the instance of the class that contains the annotated field.
    - **Entity**: This represents the entity class instance returned by the resource method. It is typically used in defining link headers.
    - **Resource**: This represents the resource class instance that returns the entity.

- resource: The resource element specifies a resource class whose @Path URI template will be used to build the injected URI.

- bindings: The binding element specifies the runtime binding for embedded URI template parameters. For instance, bindings = @Binding(name = "id", value = "${instance.departmentId}") indicates that the template parameter id is bound to the EL ${instance.departmentId} and value for id can be resolved from the EL that it is bound to.

- condition: The condition element specifies a Boolean EL expression whose value determines whether a Link value can be injected onto the resource.

- style: This defines the style of the URI to inject, such as the relative path or the absolute path.

- rel: This specifies the relationship with the target resource.

- type: This specifies the media type for the referenced resource content, for example, application/json.

- hreflang: This indicates the language for the referenced resource, for example, hreflang="en".

See the API doc to learn about all the elements available with @InjectLink:
https://jersey.java.net/apidocs/latest/jersey/org/glassfish/jersey/linking/InjectLink.html.

Grouping multiple links using @InjectLinks

You can use the @org.glassfish.jersey.linking.InjectLinks annotation to group multiple hypermedia links as an array and inject it to the List or Link[] property present in the resource representation class. Here is an example:

```
@InjectLinks({
        @InjectLink(
                value = "{id}/employees",
                style = Style.RELATIVE_PATH,
                bindings = @Binding(name = "id", value =
                            "${instance.departmentId}"),
                rel = "employees"
        ),
        @InjectLink(
                value = "{id}/employees/{managerId}",
                style = Style.RELATIVE_PATH,
                bindings = {
```

```
             @Binding(name = "id", value =
                 "${instance.departmentId}"),
             @Binding(name = "managerId", value =
                 "${instance.managerId}")},
          rel = "manager"
    )})
@XmlJavaTypeAdapter(LinkAdaptor.class)
@XmlElement(name = "links")
List<Link> links;
```

The sample resource link produced by the preceding definition may look like the following:

```
"links":[{"href":"300/employees","rel":"employees"},
      {"href":"300/employees/200","rel":"manager"}]
```

Declaratively building HTTP link headers using @InjectLinks

You can use @InjectLinks to add HTTP link headers as well. Here is an example:

```
@InjectLinks({
  @InjectLink(
    value = "{id}/employees/{managerId}",
    style = Style.RELATIVE_PATH,
    bindings = {
      @Binding(name = "id", value =
        "${instance.departmentId}"),
      @Binding(name = "managerId", value =
        "${instance.managerId}")},
    rel = "manager"
  )})@XmlRootElement
public class DepartmentRepresentation {
....
}
```

This generates the following link header at runtime:

```
Link: <300/employees/24170>; rel="manager"
```

Reading and writing binary large objects using Jersey APIs

When you work on enterprise-grade business applications, often you may want to build RESTful web APIs for reading and writing large binary objects such as images, documents, and various types of media files. Unfortunately, the JAX-RS API does not have standardized APIs for dealing with large binary files. In this section, we will see offerings from the Jersey framework to store and retrieve images files. These APIs are generic in nature and can be used with any large binary file.

Building RESTful web service for storing images

Let us build a REST API to store the image sent by the client. We will start with the client and then move on to the server-side implementation.

This example uses an HTML client to upload images to the REST API. When you make a POST request to the server, you have to encode the data that forms the body of the request. You can use the multipart/form-data encoding to deal with a large binary object uploaded via <input type="file">. The client-side HTML code may look like the following:

```html
<html>
  <head>
   <title>File upload</title>
   <meta charset="UTF-8">
  </head>
  <body>
   <form action="employees/100/image"
     method="post" enctype="multipart/form-data">
     Choose photo for employee# 100 :
     <input type="file" name="empImgFile" />
     <br>
     <input type="submit" value="Upload Image" />
   </form>
  </body>
</html>
```

This HTML client uploads images for an employee identified by id=100.
The RESTful web API for storing images is located at URI: employees/100/image.
The client code for uploading an image to the RESTful web API is in place now.

As the next step, we will build a RESTful web API that accepts an uploaded image and stores it in a database. Jersey makes it simple by offering many binding annotations for method parameters to extract the desired value from the request body. For instance, it offers the `@org.glassfish.jersey.media.multipart.` `FormDataParam` annotation, which can be used for binding the named body part(s) of a `multipart/form-data` request body to a method parameter or a class member variable, as appropriate. We will use this annotation in conjunction with the request content encoded with `multipart/form-data` for consuming forms that contain files, non-ASCII data, and binary data. Jersey allows you to inject `@FormDataParam` onto the following parameter types:

- Any type of parameter for which a message body reader is available. The following example binds an input stream present in the first named body part `empImageFile` with an `inputStream` object: `@FormDataParam("empImgFile")` `InputStream inputStream`.

- `org.glassfish.jersey.media.multipart.FormDataBodyPart`: This object can be used for reading the value of a parameter that represents the first named body part present in the request body. You can also use `List` or `Collection` of `FormDataBodyPart` to read the values of multiple body parts with the same name. An example is `@FormDataParam("p1")` `List<FormDataBodyPart> values`.

- `org.glassfish.jersey.media.multipart.FormDataContentDisposition`: This represents the `form-data` content disposition header in the incoming payload. You can use it for retrieving details about the uploaded file, such as its name and size.

When you use `@FormDataParam` on a field, the entity provider will inject content from the incoming message body to the annotated fields, as appropriate.

The following code snippet demonstrates how you can use `@FormDataParam` for building a REST API that reads an image uploaded by a client. Note that the name parameter set for `@FormDataParam(...)` must match with file input component present in the request payload. In this example, we name the input file component `empImgFile` in the HTML `<input type="file" name="empImgFile" />`. You must use the same name as the parameter for `@FormDataParam("empImgFile")` to read the uploaded file content present in the payload posted to the server. This example uses JPA to persist the data:

```
//Other imports are not shown for brevity
import org.glassfish.jersey.media.multipart.
        FormDataContentDisposition;
import org.glassfish.jersey.media.multipart.FormDataParam;
```

```
@Stateless
@Path("employees")
public class EmployeeResource {
    //Name of the persistence unit from persistence.xml
    @PersistenceContext(unitName = "EMP_PU")
    private EntityManager entityManager;

    @POST
    @Path("{empId}/image")
    @Consumes(MediaType.MULTIPART_FORM_DATA)
    public void uploadImage(@Context HttpServletRequest request,
        @FormDataParam("empImgFile") InputStream in,
        @FormDataParam("empImgFile") FormDataContentDisposition
        fileDetail,
        @PathParam("empId") Integer empId) throws Exception {

        ByteArrayOutputStream bos = new ByteArrayOutputStream();
        int size = request.getContentLength();
        byte[] buffer = new byte[size];
        int len=0;
        while ((len = in.read(buffer, 0, 10240)) != -1) {
    bos.write(buffer, 0, len);
        }
        byte[] imgBytes = bos.toByteArray();
        //Pass the image to underlying entity
         //to persist the content
        EmployeeImage empImg = findEmployeeImageEntity(empId);
        empImg.setImage(imgBytes);
        entityManager.merge(empImg);
    }
//Other methods are not shown for brevity
}
```

Before ending this section on REST support for handling binary files, let us take a quick look at the code snippet for reading binary files (or images) as well.

Building RESTful web service for reading images

The following method reads the binary representation of an image from the database and streams the content by using the `javax.ws.rs.core.StreamingOutput` class. The method is annotated with `@Produces(MediaType.APPLICATION_OCTET_STREAM)` to indicate that the response is in a binary form:

```java
//Other imports are omitted for brevity
import javax.ws.rs.core.StreamingOutput;

@GET
@Path("/{empId}/image")
@Produces(MediaType.APPLICATION_OCTET_STREAM)
public StreamingOutput getImage(final @PathParam("empId")
    Integer id) throws Exception {

  return new StreamingOutput() {

    @Override
    Public void write(OutputStream output)
        throws IOException {
    EmployeeImage empImg = findEmployeeImageEntity(id);
    byte[] buf = empImg.getImage();
    output.write(buf);
    output.flush();
      }
  };
}
```

You can use the preceding RESTful web API directly with the `<img>` component present in the HTML page as shown in the following HTML snippet. The `employees/100/image` URI points to the RESTful web API that we built for reading the image content:

```html
<img alt="Employee image" src="employees/100/image" id="id"/>
```

Generating chunked output using Jersey APIs

A chunked response means that instead of waiting for the entire result, split the result into chunks (partial results) and send one after the other. Sending a response in chunks is useful for a RESTful web API if the resource returned by the API is huge in size.

With Jersey, you can use can use the `org.glassfish.jersey.server.` `ChunkedOutput` class as the return type to send the response to a client in chunks. The chunked output content can be any data type for which a `MessageBodyWriter<T>` (entity provider) is available.

When you specify `ChunkedOutput` as the return type for a REST resource method, it tells the runtime that the response will be chunked and sent one by one to the client. Seeing `ChunkedOutput` as the return type for a method, Jersey will switch to the asynchronous processing mode while processing this method at runtime, without you having to explicitly use `AsyncResponse` in the method signature. Further, when the response content is generated for this method, Jersey will set `Transfer-Encoding: chunked` in the response header. The chunked transfer encoding allows the server to maintain an HTTP-persistent connection for sending the result to the client in a series of chunks as and when they become available.

The following example shows how you can use `ChunkedOutput` to return a large amount of data. Here is a quick summary of this example:

- This example uses a JPA entity to read an employee record from the database. The employee entity definition is not listed in the code snippet in order to save space. We use `org.eclipse.persistence.queries.` `CursoredStream` to read records in batches from the database. Under the cover, `CursoredStream` wraps a database result set cursor to provide a stream on the resulting selected objects.

- This example defines the `ChunkedOutput<List<Employee>>` `findAllInChunk()` method to return the employee collection in a series of chunks.

- Jersey will process the resource method that returns `ChunkedOutput` asynchronously. This is the reason why this example uses a worker thread to read records from the database. The read operation makes use of the `org.` `eclipse.persistence.queries.CursoredStream` class from `EclipseLink` (which is the JPA provider for this example) to wrap a database result set cursor to provide a stream on the resulting selected objects.

- While returning a response to the client, Jersey will add the Transfer-Encoding: chunked **response header for the** ChunkedOutput **return type.** The client now knows that the response is going to be chunked, so it reads each chunk of the response separately, processes it, and waits for more chunks to arrive on the same connection. This allows the server to maintain an HTTP-persistent connection for sending the series of chunks to clients. Once everything is done, the server closes the connection:

```java
//Other imports are omitted for brevity
import org.eclipse.persistence.queries.CursoredStream;
import org.glassfish.jersey.server.ChunkedOutput;

@Stateless
@Path("employees")
public class EmployeeResource {

  //A thread manager that manages a long-running job
    private final ExecutorService executorService =
      Executors.newCachedThreadPool();

  @GET
  @Path("chunk")
  @Produces({MediaType.APPLICATION_JSON})
  public ChunkedOutput<List<Employee>> findAllInChunk() {
      final ChunkedOutput<List<Employee>> output = new
        ChunkedOutput<List<Employee>>() {
          };
       //Execute the thread
      executorService.execute(new
        LargeCollectionResponseType(output));

      // Returns chunked output set by
      // LargeCollectionResponseType thread class
      return output;
  }

   //This thread class reads employee records from database
   //in batches. This thread is used to back up asynchronous
   //processing of the chunked output.

   class LargeCollectionResponseType implements Runnable {

      ChunkedOutput output;
      EntityManager entityManagerLocal = null;
```

```
//Stream class used to deal
//with large collections
CursoredStream cursoredStream = null;
//Page size used for reading records from DB
final int PAGE_SIZE = 50;

LargeCollectionResponseType(ChunkedOutput output) {
    this.output = output;
    //Get the entity manager instance
    EntityManagerFactory emf =
        Persistence.createEntityManagerFactory("EMP_PU");
    entityManagerLocal = emf.createEntityManager();
    //Get employee query
    //Employee entity definition is not shown for brevity
    Query empQuery = entityManagerLocal.
        createNamedQuery("Employee.findAll");
    //AScrollableCursor is enabled using query hint
    //This hint allows the client to scroll through
    //the results page by page
    empQuery.setHint("eclipselink.cursor", true);
    cursoredStream = (CursoredStream)
        empQuery.getSingleResult();
}

public void run() {
    try {
        boolean hasMore = true;
        do {
            //Scroll through the results page by page
            List<Employee> chunk = (List<Employee>)
                getNextBatch(cursoredStream, PAGE_SIZE);
            hasMore = (chunk != null && chunk.size() > 0);
            if (hasMore) {
                //Write current chunk to ChunkedOutput
                output.write(chunk);
            }
        } while (hasMore);
    } catch (IOException e) {
        // IOException thrown when writing the
        // chunks of response: Should be handled
        e.printStackTrace();
    } finally {
        try {
            output.close();
```

```
                } catch (IOException ioe) {
                    ioe.printStackTrace();
                }


            }
        }


        //CursoredStream is used to deal with large
        //collections returned from TOPLink queries
        //more efficiently
        private List<Employee> getNextBatch(CursoredStream
            cursoredStream, int pagesize) {
            List emps = null;
            if (!cursoredStream.atEnd()) {
                emps = cursoredStream.next(pagesize);
            }
            return emps;
        }
    //Rest of the code goes here
    }
```

Jersey client API for reading chunked input

To read the chunked input on the client, Jersey offers the `org.glassfish.jersey.`
`client.ChunkedInput<T>` class. Here is a client example that reads the employee
list in chunks as returned by the server:

```
//Other imports omitted for brevity
import org.glassfish.jersey.media.sse.EventInput;
import javax.ws.rs.client.ClientBuilder;

String BASE_URI = "http://localhost:8080/hr-app/api";
Client client = ClientBuilder.newClient();
Response response = client.target().path("employees")
    .path("chunk").request().get();
ChunkedInput<List<Employee>> chunks = response
    .readEntity(new GenericType<ChunkedInput<List<Employee>>>(){});
List<Employee> chunk;
while ((chunk = chunks.read()) != null) {
  //Code to process List<Employee> received in chunks goes here
}
//Close the client after use
client.close();
```

Having discussed chunked output and input, we now will move on to another exciting feature offered by the Jersey framework that allows the RESTful web APIs to push notification to clients.

Supporting Server Sent Event in RESTful web services

Server Sent Event (SSE) is a mechanism where a client (browser) receives automatic updates from a server via a long-living HTTP connection that was established when the client contacted the server for the first time. The SSE client subscribes to a stream of updates generated by a server, and whenever a new event occurs, a notification is sent to the client via the existing HTTP connection. The connection is then left open until the server has some data to send. In this section, we will discuss how the SSE technology can be used in a REST API to send continuous updates to the client.

> Server Sent Events use a single, unidirectional, persistent connection between the client and the server. This is suited for the one-way publish-subscribe model wherever the server pushes updates to clients.

In a typical HTTP client-server communication model, the client opens the connection and sends a request to the server. The server then responds back with the result and closes the connection. With SSE, the server leaves the connection open even after sending the first response back to the client. This connection will be left open as long as the server wants and can be used for sending notifications to all the connected clients.

Let us see how we can implement SSE in RESTful web services by using Jersey APIs. The following are the core Jersey classes that you may want to use while building SSE-enabled RESTful resources:

- `org.glassfish.jersey.media.sse.SseBroadcaster`: This is a utility class, used for broadcasting SSE to multiple subscribers. Each subscriber is represented by an `EventOutput` instance, which is explained next.

- `org.glassfish.jersey.media.sse.EventOutput`: One instance of this class corresponds with exactly one HTTP connection. When a client subscribes to SSEs by calling the designated REST API method, the server (Jersey application) generates `EventOutput` and returns it to the caller. When `EventOutput` is returned from the resource method, the underlying HTTP connection will be left open for later use by the server. The server can use this HTTP connection to broadcast messages whenever needed.

Let us build a simple example to learn how to enable SSE support in RESTful web services.

The first step is to add the required dependencies for SSE (the `jersey-media-sse` jar) to the project. If you use Maven for building your source, then the dependency to `jersey-media-sse` may look like the following:

```
<dependency>
   <groupId>org.glassfish.jersey.media</groupId>
   <artifactId>jersey-media-sse</artifactId>

   <!--specify right version -->
   <version>2.17</version>
   <type>jar</type>

   <!-- container(GlassFish) provides dependency
         for this example -->
   <scope>provided</scope>
</dependency>
```

The Jersey runtime will automatically discover and register the Jersey SSE module if it is found in the application class path. You do not need to do anything explicitly in order to enable this feature.

In the following example, we will use an SSE event mechanism to notify the subscribed clients whenever the department resource gets modified on the server.

Let us take a closer look at the implementation to understand how SSE is leveraged in this example via Jersey APIs:

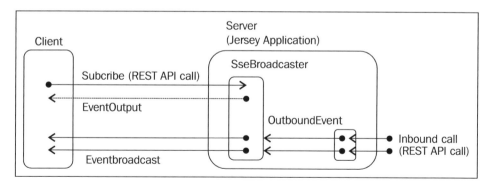

Let's understand the image in detail:

1. The client subscribes to SSEs by calling the `manageSSEEvents(...)` RESTful web service method, which is accessible via the following URI: `GET /departments/events HTTP/1.1`.

   When clients subscribe to events, we add them to the `SseBroadcaster` instance. Later, when the event needs to be broadcast, we ask `SseBroadcaster` to broadcast the events to all subscribed parties.

   This example uses a singleton resource class. The reason for us to use the singleton resource class is primarily to make sure that API calls, which need access to `SseBroadcaster`, use the same `SseBroadcaster` instance. You can improve this example by adding proper thread synchronization blocks.

2. Later, when a client updates a department resource, this example will create an `OutboundEvent` instance and broadcast it to all the listeners via the `SseBroadcaster` instance discussed in Step 1. The `OutboundEvent` object holds the relevant message about the modifications made on the department.

3. Let us see how the client deals with SSE. An SSE client keeps track of the most recently received event identifier. If the connection fails, the client will attempt to reconnect and send a special `Last-Event-ID` HTTP header containing the event ID. This header can be used as a synchronization mechanism between the client and the server in the event of a temporary connection failure. The following method used in the example processes the `Last-Event-ID` sent by the client and replays all the missed events: `public EventOutput manageSSEEvents( @HeaderParam(SseFeature.LAST_EVENT_ID_HEADER) @DefaultValue("-1") int lastEventId)`.

4. When the client closes a connection and does not respond within the reconnect delay window, then the broadcaster identifies the corresponding `EventOutput` and releases it along with all the resources associated with it.

5. Alternatively, the server can close all open connections by invoking the `closeAll()` method on the `SseBroadcaster` object.

The following is the code snippet used for building an SSE-enabled RESTful web API discussed in this example:

```
//Other imports are omitted for brevity
import org.glassfish.jersey.media.sse.EventOutput;
import org.glassfish.jersey.media.sse.OutboundEvent;
import org.glassfish.jersey.media.sse.SseBroadcaster;
import org.glassfish.jersey.media.sse.SseFeature;
```

```
@Path("departments/events")
@Singleton
public class SSEEnabledDeptResource {

    @PersistenceContext(unitName = "SSE_PU")
    private EntityManager entityManager;

    private static ArrayList<String> modifiedDepts = new
        ArrayList<String>();
    private static final SseBroadcaster broadcaster = new
        SseBroadcaster();

    // Client subscribes to SSEs by calling
    // this RESTful web service method.
    // The lastEventId param copies Last-Event-ID HTTP header
    // field sent by the client. This is used for replaying
    // missed events, if any
    @GET
    @Produces(SseFeature.SERVER_SENT_EVENTS)
    public EventOutput manageSSEEvents(
        @HeaderParam(SseFeature.LAST_EVENT_ID_HEADER)
        @DefaultValue("-1") int lastEventId) {

        EventOutput eventOutput = new EventOutput();
        if (lastEventId > 0) {
            replayMissedUpdates(lastEventId, eventOutput);
        }
        if (!broadcaster.add(eventOutput)) {
            // Let's try to force a 5-s delayed client
            // reconnect attempt
            throw new ServiceUnavailableException(5L);
        }
        return eventOutput;
    }
    //Replay all missed events since lastEventId
    private void replayMissedUpdates(final int lastEventId,
        final EventOutput eventOutput) {
      try {
        for (int i = lastEventId;
                    i < modifiedDepts.size(); i++) {
          eventOutput.write(createItemEvent(i,
                        modifiedDepts.get(i)));
        }
```

```
    } catch (IOException ex) {
      throw new InternalServerErrorException
                    ("Error replaying missed events", ex);
    }
  }


  //This method generates an SSE whenever any client
  //invokes it to modify the department resource
  //identified by path parameter
  @PUT
  @Path("{id}")
  @Consumes(MediaType.APPLICATION_JSON)
  public void edit(@PathParam("id") Short id,
      Department entity) {
      entityManager.merge(entity);
      final int modifiedListIndex = modifiedDepts.size() + 1;
      // Broadcasting an un-named SSE with payload
      // as the name of the newly added item in data
      broadcaster.broadcast(createItemEvent
          (modifiedListIndex, entity.getDepartmentName()));
      modifiedDepts.add(entity.getDepartmentName());
  }
  // A helper method to create OutboundEvent
  private OutboundEvent createItemEvent(final int eventId,
      final String name) {
       return
          new OutboundEvent.Builder()
          .id(String.valueOf(eventId))
          .data(String.class, name).build();
  }
}
```

Remember that an SSE is unidirectional by nature and is appropriate for a publish-subscribe communication model. Here are some advantages of using SSEs:

- With an SEE, a message is transported over the popular HTTP instead of a custom protocol. This keeps both the server and the client simple and easy to work on.

- HTTP has built-in support for reconnection and event-id used in an SSE.

- SSE is a simple and lightweight protocol.

Understanding the Jersey server-side configuration properties

Each application is different and must be tuned separately. Things that work for one application do not necessarily work for another. Keeping this point in mind, Jersey offers various server-side configuration properties to optimize the runtime performance of RESTful web services. The following table lists some of the core properties that you may find useful while tuning RESTful web APIs.

 To view the complete list of configuration properties offered by Jersey, visit the following *Appendix* page in Jersey User Guide: `https://jersey.java.net/documentation/latest/ appendix-properties.html`

Here are a few major configuration properties with a detailed explanation for each:

Configuration Property	Description
`jersey.config.server.subresource.cache.size`	This property takes an integer value that defines the cache size for subresource locator models. The default value is 64. Caching of subresource locator models is useful for avoiding the repeated generation of subresource models while processing the request. Runtime identifies the cached subresource with the RESTful web API URI and input parameters values.
`jersey.config.server.subresource.cache.age`	This property takes an integer value that defines the maximum age (in seconds) for cached subresource locator models. This is not enabled by default. This is useful for reducing the memory footprint when your application is idle.

Configuration Property	Description
`jersey.config.server.subresource.cache.` `jersey.resource.enabled`	This property takes a true or false value. If it is set to true, then Jersey will cache resources in addition to caching subresource locator classes and instances (which are cached by default). To leverage this feature, your resource method needs to return the same resource instances for the same input parameters. This is not enabled by default.

You can configure these properties either by extending the `org.glassfish.jersey.server.ResourceConfig` class or by using `init-param` in `web.xml` as follows:

- Configuring server-side properties by extending `ResourceConfig`:

```
@Provider
@javax.ws.rs.ApplicationPath("webresources")
public class ApplicationConfig extends ResourceConfig {

    public ApplicationConfig(@Context ServletContext
        context) {
    //Specify server-side configuration properties
    property(ServerProperties
        .SUBRESOURCE_LOCATOR_CACHE_SIZE, 1000);
    property(ServerProperties
        .SUBRESOURCE_LOCATOR_CACHE_AGE, 60 * 10);
    }
}
```

- Specifying configuration properties in `web.xml`:

```
<web-app ...>
    <servlet>
        <servlet-name>
            JerseyRestApplicationServlet
        </servlet-name>
        <servlet-class>
            org.glassfish.jersey.servlet.ServletContainer
        </servlet-class>
        <init-param>
```

```
        <param-name>
            jersey.config.server.subresource.cache.size
        </param-name>
        <param-value>1000</param-value>
    </init-param>
<init-param>
        <param-name>
            jersey.config.server.subresource.cache.age
        </param-name>
        <param-value>600</param-value>
    </init-param>
</servlet>
</web-app>
```

Monitoring RESTful web services using Jersey APIs

Jersey lets you register various event listeners to monitor the state of your JAX-RS application. Here are the two core listener interfaces that you may need to be aware of:

- `org.glassfish.jersey.server.monitoring.ApplicationEventListener`: This is a Jersey-specific provider component that listens to application events such as initialization of application, start and stop of application, and so on. The implementation class can be registered as any standard JAX-RS provider.

- `org.glassfish.jersey.server.monitoring.RequestEventListener`: The implementation of the interface will be called for request events when they occur. This is not a JAX-RS provider; an instance of `RequestEventListener` must be returned from the `ApplicationEventListener::onRequest(RequestEvent)`.

Jersey also comes with the `MonitoringStatistics` JMX bean to collect the application state, which can be enabled by setting the following configuration property: `jersey.config.server.monitoring.statistics.mbeans.enabled=true`.

> To learn more about the monitoring framework in Jersey, visit the following chapter in Jersey User Guide: `https://jersey.java.net/documentation/latest/monitoring_tracing.html`.

Summary

In this chapter, we covered some of the very useful extensions offered by the Jersey framework. These features are really useful to address specific use cases that you may see very often in real-life REST API development. Remember that all the features that we have discussed in this chapter are offered by Jersey and are not part of the JAX-RS standard (unless otherwise stated). Using the Jersey extension features directly in your code may lock down your application with a specific JAX-RS implementation. However, if the JAX-RS implementation that you choose is robust, proven, and as powerful compared to other similar products in the industry, then you are not really losing much by sticking to a specific vendor. Therefore, if your application really needs some vendor-specific offering, consider all aspects and then take a decision.

By now, you should have a good understanding of JAX-RS APIs and Jersey extensions. In the next chapter, we will learn how to secure RESTful web services.

6
Securing RESTful Web Services

Security is an important part of any enterprise application. In the era of cloud and the Internet of Things, controlling access to the application via the public web API is an essential requirement for any enterprise. The security implementation in a RESTful web service application decides who can access the RESTful web APIs and what they can do once they are logged in. This chapter describes how you can secure the REST APIs from unauthorized and malicious access.

In this chapter, we take the point of view of the architect and not of the creator of the infrastructures supporting our applications. Nevertheless, by the end of the chapter, you will have a good understanding of how to secure your web services using the HTTP basic authentication and OAuth authentication protocols. The following topics are discussed in this chapter:

- HTTP basic authentication
- HTTP digest authentication
- Securing RESTful web services with OAuth
- Authorizing the RESTful web service accesses
- Input validation

Securing and authenticating web services

Security on the Internet takes many forms. In the context of RESTful web services and this book, we are only interested in two forms of security: firstly, securing access to web services; secondly, accessing web services on behalf of our users.

What we accomplish with securing web services is the calculated control of resources. Even though most web services are publicly available, we still need to control data access and traffic throughput. We can do both by restricting access through subscription accounts. For example, Google's web service API limited the number of queries a registered user could execute daily. Similarly, many other API vendors restrict the access of their APIs.

Security has two essential elements: authentication and authorization.

- **Authentication**: It is the process of verifying the identity of the user who is trying to access the application or web service. This is typically performed by obtaining user credentials, such as username and password, and validating them against the user details configured on the server.

- **Authorization**: This is the process of verifying what an authenticated user is permitted to do in the application or service.

In this chapter, we will take a look at various approaches for authenticating and authorizing RESTful web services. We will start with HTTP basic authentication for RESTful web services, which is the simplest authentication mechanism among all.

HTTP basic authentication

Basic HTTP authentication works by sending the Base64 encoded username and the password as a pair in the HTTP authorization header. The username and password must be sent for every HTTP request made by the client. A typical HTTP basic authentication transaction can be depicted with the following sequence diagram. In this example, the client is trying to access a protected RESTful web service endpoint (/webresources/departments) to retrieve department details:

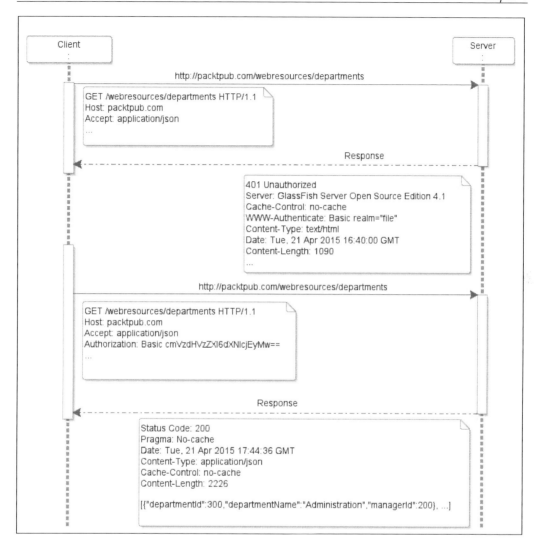

This diagram represents a whole transaction. A client begins by requesting the URI, /webresources/departments. Because the resource is secured using HTTP basic authentication and the client does not provide the required authorization credentials, the server replies with a 401 HTTP response. The client receives the response, scans through it, and prepares a new request with the necessary data needed to authenticate the user. The new request from the client will contain the authorization header set to a Base64 encoded value of column delimited username and password string, <username>:<password>. This time, the server will verify the credentials and replies with the requested resource.

As we have seen, client requests can be generated from any application that can create HTTP connections, including web browsers. Web browsers typically cache the credentials so that users do not have to type in their username and password for every secured resource request. This is viewed as a deficiency of the protocol; as unauthorized access can take place with cached credentials, and there is no way for a web service to differentiate authorized requests from unauthorized ones. Furthermore, using basic authentication is not enough for security because usernames and passwords are only encoded using Base64 encoding, which can be easily deciphered. However, the intent of Base64 is not to secure the name-value pair, but to uniformly encode characters when transferred over HTTP. Because of these reasons, it is not recommended to use basic authentication over HTTP for any application accessed over the Internet. In general, we solve this potential security hole by using HTTPS (Transport Layer security) instead of HTTP, which we will discuss later in this chapter.

Building JAX-RS clients with basic authentication

A normal client-server transaction, when using HTTP basic authentication, can take two forms. On one hand, a client makes a request to the server without authentication credentials (as depicted in the last sequence diagram). On the other hand, a client makes a request to the server with authentication credentials. Let's take a closer look at these two scenarios.

When a client makes a request without authentication credentials, the server sends a response with an HTTP error code of 401 (unauthorized access). If the request is executed from a web browser, users see the ubiquitous **Authentication Required** browser popup, as shown here:

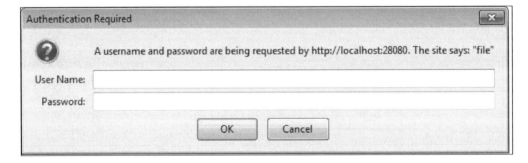

Users can then enter a valid username and password to complete the request. Note that the web browser keeps track of the 401 response, and is charged with sending the proper authentication credentials back with the original URI. This makes the transaction seamless for users. Now, if we were using a client other than a web browser, we would need to programmatically intercept the 401 response and then provide valid credentials to complete the original request.

The second scenario that comes up while using HTTP basic authentication is when we do not wait for a server's 401 response, but provide authentication credentials at the beginning itself. As we said, we provide the credentials in the HTTP header authorization. APIs for setting the HTTP headers vary with client frameworks that you use. The following JAX-RS client example uses the `javax.ws.rs.client.ClientRequestFilter` implementation to associate the HTTP header authorization with each request. If you need a quick brush up on `ClientRequestFilter`, refer to the *Modifying request and response parameters with JAX-RS filters* section, in *Chapter 4, Advanced Features in the JAX-RS API*:

```
//Other imports are removed for brevity
import java.util.Base64;
import javax.ws.rs.client.ClientRequestContext;
import javax.ws.rs.client.ClientRequestFilter;
import javax.ws.rs.core.MultivaluedMap;
import javax.ws.rs.ext.Provider;

@Provider
public class ClientAuthenticationFilter implements
    ClientRequestFilter {

    private final String user;
    private final String password;

    public ClientAuthenticationFilter(String user,
        String password) {
        this.user = user;
        this.password = password;
    }

    //The filter() method is called before a request has been
    //dispatched to a client transport layer.
    //This method is used in this example for attaching user
    //name-password token with authorization header
    public void filter(ClientRequestContext requestContext) throws
        IOException {
```

```
        MultivaluedMap<String, Object> headers =
            requestContext.getHeaders();
        final String basicAuthentication =
            getBasicAuthentication();
        headers.add("Authorization", basicAuthentication);


    }
    //Return BASE64 encoded user name and password
    private String getBasicAuthentication() {
        String token = this.user + ":" + this.password;
        try {
            byte[] encoded =
                Base64.getEncoder().encode(
                    token.getBytes("UTF-8"));
            return "BASIC " + new String(encoded);
        } catch (UnsupportedEncodingException ex) {
            throw new IllegalArgumentException(
                "Cannot encode with UTF-8", ex);
        }
    }
}
```

The next step is to register the preceding filter implementation with the JAX-RS client code that makes the REST API call. The following code snippet illustrates how to accomplish this step. This example invokes a protected RESTful web service URI, /departments/count, to read the total number of departments. The client sets the HTTP basic authentication header via ClientAuthenticationFilter:

```
//Rest of the implementation is not shown here to save space
private static final String BASE_URI =
    "http://localhost:8080/hrapp";
//This method invokes protected REST API.
//Valid username and password needs to be passed by the caller
public Integer totalDepartmnets(String username,
    String password) {

  Client client = javax.ws.rs.client.ClientBuilder.newClient();
  WebTarget webTarget = client.target(BASE_URI)
      .path("departments");
  //Register the filter with client
  ClientAuthenticationFilter filter = new
      ClientAuthenticationFilter(username, password);
  webTarget.register(filter);
```

```
Integer count= webTarget.path("count").request
    (javax.ws.rs.core.MediaType.TEXT_PLAIN).get(Integer.class);
client.close();
return count;
}
```

The JAX-RS client runtime invokes all registered filters before the request has been dispatched to the transport layer. In this example, `ClientAuthenticationFilter` adds the HTTP authentication header to each request made by the client. Because we are sending authentication credentials in the first REST API call itself, we do not expect a 401 response from the server, and the API call will proceed as any other request.

For the other HTTP request types, such as `POST`, `PUT`, and `DELETE`, the client request process cycle follows the same pattern as shown earlier. Client runtime sets the credentials and proceeds with the request and consumption of the response. Finally, every request type must include the authentication credentials or else we will have to handle, programmatically, the server's 401 response. If the client knows the type of authentication required by the target API in advance, it makes sense to attach the necessary authentication content with the very first request itself, which will help you in avoiding an extra round trip that would be otherwise required for authentication.

For details on HTTP basic authentication, see the page at `http://www.ietf.org/rfc/rfc2617.txt`.

In the next section, we will learn how to secure a JAX-RS RESTful web service application deployed on a server such as the GlassFish server.

Securing JAX-RS services with basic authentication

In this section, we cover how to configure a JAX-RS application to challenge clients for valid authentication credentials.

The basic authentication configuration depends on the web container being used. Throughout this book, we have used a GlassFish server for every application that required a Java web container; therefore, this example also assumes GlassFish as the target server for running the RESTful web APIs. We only look at the basic authentication configuration for the latest version of GlassFish (version 4.x).

The problem to solve is the restriction of access to our RESTful web services. Using basic authentication, we can do this by creating a set of users for a specific security realm. A security realm is a mechanism used for protecting application resources. It gives you the ability to protect a resource by defining security constraints and user roles that can access the protected resource. Let's see how the security realms are defined and used for securing resources deployed in a GlassFish server.

Configuring JAX-RS application for basic authentication

You can secure a Java web application, deployed in a Java EE container, via basic authentication by making appropriate security entries in the web.xml descriptor file, and also in the container (vendor) specific deployment descriptor file(glassfish-web.xml, in this example).

Let's say we want to use basic authentication for one of the JAX-RS sample web service applications that we built in previous chapters.

The first step is to modify the web.xml file to look as follows. Note that web.xml is found in the WEB-INF folder of your web application; you should generate a new one if it is found missing:

```xml
<?xml version="1.0" encoding="UTF-8"?>
<web-app ...>

    <security-constraint>
        <web-resource-collection>
            <web-resource-name>
                Protected resource
            </web-resource-name>
            <url-pattern>/*</url-pattern>
            <http-method>GET</http-method>
        </web-resource-collection>

        <auth-constraint>
            <!-- role name that authorized users belongs to-->
            <role-name>APIUser</role-name>
        </auth-constraint>
        <!-- /added -->
        <!-- Use it only if you use https -->
        <user-data-constraint>
            <transport-guarantee>
              CONFIDENTIAL
```

```
            </transport-guarantee>
          </user-data-constraint>
      </security-constraint>

      <login-config>
          <auth-method>BASIC</auth-method>
          <!-- realm name used in GlassFish -->
          <realm-name>file</realm-name>
      </login-config>
      <security-role>
          <role-name>APIUser</role-name>
      </security-role>
  </web-app>
```

Hers is a quick summary of the core elements that you saw in the preceding web.xml file:

- The <security-constraint> element in web.xml is used to secure a collection of resources by restricting access to them with the appropriate URL mapping:
    - The <web-resource-collection> subelement describes the protected resources in the application, which are identified via URL patterns and HTTP methods.
    - The subelement, <auth-constraint>, defines the user roles that are authorized to access constrained resources.
    - The subelement, <user-data-constraint>, defines how data is protected in the transmission channel. It takes the following values: CONFIDENTIAL, INTEGRAL, or NONE. CONFIDENTIAL and INTEGRAL are treated in the same way by the Java EE container, and these values imply the use of Transport Layer security (HTTPS) to all incoming requests matching the URL patterns present in <web-resource-collection>.

- The element, <login-config>, defines the login configurations used in the application.

    The subelement, <realm-name>, refers to a collection of security information that is checked for authenticating the user when a secured page (resource) is accessed at runtime. The realm name that you enter should match with the security realm that you configured on the server.

The subelement, `<auth-method>`, defines the authorization method used in the application. The possible values are as follows:

- ° `BASIC`: This is the HTTP basic authentication that we discussed a while ago.

- ° `DIGEST`: This is the same as HTTP basic authentication except that instead of a password, the client sends a cryptographic hash of user credentials along with the username.

- ° `FORM`: This uses an HTML form for login, having field names that match with specific convention. For instance, `j_username` and `j_ password` are used as names for the username and password fields respectively.

- ° `CLIENT-CERT`: This uses a certificate or other custom tokens in order to authenticate a user.

Let's get back to the configurations for basic authentication, which we were discussing. The `web.xml` file that we used for this example tells the web server that the web application uses basic authentication and that any URI access must be authenticated for the role-name, `APIUser`. This means that to access the URI, `http://localhost:8080/hrapp/departments`, the user should belong to the `APIUser` role.

We have not yet finished configuration entries for the application. The next step is to map the role that we have specified in `web.xml` (`APIUser`) to user groups that we will define on the server. This configuration is done on the vendor-specific deployment descriptor, `glassfish-web.xml`:

```xml
<?xml version="1.0" encoding="UTF-8"?>
<glassfish-web-app error-url="">
    <!-- Other entries go here -->
    <security-role-mapping>
        <!-- maps "Users" group to APIUser -->
        <role-name>APIUser</role-name>
        <group-name>Users</group-name>
    </security-role-mapping>
</glassfish-web-app>
```

While configuring the security realm on the server, we should map actual users of the application to the user groups as appropriate. This is explained in the next section. Though the basic concepts of the security configuration remain the same across various Java EE servers, the actual steps may vary. This example takes GlassFish as a server and explains the security configurations in the next section.

To learn more about securing Java web application, refer to the topic, *Security* in *The Java EE Tutorial*, available at `http://docs.oracle.com/javaee/7/tutorial/partsecurity.htm#GIJRP`.

Defining groups and users in the GlassFish server

GlassFish allows you to define users for the application using the concept of realms. As we mentioned in the last section, a security realm can be treated as a mechanism that allows us to define users and groups. GlassFish offers various credential realms, including FileRealm, JDBCRealm, JNDIRealm, LDAPRealm, and so on. In this example we will use an existing file realm that comes with GlassFish by default. Here are the steps for adding users and groups to the file realm in GlassFish:

1. Start the GlassFish server. If you are new to the GlassFish server, take a look at the tutorial at `https://glassfish.java.net/getstarted.html`.

2. Log in as the administrator to **Admin interface**.

3. Navigate to **Configurations | server-config | Security | Realms | File**. In this example, we use a file to store user information. In a real life scenario, you may use LDAP or RDBMS.

4. Click on the **Manage User** button at the top of the page.

5. On the **File Users** page, click on **New** and add a user and give a password. Set the **Group List** value as appropriate. In `web.xml`, we have configured **Users** as a group, so specify the same name as a value for **Group List**, for this example.

6. Click on **OK** to save change.

Now you can deploy the secured RESTful web service application into the server. The client can use the username and password that we configured in this section for accessing the RESTful web APIs.

The basic authentication methods described here has a fundamental security hole. It sends credentials as clear text in every HTTP request. Therefore, we need a mechanism to ensure that credentials cannot be spoofed during a transaction. The solution is to use the **Secure Socket Layer** (**SSL**) or **Transport Layer Security** (**TLS**) protocol.

SSL is the standard for securing data transfer over the Internet. HTTP over SSL (HTTPS) is used to secure connections between the Internet browser client and server. The HTTPS protocol uses certificates to ensure secure communications between the client and server. The latest version of the SSL standard is called TLS.

TLS/SSL is a well understood web protocol, and because the RESTful web services we implemented in previous chapters are nothing more than server components, all we need to do is configure GlassFish to use TLS/SSL; therefore, every request and response message between the clients and servers, assuming TLS/SSL has been configured properly, would now be encrypted.

Just remember that once TLS/SSL has been turned on, requests will be HTTPS requests, this means that URIs take the form of `https://<REST-RESOURCE-URI>` (note the `https` prefix in the address).

For the sake of brevity, we have not covered how to configure TLS/SSL in this book. The GlassFish server administration guide covers this topic in *Chapter 14, Administering Internet Connectivity*. You can download the administration guide from `https://glassfish.java.net/docs/4.0/administration-guide.pdf`.

To learn how to set up the SSL configuration on the Jersey client, take a look at *Section 5.9, Securing a Client* in the Jersey User Guide. The link to the documentation is `https://jersey.java.net/documentation/latest/client.html`.

HTTP digest authentication

The HTTP digest authentication authenticates a user based on a username and a password. However, unlike with basic authentication, the password is not transmitted in clear text between the client and the server. Instead, the client sends a one way cryptographic hash of the username, password, and a few other security related fields using the MD5 message-digest hash algorithm. When the server receives the request, it regenerates the hashed value for all the fields as done by client and compares it with the one present in the request. If the hashes match, the request is treated as authenticated and valid. To learn how to configure digest authentication realm in the GlassFish server, refer to *Chapter 2, Administering User Security in GlassFish Security Guide*, which you can download from `https://glassfish.java.net/docs/4.0/security-guide.pdf`.

If the client application uses the Jersey framework implementation, then the API to invoke RESTful web services secured via the HTTP digest authentication may look like as shown in the following code snippet:

```
//Rest of the imports are removed for brevity
import org.glassfish.jersey.client.authentication.
    HTTP_AUTHENTICATION_DIGEST_USERNAME;
import org.glassfish.jersey.client.authentication.
    HTTP_AUTHENTICATION_DIGEST_PASSWORD;

//Client code goes here
final String RESOURCE_URI =
    "http://localhost:8080/hrapp/departments";
Client client = javax.ws.rs.client.ClientBuilder.newClient();
//Provide the username and password, and invoke method
Response response = client.target(RESOURCE_URI).request()
  .property(HTTP_AUTHENTICATION_DIGEST_USERNAME, "<Username>")
  .property(HTTP_AUTHENTICATION_DIGEST_PASSWORD, "<Password>")
  .get();
```

Securing RESTful web services with OAuth

OAuth is an open standard for authorization, used by many enterprises and service providers to protect resources. OAuth solves a different security problem than what HTTP basic authentication has been used for. OAuth protocol allows client applications to access protected resources on behalf of the resource owner (typically, the application user).

If we look at the history of this protocol, the OAuth Version 1.0 was published as RFC 5849 in 2010. Later, the next evolution of OAuth, Version 2.0, was published as RFC 6749 in 2012. Note that these two versions are different in their implementations and do not have many things in common. In this section, we will see what the OAuth protocol and its details are. We will also discuss how a RESTful web service client can access OAuth-protected RESTful web APIs.

Understanding the OAuth 1.0 protocol

The OAuth protocol specifies a process for resource owners to authorize third-party applications to access their server resources without sharing their credentials.

Consider a scenario where Jane (the user of an application) wants to let an application access her private data that is stored in a third-party service provider. Before OAuth 1.0 or other similar open source protocols, such as Google AuthSub and FlickrAuth, if Jane wanted to let a consumer service use her data stored on some third-party service provider, she would need to give her user credentials to the consumer service to access data from the third party service via appropriate service calls. Instead of Jane passing her login information to multiple consumer applications, OAuth 1.0 solves this problem by letting the consumer applications request authorization from the service provider on Jane's behalf. Jane does not divulge her login information; authorization is granted from the service provider, where both her data and credentials are stored. The consumer application (or consumer service) only receives an authorization token that can be used to access data from the service provider. Note that the user (Jane) has full control of the transaction and can invalidate the authorization token at any time during the signup process, or even after the two services have been used together.

The typical example used to explain OAuth 1.0 is that of a service provider that stores pictures on the Web (let's call the service StorageInc), and a fictional consumer service that is a picture printing service (let's call the service PrintInc). On its own, PrintInc is a full-blown web service but it does not offer picture storage, its business is only printing pictures. For convenience, PrintInc has created a web service that lets its users download their pictures from StorageInc for printing.

This is what happens when a user (the resource owner) decides to use PrintInc (the client application) to print his/her images stored in StorageInc (the service provider):

1. The user creates an account in PrintInc. Let's call the user Jane, to keep things simple.

2. PrintInc asks if Jane wants to use her pictures stored in StorageInc and presents a link to get authorization to download her pictures (the protected resources). Jane is the resource owner here.

3. Jane decides to let PrintInc connect to StorageInc on her behalf and clicks on the authorization link.

4. Both PrintInc and StorageInc have implemented the OAuth protocol, so StorageInc asks Jane if she wants to let PrintInc use her pictures. If she says yes, then StorageInc asks Jane to provide her username and password. Note, however, that her credentials are being used at StorageInc's site, and that PrintInc has no knowledge of her credentials.

5. Once Jane provides her credentials, StorageInc passes PrintInc an authorization token, which is stored as a part of Jane's account on PrintInc.

6. Now we are back at PrintInc's web application and Jane can now print any of her pictures stored in StorageInc's web service.

7. Finally, every time Jane wants to print more pictures, all she needs to do is come back to PrintInc's website and download her pictures from StorageInc. Note that she does not need to provide her username and password again, as she has already authorized these two web services to exchange data on her behalf.

The preceding example clearly portrays the authorization flow in OAuth 1.0 protocol. Before getting deeper into OAuth 1.0, here is the brief overview of the common terminologies and roles that we have seen in this example:

- **Client (consumer)**: This refers to an application (service) that tries to access protected resource on behalf of the resource owner and with the resource owner's consent. A client can be a business service, mobile, web, or desktop application. In the previous example, PrintInc is the client application.

- **Server (service provider)**: This refers to an HTTP server that understands the OAuth protocol. It accepts and responds to requests authenticated with the OAuth protocol from various client applications (consumers). If you relate this with the previous example, StorageInc is the service provider.

- **Protected resource**: Protected resources are resources hosted on servers (the service providers) that are access restricted. The server validates all incoming requests and grants access to the resource as appropriate.

- **Resource owner**: This refers to an entity capable of granting access to a protected resource. Mostly, it refers to an end user who owns the protected resource. In the previous example, Jane is the resource owner.

- **Consumer key and secret (client credentials)**: These two strings are used to identify and authenticate the client application (the consumer) making the request.

- **Request token and secret (temporary credentials)**: This is the temporary credential returned by the server when the resource owner authorizes the client application to use the resource. As the next step, the client will send this request token to the server to get authorized. On successful authorization, the server returns an access token. The access token is explained next.

- **Access token and secret (token credentials)**: The server returns an access token to the client when the client submits temporary credentials obtained from the server during the resource grant approval by the user. The access token is a string that identifies a client that is requesting for protected resources. Once the access token is obtained, the client passes it along with each resource request to the server. The server can then verify the identity of the client by checking this access token.

The following sequence diagram shows the interactions between the various parties involved in the OAuth 1.0 protocol:

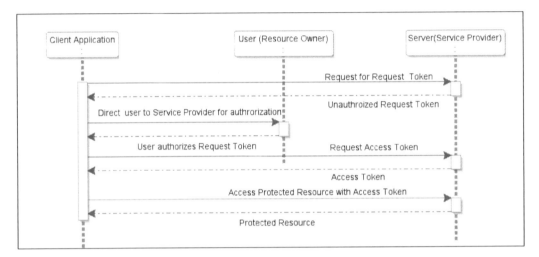

 You can get more information about OAuth 1.0 protocol at `http://tools.ietf.org/html/rfc5849`, which is their official website.

Building the OAuth 1.0 client using Jersey APIs

Let's build a simple client to understand the API usage for accessing the OAuth 1.0 protected resource. Note that the JAX-RS specification has not yet standardized APIs for the OAuth client. This example uses the Jersey API to build the OAuth 1.0 client.

 The complete source code for this example is available on the Packt Publishing website. You can download the example from the Packt Publishing website link that we mentioned at the beginning of this book, in the *Preface* section. In the downloaded source code, see the project, `rest-chapter6-oauth1-client`.

You should start by specifying the dependency to the `oauth1-client` jar file in the client application. If you use Maven to build the client, the dependency entry in `pom.xml` may look like as shown here:

```
<dependency>
    <groupId>org.glassfish.jersey.security</groupId>
    <artifactId>oauth1-client</artifactId>
    <!-- specify appropriate version -->
    <version>2.17</version>
</dependency>
```

Here are the detailed steps for accessing the OAuth 1.0 protected resource:

1. OAuth 1.0 includes a consumer key and matching consumer secret that together authenticate the client application to the service provider. You may want to obtain these credentials from the respective service provider for use in the client code. The `org.glassfish.jersey.client.oauth1.OAuth1ClientSupport` is the starter class to build the support for OAuth 1.0 into the Jersey client. The `OAuth1Builder` object obtained from `OAuth1ClientSupport` can be used to build `OAuth1AuthorizationFlow` by calling the `authorizationFlow()` method. The `authorizationFlow()` method takes the following end points (these values can be obtained from the service provider):

    ○   **Request token URI**: This is the URI of the endpoint on the authorization server, where the request token can be obtained.

    ○   **Access token URI**: This is the URI of the endpoint on the authorization server, where the access token can be obtained.

    ○   **Authorization URI**: This is the URI of the endpoint on the authorization server to which the user (the resource owner) should be redirected in order to grant access to this application (our consumer).

    The following code snippet illustrates the previously discussed steps. This example tries to access the Twitter API protected with OAuth 1.0:

```
//Other imports are not shown for brevity
import javax.ws.rs.client.Client;
import javax.ws.rs.client.ClientBuilder;
import javax.ws.rs.core.Feature;
import org.glassfish.jersey.client.oauth1.ConsumerCredentials;
import org.glassfish.jersey.client.oauth1.OAuth1AuthorizationFlow;
import org.glassfish.jersey.client.oauth1.OAuth1ClientSupport;

// Read consumer key/secret from API provider
```

```
// You should obtain these keys from appropriate
// service provider (e.g. Twitter)
final String CONSUMER_KEY = "e4piTL0EFrS2K6TLUyAdc5R6l";
final String CONSUMER_SECRET =
    "E6r9PvI3g0noBOTDx55TtLU3IXP782wvyF48O1DrHF8E1NVlC";
// ConsumerCredentials stores client secret as
// byte array to improve security.
final ConsumerCredentials consumerCredentials = new
    ConsumerCredentials( CONSUMER_KEY,  CONSUMER_SECRET);
//Build the OAuth1AuthorizationFlow by supplying URI for
//reading request token, access token and authorize token
//This client reads Tweets on behalf of the end user
final OAuth1AuthorizationFlow oauth1AuthoriznFlow =
    OAuth1ClientSupport.builder(consumerCredentials)
        .authorizationFlow(
            "https://api.twitter.com/oauth/request_token",
            "https://api.twitter.com/oauth/access_token",
            "https://api.twitter.com/oauth/authorize")
        .build();
```

2. Once you have the `org.glassfish.jersey.client.oauth1.`
   `OAuth1AuthorizationFlow` instance ready, you can kick off the
   authorization process. To start the authorization process, call the `start()`
   method on the `OAuth1AuthorizationFlow` instance. Under the cover, the
   `start()` method makes a request to the request token URI and gets the
   request token that will be used for the authorization process. The method
   returns the authorization URI as a string:

```
//Get authorization URI
String authorizationUri = oauth1AuthoriznFlow
    .start();
```

3. The next step in the authorization flow is to redirect the user to the
   authorization URI returned by the `start()` method. If the client is a
   web application, you can use servlet APIs or JAX-RS APIs to implement
   redirection.

4. After successful authorization, the authorization server redirects the user
   back to the URI specified by `OAuth1Builder.FlowBuilder::callbackU`
   `ri(String)` and also provides `oauth_verifier` as a query parameter in
   the call back URI. The client should extract this parameter from the request
   and finish the authorization flow by calling the `finish(verifier)` method.
   The `finish()` method will internally request the access token from the
   authorization server and return it:

```
//Get the access token and finish the authorization flow
```

```
AccessToken accessToken = oauth1AuthoriznFlow
        .finish(verifier);
```

 OAuth 1.0 works by ensuring that both the client and server share an OAuth token and a consumer secret. The client must generate a signature on every request (or REST API call) by encrypting a bunch of unique information using the consumer secret. The server must generate the same signature, and only grant access if both the signatures match.

5. The OAuth client application used in this example, will use the access token obtained from the `AccessToken` instance together with the client secret from the `org.glassfish.jersey.client.oauth1.ConsumerCredentials` object to perform OAuth authenticated requests to the service provider. Remember that we have created the `ConsumerCredentials` instance at the beginning of this example, as a part of the `OAuth1AuthorizationFlow` initialization, by passing the consumer key and secret.

6. The OAuth1 filter feature obtained by calling `getOAuth1Feature()` on the `OAuth1AuthorizationFlow` object can be used to configure client instances to perform authenticated requests to the server. This filter feature will prepare all the requests from the client compatible to OAuth 1.0. The following code snippet illustrates the use of the OAuth filter feature to access the protected resources from the service provider:

```
//See the code snippet at the beginning of this section
//to know how we created oauth1AuthoriznFlow object
Feature filterFeature = oauth1AuthoriznFlow.getOAuth1Feature();
//create a new Jersey client and register filter
//feature that will add OAuth signatures and  access token
Client client = ClientBuilder.newBuilder()
            .register(filterFeature)
            .build();

// Protected REST API URI that application wants to access:
//https://<service-provider>/<resource>"
//This example access following twitter API
final String PROTECTED_RESOURCE_URI =
    "https://api.twitter.com/1.1/statuses/home_timeline.json";

  // make requests to protected resources
  final Response response =
        client.target(PROTECTED_RESOURCE_URI).request().get();
```

```
if (response.getStatus() != 200) {
  String errorEntity = null;
  if (response.hasEntity()) {
    errorEntity = response.readEntity(String.class);
  }
  throw new RuntimeException(
      "Request to protected resource was not successful");
}else{
    //Code for processing the response goes here
    String result = response.readEntity(String.class);
}
```

After having understood the OAuth 1.0 protocol and its usage, let's move on to the OAuth 2.0 protocol. The next section discusses this topic in detail.

Understanding the OAuth 2.0 protocol

OAuth 2.0 is the latest release of the OAuth protocol, mainly focused on simplifying the client side development. Note that OAuth 2.0 is a completely new protocol and this release is not backwards-compatible with OAuth 1.0. It offers specific authorization flows for web applications, desktop applications, mobile phones, and living room devices. Following are some of the major improvements in OAuth 2.0, as compared to the previous release:

- **The complexity involved in signing each request**: OAuth 1.0 mandates that the client must generate a signature on every API call to the server resource using the token secret. On the receiving end, the server must regenerate the same signature and the client will be given access only if both the signatures match. OAuth 2.0 requires neither the client nor server to generate any signature for securing the messages. Security is enforced via the use of TLS/ SSL (HTTPS) for all communication.

- **Addressing non-browser client applications**: Many features of OAuth 1.0 are designed by considering the way a web client application interacts with the inbound and outbound messages. This has proven to be inefficient while using it with non-browser clients such as on-device mobile applications. OAuth 2.0 addresses this issue by accommodating more authorization flows suitable for specific client needs that do not use any web UI, such as on-device (or native) mobile applications or API services. This makes the protocol very flexible.

- **The separation of roles**: OAuth 2.0 clearly defines the roles for all parties involved in the communication, such as the client, resource owner, resource server, and authorization server. The specification is clear on which parts of the protocol are expected to be implemented by the resource owner, authorization server, and resource server.

- **The short lived access token**: Unlike in the previous version, the access token in OAuth 2.0 can contain the expiration time, which improves the security and reduces chances of illegal access.

- **The refresh token**: OAuth 2.0 offers a refresh token that can be used for getting a new access token on the expiry of the current one, without going through the entire authorization process once again.

Before we get into the details of OAuth 2.0, let's take a quick look at how OAuth 2.0 defines roles for each party involved in the authorization process. Though you might have seen similar roles while discussing OAuth 1.0 in last section, it does not clearly define what part of the protocol is expected to be implemented by each one:

- **The resource owner**: This refers to an entity capable of granting access to a protected resource. In a real life scenario, this can be an end user who owns the resource.

- **The resource server**: This hosts the protected resources. The resource server validates and authorizes the incoming requests for the protected resource by contacting the authorization server.

- **The client (consumer)**: This refers to an application that tries to access protected resources on behalf of the resource owner. It can be a business service, mobile, web, or desktop application.

- **Authorization server**: This, as the name suggests, is responsible for authorizing the client that needs access to a resource. It issues access tokens to the client after successfully authenticating the resource owner and obtaining authorization. In a real life scenario, the authorization server may be either the same as the resource server, or a separate entity altogether. The OAuth 2.0 specification does not really enforce anything on this part.

It would be interesting to learn how these entities talk with each other to complete the authorization flow. Following is a quick summary of the authorization flow in a typical OAuth 2.0 implementation:

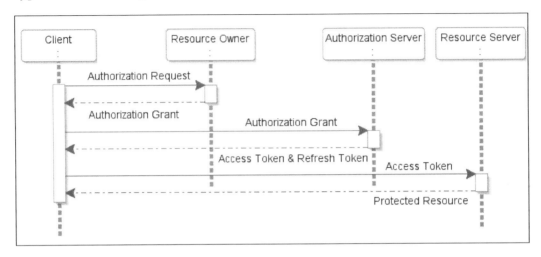

Let's understand the diagram in more detail:

- The client application requests authorization to access protected resources from the resource owner (user). The client can either directly make the authorization request to the resource owner, or via the authorization server by redirecting the resource owner to the authorization server endpoint.

- The resource owner authenticates and authorizes the resource access request from the client application and returns the authorization grant to the client. The authorization grant type returned by the resource owner depends on the type of client application that tries to access the OAuth protected resource. Note that OAuth 2.0 protocol defines four types of grants in order to authorize access to protected resources. To learn more on grant types, please take a look at the section, *Understanding the grant types in OAuth 2.0*.

- The client application requests an access token from the authorization server by passing the authorization grant along with other details for authentication, such as the client ID, client secret, and grant type.

- The authorization server authenticates the client and validates the authorization grant present in the request. On successful authentication, the authorization server issues an access token (and optionally, a refresh token) to the client application.

- The client application requests the protected resource (RESTful web API) from the resource server by presenting the access token for authentication.

- On successful authentication of the client request, the resource server returns the requested resource.

The sequence of interaction that we just discussed are of a very high level. Depending upon the grant type used by the client, details of the interaction may change. The following section will help you understand the basics of grant types.

Understanding the grant types in OAuth 2.0

Grant types in the OAuth 2.0 protocol are, in essence, different ways to authorize access to protected resources using different security credentials (for each type). The OAuth 2.0 protocol defines four types of grants, as listed in the following; each can be used in different scenarios, as appropriate:

- **Authorization code**: The authorization code is obtained from the authentication server instead of directly requesting it from the resource owner. In this case, the client directs the resource owner to the authorization server. The authorization server authenticates the user, obtains authorization, and returns the authorization code to the client. In this mode, the resource owner's credentials are never shared with the client. This is very similar to OAuth 1.0, except that the cryptographic signing of messages is not required in OAuth 2.0.

- **Implicit**: The implicit grant is a simplified version of the authorization code grant type flow. In the implicit grant flow, the client is issued an access token directly as the result of the resource owner's authorization. This is less secure as the client is not authenticated. This is commonly used for client-side devices, such as mobile, where the client credentials cannot be stored securely.

- **Resource owner password credentials**: The resource owner's credentials, such as username and password, are used by the client for directly obtaining the access token during the authorization flow. The access code is used thereafter for accessing resources. This grant type is only used with trusted client applications. This is suitable for legacy applications that use the HTTP Basic authentication to incrementally transition to OAuth 2.0.

- **Client credential**: Client credentials are used directly for getting access tokens. This grant type is used when the client is also the resources owner. This is commonly used for embedded services and backend applications, where the client has an account (direct access rights).

 A very detailed discussion of the authorization flow for each grant type in OAuth 2.0 is not in the scope of this book. You can learn more about OAuth 2.0 at https://tools.ietf. org/html/rfc6749.

Building the OAuth 2.0 client using Jersey APIs

Let's build a simple OAuth 2.0 client using Jersey APIs to understand the API usage pattern.

 The complete source code for this example is available on the Packt Publishing website. You can download the example from the Packt Publishing website link that we mentioned at the beginning of this book, in the *Preface* section. In the downloaded source code, take a look at the project, rest-chapter6-oauth2-webclient.

To use the Jersey OAuth 2.0 client APIs in your application, you need to add dependency to the oauth2-client jar file. If you use Maven, the dependency entry in pom.xml may look as shown in the following lines:

```
<dependency>
  <groupId>org.glassfish.jersey.security</groupId>
  <artifactId>oauth2-client</artifactId>
  <version>2.17</version>
</dependency>
```

 The Jersey framework (version 2.17), which is the latest release available at the time of writing this book, does not offer any server API for protecting services via the OAuth 2.0 protocol. Also, Jersey OAuth 2.0 client APIs version 2.17 supports only the authorization code grant type.

As OAuth 2.0 is not a strictly defined protocol, you may not find a generic client API solution that works with all implementations of OAuth 2.0 (by different vendors). The `org.glassfish.jersey.client.oauth2.OAuth2ClientSupport` is the main starting class for an OAuth 2.0 client. You will use this as the starting class for building the OAuth 2.0 authorization flow. The current release of the `OAuth2ClientSupport` class (version 2.17) provides dedicated methods for building authorization grant flow for accessing the OAuth 2.0 protected RESTful web APIs from vendors such as Google and Facebook. Following are the steps for building a Jersey client for Google Tasks APIs:

1. To start with the authorization code grant flow, generate an instance of `org.glassfish.jersey.client.oauth2.ClientIdentifier` by passing the client ID and client secret obtained from the service provider (authorization server). This is usually obtained while registering the client with the server. This example access Google Tasks API. Note that the Google Tasks API lets you search, read, and update Google Tasks contents. Remember that the Jersey OAuth 2.0 client supports only the authorization code grant type, and so, this example also uses the same grant type.

    The following link will help you with details for accessing the OAuth 2.0 protected Google APIs: `https://developers.google.com/identity/protocols/OAuth2`.

    High level steps for obtaining the client ID and client secret are available at `https://developers.google.com/console/help/new/`.

2. Once you have the `ClientIdentifier` instance ready, the next step is to start building the authorization code grant flow for accessing the Google Tasks API by calling the `googleFlowBuilder()` method. This method has the following signature:

    ```
    OAuth2ClientSupport::googleFlowBuilder(
        ClientIdentifier clientIdentifier, String redirectURI,
        String scope)
    ```

    This call returns the `org.glassfish.jersey.client.oauth2.OAuth2FlowGoogleBuilder` object that can be directly used to generate the authorization code grant flow defined by Google. Here is the quick summary of parameters for the `googleFlowBuilder` method:

    °   `clientIdentifier`: This is the `ClientIdentifier` instance created using the client ID and client secret issued by the service provider.

- ○ redirectURI: This is the URI to which the user (the resource owner) should be redirected to after the user grants access to the consumer application. It will pass null if the application does not support redirection (for example, if it is not a web application).

- ○ scope: The API to which an access is requested (for example, Google Tasks).

3. To start the authorization flow get an instance of org.glassfish.jersey.client.oauth2.OAuth2CodeGrantFlow by calling the build() method on OAuth2FlowGoogleBuilder. The OAuth2CodeGrantFlow instance is capable of authorizing the user using the "Authorization Code Grant Flow". The following code snippet demonstrates the API usage for generating OAuth2CodeGrantFlow to access the Google Tasks API:

```
//Other imports are not shown for brevity
import org.glassfish.jersey.client.oauth2.OAuth2ClientSupport;
import org.glassfish.jersey.client.oauth2.OAuth2CodeGrantFlow;
import org.glassfish.jersey.client.oauth2.OAuth2FlowGoogleBuilder;
import org.glassfish.jersey.client.oauth2.ClientIdentifier;
import org.glassfish.jersey.client.oauth2.TokenResult;

final String CLIENT_ID =
    "679110343pm.apps.googleusercontent.com";
final String CLIENT_SECRET = "JNA68GMPo9UncOmtPlnGxItq ";
//Protected ApI that needs to be accessed by client app
String SCOPE = "https://www.googleapis.com/auth/tasks.readonly";

//On successful authorization user
//is redirected to this URI
String redirectURI =
    "http://localhost:8080/hrapp/api/oauth2/authorize";

ClientIdentifier clientIdentifier = new
    ClientIdentifier(CLIENT_ID, CLIENT_SECRET);
final OAuth2CodeGrantFlow oauth2CodeGrantflow =
    OAuth2ClientSupport.googleFlowBuilder(
        clientIdentifier,  redirectURI, SCOPE)
            .prompt(OAuth2FlowGoogleBuilder.Prompt.CONSENT)
            .build();
```

4. The `OAuth2CodeGrantFlow` instance is ready to use. Let's start the authorization process. The `OAuth2CodeGrantFlow` object defines the OAuth 2.0 authorization code grant flow for the client. You can start the flow by calling the `start()` method:

```
//Get the authorization URI
String authorizationUri = oauth2CodeGrantflow.start();
```

This call triggers the authorization process and returns an authorization URI on which the user should give consent to client application to access resources. The client application should redirect the user to the authorization URI. The resource owner should authorize the client application on the authorization URI to proceed further. On successful authorization, the authorization server automatically redirects the user back to the redirect URI specified while building `OAuth2CodeGrantFlow`. The authorization server also provides the code and state as a request query parameter for the redirect URI. The client application needs to extract code and state parameters from the request to use it with the access token request. The state parameter is used for preventing cross-site request forgery.

5. To finish the authorization process, call `OAuth2CodeGrantFlow::finish(String code, String state)` by supplying the code and state returned by the authorization server on authorization. The method will internally request the access token from the authorization server and return the result as a `TokenResult` object. The `TokenResult` object contains the result of the authorization flow including the access token.

6. Later, you can call `OAuth2CodeGrantFlow::getAuthorizedClient()` to get the JAX-RS client that is configured to perform authorized requests to the service provider. The returned JAX-RS client has all the necessary information about the consumer credentials and access token that were received during authorization process. You can directly use this client to access the protected resources. The following code snippet illustrates the usage of client APIs, as explained in steps 5-6:

```
//Step 5: code and state are returned by authorization server
TokenResult tokenResult = oauth2CodeGrantflow.finish(code, state);
//Step 6: Get the authorized client
Client client = oauth2CodeGrantflow.getAuthorizedClient();
String GOOGLE_TAKS_URI =
    "https://www.googleapis.com/tasks/v1/users/@me/lists";
//Prepare client to call Google Tasks API
```

```
WebTarget service = client.target(GOOGLE_TAKS_URI);
//Get the response object and work on it
Response response =  service.request().get();
if(response.getStatus() == 200){
//Code for processing response such as building
//Java model etc goes here
    String output = response.getEntity(String.class);
}
```

With this, we have finished the discussion on OAuth. In the next section, you will learn how to control access to RESTful resources via security APIs.

Building OAuth 2.0 compliant services

If you feel that support for OAuth in the current Jersey release is not enough to meet your use cases, you can look at other OAuth implementations available in Java. Apache Oltu is one of the popular OAuth protocol implementations available today. You can learn more about Apache Oltu at `https://oltu.apache.org`.

Note that the Jersey framework (version 2.17), which is the latest release available at the time of writing this book, does not offer any server API for protecting your RESTful web services via OAuth 2.0. However, with Apache Oltu, you can easily create OAuth 2.0 compliant server endpoints. More details can be found at `https://cwiki.apache.org/confluence/display/OLTU/ OAuth+2.0+Authorization+Server`.

Authorizing the RESTful web service accesses via the security APIs

The authorization process verifies whether the client who has requested or initiated an action has the right to do so. In this section, we will see how to use the JAX-RS APIs for authorizing incoming REST API calls from various clients.

Using SecurityContext APIs to control access

We started off this chapter by discussing how an application authenticates a user who is trying to access a secured resource. When a client accesses a secured resource, the server identifies and validates the requester, and on successful authentication, the requester is allowed to get inside the application. During this process, the underlying security framework generates a `javax.ws.rs.core.SecurityContext` object that holds security related information pertaining to the requester. The JAX-RS framework allows you to access the `SecurityContext` object in the code in order to perform security checks in the code.

Some of the frequently used methods exposed by `SecurityContext` are given as follows:

- `getAuthenticationScheme()`: This method returns the authentication scheme used for protecting resources, such as HTTP basic, HTTP digest, NTLM, and so on

- `getUserPrincipal()`: This method returns the logged-in username

- `isSecure()`: This returns true if the request is made through a secure channel (HTTPS)

- `isUserInRole(String role)`: This returns true if the logged-in user is included in the role, which is supplied as a parameter for this method

> Please refer to the following API doc to learn more about `SecurityContext`: http://docs.oracle.com/javaee/7/api/javax/ws/rs/core/SecurityContext.html.

You can access `SecurityContext` in the JAX-RS resource methods and call appropriate APIs on it to perform the authorization of the requester. Following is an example demonstrating the usage of `SecurityContext::isUserInRole(String)`. In this example, system information is returned to the caller but only if the requested user (client) is in an admin role:

```
//Other imports are not shown for brevity
import javax.ws.rs.core.Context;
import javax.ws.rs.core.MediaType;
import javax.ws.rs.core.Response;
import javax.ws.rs.core.SecurityContext;

@Path("system")
```

```
public class SystemResource {
    @GET
    @Path("info")
    public Response getSystemInfo(@Context SecurityContext
        securityContext) {
        String adminGroup = "admin";
        if (securityContext.isUserInRole(adminGroup)) {
            // getSystemInfo reads system info - not shown here
            SystemInfo sysInfo=getSystemInfo();
            return Response.ok(sysInfo,
                MediaType.APPLICATION_JSON).build();
        } else {
            return
                Response.status(Response.Status.FORBIDDEN).build();
        }
    }
}
```

Using the javax.annotation.security annotations to control access with the Jersey framework

The javax.annotation.security annotations available with Java EE simplify the coding effort for adding authentication and authorization checks for an application. Jersey framework allows you to use the following javax.annotation.security annotations, on the JAX-RS resource class or methods, to control the access based on the user role:

- javax.annotation.security.DenyAl: With this, no roles can invoke the annotated resource class or method

- javax.annotation.security.PermitAll: With this, all security roles are allowed to invoke the annotated resource method(s)

- javax.annotation.security.RolesAllowed: This specifies the list of roles permitted to access method(s) in an application

 The security annotation support that we discussed in this section is brought into the RESTful web service resources via the Jersey framework, and you may not find it working in the same way with other implementations of JAX-RS.

To use the preceding annotations in your JAX-RS resource class or methods, you need to register the following dynamic feature provider offered by the Jersey framework: `org.glassfish.jersey.server.filter.RolesAllowedDynamicFeature`. The following code snippet uses subclass of `javax.ws.rs.core.Application` to register the `RolesAllowedDynamicFeature` provider:

```
//Other imports are removed for brevity
import org.glassfish.jersey.server.filter.RolesAllowedDynamicFeature;

@javax.ws.rs.ApplicationPath("webresources")
public class ApplicationConfig extends Application {
    @Override
    public Set<Class<?>> getClasses() {
        Set<Class<?>> resources = new java.util.HashSet<>();
        //Rest of the code goes here
        resources.add(RolesAllowedDynamicFeature.class);
        return resources;
    }
}
```

Let's see how to use the security annotation with a JAX-RS service to prevent unauthorized access. The following code snippet uses the `@RolesAllowed` security annotation to restrict access to the resource method. This example uses `@RolesAllowed("admin")` on the resource method to let only users with an admin role access this API at runtime:

```
import javax.annotation.security.RolesAllowed;

@GET
@Path("security")
@RolesAllowed("admin")
public Response getSystemInfo() {
    // getSystemInfo reads system info
    //method definition is not shown here to save space
    SystemInfo sysInfo=getSystemInfo();
    return Response.ok(sysInfo,
        MediaType.APPLICATION_JSON).build();
}
```

Using Jersey's role-based entity data filtering

The entity filtering feature offered by the Jersey framework allows you to conveniently filter out any non-relevant data from the response entity. To use this feature, create custom entity filtering annotations based on `@org.glassfish.jersey.message.filtering.EntityFiltering` and apply them on model entity fields that you want to filter out conditionally. Later, while generating a response for the REST API call, runtime will match the entity filtering annotation present on the resource method with the annotation present on the entity fields, and include only those matching fields in the response content.

 To learn more about entity filtering offerings in Jersey framework, read the following section in the Jersey User Guide available at `https://jersey.java.net/documentation/latest/user-guide.html#entity-filtering`.

The Jersey framework has extended this filtering feature to use with security annotations. You can filter out entities, or specific entity attributes, from the response body by using security annotations (`@PermitAll`, `@RolesAllowed`, and `@DenyAll`). Jersey offers this support via the `org.glassfish.jersey.message.filtering.SecurityEntityFilteringFeature` provider. Let's take an example that uses this feature to shape the response content based on user roles.

The very first step is to add dependency to the Jersey entity filtering jar. If you use Maven, the dependency entry in `pom.xml` may look like the following:

```
<dependency>
    <groupId>org.glassfish.jersey.ext</groupId>
    <artifactId>jersey-entity-filtering</artifactId>
    <version>2.17</version>
</dependency>
```

The next step is to register the `SecurityEntityFilteringFeature` provider in the application. Here is an example:

```
//Other imports are not shown for brevity
import org.glassfish.jersey.server.ResourceConfig;

@javax.ws.rs.ApplicationPath("webresources")
public class ApplicationConfig extends ResourceConfig {
    public ApplicationConfig() {

    register(org.glassfish.jersey.message.filtering.
        SecurityEntityFilteringFeature.class);
```

```
//Rest of the code goes here
register("com.packtpub.rest.ch6.security.resources");
register(org.glassfish.jersey.server.filter.
    RolesAllowedDynamicFeature.class);
    }
}
```

Once you have configured the required provider components, the next step is to identify the field in the response entity object class definition that needs to be filtered out based on the user role. For instance, in the following example, you want to include the `totalEmployees` field of the `Department` entity in the response object only if the requesting user is in an administrator's or manager's role. You can declaratively achieve this by annotating the `getTotalEmployees()` method that returns `totalEmployees`, with the `@RolesAllowed({"manager", "admin"})` annotation, as shown in the following lines:

```
//imports are omitted for brevity
@XmlRootElement
public class Department implements Serializable {
  private Short departmentId;
  private String departmentName;
  private Integer totalEmployees;
  private Integer managerId;

  @RolesAllowed({"manager", "admin"})
   public Integer getTotalEmployees() {
       return totalEmployees;
   }
  //All other getters and setters are not shown for brevity

}
```

The REST API method returning the `Department` entity discussed earlier may be as shown here:

```
@GET
@Path("departments/{id}")
@RolesAllowed({"users","manager","admin"})
@Produces("application/json")
public Department findDepartment(@PathParam("id") Short id) {
   Department dept= findDepartmentEntity(id);
   return dept;
}
```

At runtime, when a request for a department resource reaches the application (for example, /departments/10), the security entity filtering feature will check for user roles, and the attribute, totalEmployees, will be included in the entity response body only if the user role matches with the values given for the @RolesAllowed annotation that we had set on the getTotalEmployees() method in the Department model class.

For instance, with the previously described settings, when a normal user (*not* belonging to a manager's or admin's role) accesses the REST resource URI, departments/300, the attribute, totalEmployees, will not be rendered in the response entity body:

```
{"departmentId":300,"departmentName":"Administration",
"managerId":200}
```

Input validation

Input validation is the process of ensuring the completeness and sanity of input data before posting it to the underlying data source. It is considered as an outer, defensive perimeter for your RESTful web APIs. JAX-RS 2.0 lets you use bean validation to declaratively specify the validation constraints on an object model. If you need a quick brush up on bean validation support for the JAX-RS resource class, refer to the *Introducing validations in JAX-RS applications* section in *Chapter 4, Advanced Features in the JAX-RS API*.

You can log input validation failures for business critical APIs. This may help you detect malformed and malicious input to the application.

Summary

In this chapter, we covered the important topics of RESTful web service application development and security, albeit from a higher point of view than we have done in previous chapters. Because these topics require highly specialized knowledge, we only covered enough of them to be able to make pragmatic decisions during development. In all likelihood, the supporting environments for our web services will be managed by third party vendors or internal IT departments. Nonetheless, as well rounded developers, we should understand what it takes to engineer secure, scalable, and highly available web applications.

In the next chapter, we will discuss various solutions for describing, producing, consuming, and visualizing RESTful web services.

7
The Description
and Discovery of
RESTful Web Services

In earlier days, many software solution providers did not really pay enough attention to documenting their RESTful web APIs. However, soon they realized the need for a good API documentation solution in order to accelerate the adoption of their REST API services by customers. As a result, many REST API metadata standards have emerged in the recent past.

Today, you will find a variety of approaches to document RESTful web APIs. This chapter describes some of the popular solutions available today for describing, producing, consuming, and visualizing RESTful web services. This learning will definitely help you to quickly learn and use the other API documentation solutions available in the market.

The following solutions are covered in this chapter:

- Web Application Description Language
- RESTful API Modeling Language
- Swagger

Introduction to RESTful web services

The API documentation for RESTful web services provides a standard language-independent interface, which can be used by both humans and machines to discover the capabilities of APIs without accessing the source code. This chapter introduces a few of the various API documentation tools and options that you might choose from.

Let's start by discussing one of the earliest solutions for RESTful web API documentation—Web Application Description Language.

Web Application Description Language

Web Application Description Language (WADL) is an XML description of HTTP-based web applications such as RESTful web services. WADL was submitted to the **World Wide Web Consortium (W3C)** by Sun in 2009 but has not been standardized yet.

WADL models the resources provided by a RESTful web service with relationships between the resources. It also allows you to clearly represent the media types used for the request and response contents.

An overview of the WADL structure

The WADL schema that you use for building a WADL file is based on the WADL specification. Here is a quick overview of the WADL file content that describes RESTful web APIs.

The top-level element in a WADL document is the application. It contains global information about RESTful web services, such as links to schema definition and documentation. Here is a quick summary of the elements that you see in WADL:

- `<resources>`: This element comes as wrapper for all resources exposed by a RESTful web application. The `base` attribute for resources identifies the base path of all resources in the API.

- `<resource>`: This element appears as a child of the resources element. This element is used for describing a set of resources, each identified by a URI. This element can optionally have `<param>` to describe the path parameters present in the request, if any.

- `<method>`: A resource may have one or more `<method>` definitions. This element defines the HTTP methods, such as GET, POST, PUT, and DELETE, available to the resource. Note that the presence of this element in WADL represents a REST `resource` method in a RESTful web service.

- `<request>`: A `<method>` definition can optionally include this element that describes an input to the `resource` method. A request can have one or more of the following elements as its child:
    - `<doc>`: This element is used for documenting the parameters
    - `<representation>`: This element specifies the Internet media type for the payload present in the body of the request
    - `<param>`: This element specifies the query or header parameter present in the request

- `<response>`: This element specifies the result of invoking an HTTP method on a resource. The optional status code present in the response describes the list of the HTTP status codes associated with the response. A response can have one or more of the following elements as its child:
    - `<doc>`: This element is used for documenting the `<response>` header parameters
    - `<representation>`: This element describes the Internet media type for the response content returned by the API
    - `<param>`: This element specifies the HTTP header parameters present in the response.

 To learn more about the WADL specification, visit `http://www.w3.org/Submission/wadl`.

Let's take a look at a simple WADL example before proceeding further. See the following code snippet. This method returns a `Department` object for the department ID passed by the client.

```
@GET
@Path("{id}")
@Produces("application/json")
public Department findDepartment(@PathParam("id")
    Short id){
    //Method body is omitted for brevity
}
```

Wondering how the preceding REST API can be described in WADL?

The following WADL code answers this question. You do not need to spend much time on understanding this WADL file structure at this point in time. We will discuss the generation of WADL from the JAX-RS resource class in detail later.

```
<application xmlns="http://wadl.dev.java.net/2009/02">
<doc xmlns:jersey="http://jersey.java.net/"
    jersey:generatedBy="Jersey: 2.10.4 2014-08-08 15:09:00"/>
<grammars/>
<resources base=
    "http://localhost:8080/hrapp/webresources/">
    <resource path="{id}">
        <param xmlns:xs="http://www.w3.org/2001/XMLSchema"
            name="id"
        style="template" type="xs:short"/>
            <method id="findDepartment" name="GET">
                <response>
                    <ns2:representation
                        xmlns:ns2=
                            "http://wadl.dev.java.net/2009/02"
                                xmlns=""
                    element="department"
                        mediaType="application/json"/>
                </response>
            </method>
        </resource>
    </resources>
</application>
```

Generating WADL from JAX-RS

The Jersey framework has built-in support for generating the WADL file for your JAX-RS applications. In this section, we will discuss the Jersey support for generating the WADL file from the JAX-RS resource classes.

Consider the following JAX-RS web service implementation. The REST resource used in this example exposes APIs for reading the list of departments, creating a department, and editing a department identified by the ID:

```
//Imports are removed for brevity
@Stateless
@Path("departments")
public class DepartmentResource{
```

```
//Returns departments in the range specified via query params
@GET
@Produces("application/json")
public List<Department> findAllDepartments(@QueryParam("from")
    Integer from, @QueryParam("to") Integer to) {
    return findAllDepartmentEntities(from, to);
}

//Creates department with data present in the request body
@POST
@Consumes("application/json")
public void createDepartment(Department entity) {
    createDepartmentEntity(entity);
}

//Edits department with data present in the request body
@PUT
@Path("{id}")
@Consumes("application/json")
public void editDepartment(@PathParam("id") Short id,
    Department entity) {
    editDepartmentEntity(entity);
}

//Rest of the implementation is removed for brevity
}
```

The Department class used in this example will look like the following code:

```
//Other imports are removed for brevity
import javax.xml.bind.annotation.XmlRootElement;
@XmlRootElement
public class Department implements Serializable {
    private Short departmentId;
    private String departmentName;
    private Integer managerId;
    private Short locationId;
//Getters and setters for the attributes are removed for brevity
}
```

The WADL generation feature is enabled in the Jersey framework by default. For instance, when you deploy the preceding JAX-RS application to a web server, the Jersey framework automatically generates WADL for all JAX-RS resource classes present in the application. The generated WADL file is accessible via the following URI: `http://<host>:<port>/<application-name>/<application-path>/application.wadl`. The URI for accessing WADL for this example is as follows: `http://localhost:8080/hrapp/webresources/application.wadl`.

The JAX-RS annotations present on the resource class decide how the APIs need to be represented in the WADL.

Every unique `@Path` value present in the resource class results in a new `<resource>` element in the generated WADL. Following this rule, this example adds the `findAllDepartments` and `createDepartment` methods as children to a common resource element. Whereas the `editDepartment` method uses a path parameter, due to which this method is added as a child to a separate resource. In a nutshell, multiple `resource` methods having different HTTP methods but sharing the same `@Path` value will have the same parent `<resource>` element.

Here is the WADL file generated by the Jersey framework for the `DepartmentResource` resource shown in the preceding code:

```
<application xmlns="http://wadl.dev.java.net/2009/02">
    <doc xmlns:jersey="http://jersey.java.net/"
        jersey:generatedBy="Jersey: 2.10.4 2014-08-08 15:09:00"/>
    <grammars/>
    <resources base=
        "http://localhost:8080/hrapp/webresources/">
        <resource path="departments">
            <method id="findAllDepartments" name="GET">
                <request>
                    <param xmlns:xs=
                        "http://www.w3.org/2001/XMLSchema"
                            name="from"
                            style="query" type="xs:int"/>
                    <param xmlns:xs=
                        "http://www.w3.org/2001/XMLSchema"
                            name="to" style="query"
                            type="xs:int"/>
                </request>
                <response>
                    <ns2:representation
                        xmlns:ns2=
                            "http://wadl.dev.java.net/2009/02"
```

```
                    xmlns="" element="departments"
                    mediaType="application/json"/>
            </response>
        </method>
        <method id="createDepartment" name="POST">
            <request>
                <ns2:representation
                    xmlns:ns2=
                        "http://wadl.dev.java.net/2009/02"
                    xmlns="" element="department"
                    mediaType="application/json"/>
            </request>
        </method>
        <resource path="{id}">
            <param xmlns:xs="http://www.w3.org/2001/XMLSchema"
                name="id"
                style="template" type="xs:short"/>
            <method id="editDepartment" name="PUT">
                <request>
                    <ns2:representation
                        xmlns:ns2=
                            "http://wadl.dev.java.net/2009/02"
                        xmlns="" element="department"
                        mediaType="application/json"/>
                </request>
            </method>
        </resource>
    </resource>
  </resources>
</application>
```

If you want to disable the automatic generation of WADL in Jersey, configure `jersey.config.server.wadl.disableWadl` to `true`. This configuration parameter can be set in either of the following ways:

- By setting the `init-param` value, `jersey.config.server.wadl.disableWadl`, to `true` for the Jersey servlet (`org.glassfish.jersey.servlet.ServletContainer`) in `web.xml`

- By overriding `javax.ws.rs.core.Application::getProperties()` to return the map containing `jersey.config.server.wadl.disableWadl=true` as the property name and value

The default support for WADL in Jersey works for many use cases. However, it may fail to generate proper documentation in specific scenarios, as explained here:

- If the `resource` method returns the `javax.ws.rs.core.Response` object, Jersey will not be able to infer the HTTP response content and HTTP status codes returned by the method from the method signature

- Similarly, Jersey will not be able to identify the header parameters present in the `Response` object by just scanning through the method signature

The solution for the preceding scenario is to intercept the default WADL generation process and pass the necessary data about the return types. Jersey allows you to do so by extending `org.glassfish.jersey.server.wadl.config.WadlGeneratorConfig`. We will not be covering this topic in this book; you can learn about this feature at `https://wikis.oracle.com/display/Jersey/WADL`.

Generating the Java client from WADL

You can generate the Java client for a WADL file by using the `wadl2java` tool. To download the ZIP file containing `wadl2java`, go to `https://wadl.java.net/`.

After downloading the ZIP file, perform the following steps:

1. Extract the contents and set the path to the `bin` folder that contains the `wadl2java.bat` file (for example, `<wadl-dist-1.1.6>/bin`).

2. Set `JAVA_HOME` pointing to a valid JDK home folder.

3. Now, execute `wadl2java` as follows:

   ```
   wadl2java -o outputDir -p package [-a] [-s jaxrs20] [-c
   customization]  outputfile.wadl
   ```

Here is a brief description of arguments used for `wadl2java`:

- `-o outputDir`: This argument specifies the target folder for storing the generated client source.

- `-p package`: This argument specifies the Java package name for the generated client source.

- `-a`: If you specify this parameter, each schema namespace name is mapped to a package, and the element types for namespace are generated in appropriate packages.

- `-c customization`: This argument specifies the path or URL of a JAXB binding customization file.

- `-s jaxrs20`: This argument specifies that the client code should be compatible with JAXRS2.0. The default value is `jersey1x`.

- `outputfile.wadl`: Here, you can specify the path or the URL of the WADL file to process.

The following example uses the `wadl2java` tool to generate the Java client for the WADL file located at `http://localhost:8080/hrapp/webresources/application.wadl`:

```
wadl2java -o gen-src -p com.packtpub.demo.client -s jaxrs20 http://
localhost:8080/demo/webresources/application.wadl
```

Market adoption of WADL

Many API vendors like WADL for its simplicity and tooling support. It is easy to read, understand, and implement.

However, the software industry has not yet considered it to be an actual standard for describing RESTful web APIs. Further, WADL does not cover authentication constructs for REST APIs. Some vendors think that XML is not the right way to go for describing RESTful web APIs because of the complexity involved in parsing XMLs, particularly when used in mobile clients or in JavaScript clients.

With this, we end our discussion on WADL. In the next section, we will discuss the RESTful API Modeling Language, which is a YAML-based language for describing RESTful APIs.

RESTful API Modeling Language

RESTful API Modeling Language (RAML) provides human-readable and machine-processable documentation for your RESTful web services. It helps you to clearly document resources, methods, parameters, responses, media types, and other HTTP constructs that form the basis for a RESTful web service. RAML was first proposed in 2013 by RAML Workgroup. Today, RAML Workgroup includes technology leaders from various software vendors such as MulesSoft Inc., PayPal Inc., Intuit Inc., and Cisco.

RAML is built on standards such as **Yaml Ain't Markup Language (YAML)**. YAML is a human-friendly data serialization standard that works with any programming language. If you are not familiar with YAML, go through the wiki page available at `http://en.wikipedia.org/wiki/YAML`.

An overview of the RAML structure

Let's take a quick look at the RAML file structure that describes RESTful web services. An RAML file is a text file with the recommended extension of `.raml`. It uses spaces as indentation; you can use two or four spaces for indentation. The details of the content that you will find in a typical RAML file are as follows:

We are grouping the contents into different logical sections to keep this discussion simple and easy to follow:

- **Basic information**: An RAML file starts with the basic information of the RESTful web APIs that you want to describe. This information is listed in the root portion of the document. The basic information includes information about REST APIs, such as the API title, version, base URI, base URI parameters, and schema definition for resources, protocols, and default media type.

  Optionally, the root portion can also include a variety of user documentation that serve as a user guide and reference documentation for the API. Such documentation details how the API works.

- **Security**: Mostly, the REST APIs that you see today are secure. You can have security scheme definitions for accessing APIs in the RAML file towards the beginning of the contents, alongside the basic information.

- **Resources and nested resources**: The next step is to outline the resources and nested resources exposed via REST APIs. Resources are identified by their relative URI. A nested resource (child resource) is a resource defined as a child of a parent resource. Nested resources are useful if you want to access a subset from a collection of resources (which is identified as the parent resource). The `uriParameters` property is used for describing the `path` parameter used for accessing the child resources.

- **HTTP methods**: Once you have all RESTful resources defined in RAML, the next step is to define the HTTP methods, such as GET, POST, PUT, and DELETE, which a client can perform on resources. The HTTP method may have following sections:

  ○ **Query parameters**: If the REST `resource` method takes the query parameters, RAML lets you specify them along with HTTP methods via the `queryParameters` attribute, typically used with the HTTP GET method.

  ○ **Request data**: The request payload definition is also allowed in RAML. The request payload specifies the media type and form parameters present in the request, typically used with the HTTP PUT and POST methods.

- **Response**: The definitions of the REST resource and the HTTP operations on them give a high-level overview of the REST APIs. However, to really consume these APIs in real life, the client application must be aware of the response codes and content type returned by the REST calls. RAML defines the response types for each `resource` method. This includes the HTTP status codes, descriptions, examples, or schemas.

Here is a simple RAML example. See the following JAX-RS `resource` method that returns a `Department` object. Let's see how this JAX-RS resource can be represented in RAML:

```
@GET
@Path("{id}")
@Produces("application/json")
public Department findDepartment(@PathParam("id") Short id){
    //Method body is omitted for brevity...
}
```

The RAML file describing the preceding `resource` method will look like the following code:

```
#%RAML 0.8
title: department resource
version: 1.0
baseUri: "http://localhost:8080/hrapp/webresources"
schemas:
  - department: !include schemas/department.xsd
  - department-jsonschema: !include schemas/department-jsonschema.json
/departments:
  get:
  /{id}:
    uriParameters:
      id:
        type: integer
    get:
      responses:
        200:
          body:
            application/json:
              schema: department-jsonschema
              example: !include examples/department.json
```

A detailed tutorial on RAML is available at `http://raml.org/docs.html`. Here is the link to complete the RAML specification: `https://github.com/raml-org/raml-spec`.

Generating RAML from JAX-RS

In this section, we will learn how to generate the RAML file for your JAX-RS application. To generate the RAML file for JAX-RS, we use the `jaxrs-raml-maven-plugin` Maven plugin that comes as a part of RAML for the JAX-RS project (from MuleSoft Inc.). The source for RAML for JAX-RS is available at `https://github.com/mulesoft/raml-for-jax-rs`.

The `jaxrs-raml-maven-plugin` Maven plugin is capable of identifying the JAX-RS annotation, which you set on the resource class, resource methods, and fields, and uses this metadata to generate the RAML file while building the source. The `jaxrs-raml-maven-plugin` Maven plugin supports the following set of the JAX-RS annotations `@Path`, `@Consumes`, `@Produces`, `@QueryParam`, `@FormParam`, `@PathParam`, `@HeaderParam`, `@DELETE`, `@GET`, `@HEAD`, `@OPTIONS`, `@POST`, `@PUT`, and `@DefaultValue`.

The JAXB annotated (`@XmlRootElement`) classes that appear in the `resource` method signature will be represented using JSON or XML (depending on the media type set for the method) schemas in the RAML file.

The steps that you will perform for using JAX-RS to RAML Maven plugin in a JAX-RS application are as follows:

1. The `jaxrs-raml-maven-plugin` maven plugin is available in the Maven central repository. If you do not see the latest released version in the Maven central repository, clone this Git repository, `https://github.com/mulesoft/raml-for-jax-rs`, locally, and build the `raml-for-jax-rs/jaxrs-to-raml` project by executing `mvn install`.

2. Go to the project where you have all JAX-RS resource classes defined, and include `jaxrs-raml-maven-plugin` in the project's `pom.xml` file. The `<plugin>` entry in the `pom.xml` file will look like the following:

```
<build>
<plugins>
    <plugin>
        <groupId>org.raml.plugins</groupId>
        <artifactId>jaxrs-raml-maven-plugin</artifactId>
```

```
<!-- Specify the appropriate version -->
<version>1.3.3</version>
<configuration>
    <sourceDirectory>
        ${basedir}/src/main/java
    </sourceDirectory>
    <baseUrl>
        http://localhost:8080/hrapp/webresources
    </baseUrl>
    <title>Department Resource</title>
    <outputFile>
        ${project.build.directory}/
            generated-sources/dept-api.raml
    </outputFile>
    <removeOldOutput>true</removeOldOutput>
</configuration>
<executions>
    <execution>
        <goals>
            <goal>generate-raml</goal>
        </goals>
        <phase>process-classes</phase>
    </execution>
</executions>
</plugin>
<!-- Other plugin entries go here -->
</plugins>
</build>
```

3. You are now done with the setup. When you run mvn compile or mvn package, jaxrs-raml-maven-plugin, which you added in the previous step, it will generate the RAML file in Maven's generated-sources folder for all the JAX-RS resource classes found in the Maven source folder.

The complete source code for this example is available at the Packt website. You can download the example from the Packt website link that we mentioned at the beginning of this book in the *Preface* section. In the downloaded source code, see the rest-chapter7-service-doctools/rest-chapter7-jaxrs2raml project.

It is now time for us to see `jaxrs-raml-maven-plugin` in action. The RAML file generated for the `DepartmentResource` class, which we discussed a while ago in the *Generating WADL from JAX-RS* section, is shown here:

```
#%RAML 0.8
title: Department Resource
baseUri: "http://localhost:8080/hrapp/webresources"
schemas:
  - department: !include schemas/department.xsd
  - department-jsonschema: !include schemas/
    department-jsonschema.json
/departments:
  post:
    body:
      application/json:
        schema: department-jsonschema
        example: !include examples/department.json
    responses:
      200:
  get:
    queryParameters:
      from:
        type: integer
      to:
        type: integer
    responses:
      200:
        body:
          application/json:
  /{id}:
    uriParameters:
      id:
        type: integer
    put:
      body:
        application/json:
          schema: department-jsonschema
          example: !include examples/department.json
      responses:
        200:
```

Generating RAML from JAX-RS via CLI

In addition to the Maven plugin, RAML for the JAX-RS project also has a
command-line interface (CLI) tool for generating RAML from the JAX-RS
resources. Its usage is as follows:

1. Download the CLI tool from `http://raml-tools.mulesoft.com/raml-`
    `for-jax-rs/CLI/jax-rs-to-raml.jar`. Alternatively, you can clone
    the `https://github.com/mulesoft/raml-for-jax-rs` project and
    build it locally.

2. To generate the RAML code, perform `javac` with the following arguments:

    ```
    javac [space delimited JAX-RS Java class files ]
          -sourcepath [path-to-your-java-source-code]
          -classpath [your-classpath]
          -processorpath <path-to-your-jar>/jax-rs-to-raml.jar
          -processor com.mulesoft.jaxrs.raml.annotation.model.apt.
    RAMLAnnotationProcessor
          -Aramlpath=[folder-for-generated-raml]
          -implicit:class
    ```

>
> To learn more about the CLI tool for generating RAML, visit
> `https://github.com/mulesoft/raml-for-jax-rs/`
> `blob/master/command-line.md`.

Generating JAX-RS from RAML

In the previous section, we have seen how to generate the RAML documentation for
the REST resources classes present in a JAX-RS application. In this section, we will
learn how to generate the JAX-RS resources classes from an RAML documentation
file. This feature is enabled via the `raml-jaxrs-maven-plugin` Maven plugin.

Perform the following steps for using RAML to the JAX-RS Maven plugin in a
maven project:

1. The `raml-jaxrs-maven-plugin` Maven plugin is available in the Maven
    central repository. If you do not see the latest release here, clone the Git
    repository available at `https://github.com/mulesoft/raml-for-jax-rs`,
    and build the `raml-for-jax-rs/raml-to-jaxrs` project by executing `mvn`
    `install`.

2. Go to the Maven project where you want to generate the JAX-RS resource classes from the RAML file. Include `raml-jaxrs-maven-plugin` in the project's `pom.xml` file. The `<plugin>` entry in the `pom.xml` file will look like the following:

```
<plugins>
  <plugin>
    <groupId>org.raml.plugins</groupId>
    <artifactId>raml-jaxrs-maven-plugin</artifactId>
    <version>1.3.3</version>
    <configuration>
      <sourceDirectory>
        ${basedir}/src/main/resources/raml
      </sourceDirectory>
      <basePackageName>
        com.packtpub.rest.ch7.service
      </basePackageName>
      <jaxrsVersion>2.0</jaxrsVersion>
      <useJsr303Annotations>false</useJsr303Annotations>
      <jsonMapper>jackson2</jsonMapper>
      <removeOldOutput>true</removeOldOutput>
    </configuration>
    <executions>
      <execution>
        <goals>
          <goal>generate</goal>
        </goals>
        <phase>generate-sources</phase>
      </execution>
    </executions>
  </plugin>
  <!-- other plugins go here -->
</plugins>
```

3. Keep the RAML file that you want to convert into JAX-RS in the `resources` folder of the Maven project. The plugin configuration lets you specify the source folder via the `<sourceDirectory>` element.

4. Run `mvn compile` or `mvn package`, which will result in generating the JAX-RS resource classes for the RAML file present in the source folder. You can find the newly generated source files in the `generated-sources` folder under Maven's `target` folder.

Note that all generated JAX-RS resource classes that you see here are just template classes derived from the RAML file. It is your responsibility to add the appropriate business logic to each `resource` method and make the necessary changes to make it production-ready.

Generating JAX-RS from RAML via CLI

In addition to the maven plugin, RAML for the JAX-RS project has a CLI tool for generating the JAX-RS resource classes from RAML. Its usage is as follows:

1. Download the CLI tool from `http://raml-tools.mulesoft.com/raml-for-jax-rs/CLI/raml-to-jax-rs.jar`. Alternatively, you can clone the `https://github.com/mulesoft/raml-for-jax-rs` project and build it locally.

2. To generate the JAX-RS code, run the following command:

    ```
    java -cp [class-path-to-the-jar] org.raml.jaxrs.codegen.core.
    Launcher
      -basePackageName [package-name-for-generated-sources]
      -outputDirectory [output-directory-for-generated-source]
      -sourceDirectory [raml-file-location]
    ```

 To learn more about the CLI tool for generating JAX-RS, visit `https://github.com/mulesoft/raml-for-jax-rs/blob/master/command-line.md`.

A glance at the market adoption of RAML

RAML is simple and easy to use for describing RESTful web APIs. It comes with advanced language constructs and good online design tool support, which eases the job of describing APIs. You can build RAML even during the design phase of the application describing the APIs. Later, during the development phase, you can use the RAML definitions of APIs to generate high-level resource class definitions.

During development, RAML allows you to develop and test the API client independent of the actual RESTful web service implementation.

Although RAML has many good features, market adoption is less than that of other competing products. This is mainly because it came late in the game. However, this tool looks promising in the long run because the community is quite active and there is a wide range of tools available today to support RAML.

In the next section, we will discuss Swagger. Swagger is not just yet another REST API documentation tool; rather, it offers many features in addition to the API documentation.

Swagger

Swagger offers a specification and complete framework implementation for describing, producing, consuming, and visualizing RESTful web services. The Swagger framework works with many of the popular programming languages, such as Java, Scala, Clojure, Groovy, JavaScript, and .Net.

Swagger was initially developed by Wordnik (a property of Reverb) for meeting their in-house requirements, and the first version was released in 2011. The current release is Swagger 2.0, and it is 100 percent open source, supported by many vendors, such as PayPal, Apigee, and 3scale.

The Swagger framework has the following three major components:

- **Server**: This component hosts the RESTful web API descriptions for the services that clients want to use
- **Client**: This component uses the RESTful web API descriptions from the server to provide an automated interfacing mechanism to invoke the REST APIs
- **User interface**: This part of the framework reads a description of the APIs from the server and renders it as a web page and provides an interactive sandbox to test the APIs

A quick overview of Swagger's structure

Let's take a quick look at the Swagger file structure before moving further. The Swagger 1.x file contents that describe the RESTful APIs are represented as the JSON objects. With the Swagger 2.0 release, you can also use the YAML format to describe the RESTful web APIs.

This section discusses the Swagger file contents represented as JSON. The basic constructs that we discuss in this section for JSON are also applicable for the YAML representation of APIs, although the syntax differs.

When using the JSON structure for describing the REST APIs, the Swagger file uses a Swagger object as the root document object for describing APIs. Here is a quick overview of various properties that you will find in the Swagger object:

- The following properties describe the basic information about the RESTful web application:

    ○ `swagger`: This property specifies the Swagger version.

    ○ `info`: This property provides metadata about the API.

    ○ `host`: This property locates the server where APIs are hosted.

    ○ `basePath`: This property is the base path for the API. This property is relative to the value set for the `host` field.

    ○ `schemes`: This property transfers the protocol for a RESTful web API such as HTTP and HTTPS.

- The following properties allow you to specify the default values at the application level, which can be optionally overridden for each operation:

    ○ `consumes`: This property specifies the default Internet media types that the APIs consume. It can be overridden at the API level.

    ○ `produces`: This property specifies the default Internet media types that the APIs produce. It can be overridden at the API level.

    ○ `securityDefinitions`: This property globally defines the security schemes for the document. These definitions can be referred from the security schemes specified for each API.

- The following properties describe the operations (REST APIs):

    ○ `paths`: This property specifies the path to the API or the resources. The path must be appended to the `basePath` property in order to get the full URI.

    ○ `definitions`: This property specifies the input and output entity types for the operations on the REST resources (APIs).

    ○ `parameters`: This property specifies the parameter details for an operation.

    ○ `responses`: This property specifies the response type for an operation.

    ○ `security`: This property specifies the security schemes in order to execute this operation.

    ○ `externalDocs`: This property links to the external documentation.

A complete Swagger 2.0 specification is available at `https://github.com/swagger-api/swagger-spec/blob/master/versions/2.0.md`.

An overview of Swagger APIs

The Swagger framework consists of five subprojects, each built with a specific purpose. Here is a quick summary of the Swagger projects that you will see in the Git repository at `https://github.com/swagger-api`:

- `swagger-spec`: This repository contains the Swagger specification and the project in general.
- `swagger-ui`: This project is an interactive tool to display and execute the Swagger specification files. It is based on `swagger-js` (JavaScript library).
- `swagger-editor`: This project allows you to edit the YAML files. It is released as a part of Swagger 2.0.
- `swagger-core`: This project provides the `scala` and `java` library to generate the Swagger specifications directly from the code. It supports JAX-RS, Servlet APIs, and the Play framework.
- `swagger-codegen`: This project provides a tool that can read the Swagger specification files and generate the client and server code that consumes and produces the specifications.

In the next section, we will learn how to use the `swagger-core` project offerings to generate the Swagger file for a JAX-RS application.

Generating Swagger from JAX-RS

Both WADL and RAML tools, discussed in the previous sections, use the JAX-RS annotations metadata to generate the documentation for the APIs. The Swagger framework does not fully rely on the JAX-RS annotations but offers a set of proprietary annotations for describing the resources. This helps in the following scenarios:

- The Swagger core annotations provide more flexibility for generating documentation compliant with Swagger specifications
- It allows you to use Swagger for generating documentation for web components that do not use the JAX-RS annotations, such as servlet and servlet filter

The Swagger annotations are designed to work with JAX-RS, improving the quality of the API documentation generated by the framework. Note that the `swagger-core` project is currently supported on the Jersey and Restlet implementations. If you are considering any other runtime for your JAX-RS application, check the respective product manual and ensure the support before you start using Swagger for describing APIs.

Some of the commonly used Swagger annotations are as follows:

- Annotations that declare a resource are as follows:
  - `@com.wordnik.swagger.annotations.Api`: This annotation marks a class as a Swagger resource. Note that only classes that are annotated with `@Api` will be considered for generating documentation. The `@Api` annotation is used along with class-level JAX-RS annotations such as `@Produces` and `@Path`

- Annotations that declare an operation are as follows:
  - `@com.wordnik.swagger.annotations.ApiOperation`: This annotation describes a `resource` method (operation) that is designated for responding to HTTP action methods such as `GET`, `PUT`, `POST`, and `DELETE`.
  - `@com.wordnik.swagger.annotations.ApiParam`: This annotation is used for describing parameters used in an operation. This is designed for use in conjunction with the JAX-RS parameters such as `@Path`, `@PathParam`, `@QueryParam`, `@HeaderParam`, `@FormParam`, and `@BeanParam`.
  - `@com.wordnik.swagger.annotations.ApiImplicitParam`: This annotation allows you to define the operation parameters manually. You can use this to override the `@PathParam` or `@QueryParam` values specified on a `resource` method with custom values. If you have multiple `ImplicitParam` for an operation, wrap them with `@ApiImplicitParams`.
  - `@com.wordnik.swagger.annotations.ApiResponse`: This annotation describes the status codes returned by an operation. If you have multiple responses, wrap them by using `@ApiResponses`.
  - `@com.wordnik.swagger.annotations.ResponseHeader`: This annotation describes a header that can be provided as part of the response.
  - `@com.wordnik.swagger.annotations.Authorization`: This annotation is used within either `Api` or `ApiOperation` to describe the authorization scheme used on a resource or an operation.

- Annotations that declare API models are as follows:

    ○ `@com.wordnik.swagger.annotations.ApiModel`: This annotation describes the model objects used in the application

    ○ `@com.wordnik.swagger.annotations.ApiModelProperty`: This annotation describes the properties present in the `ApiModel` object

 A complete list of the Swagger core annotations is available at `https://github.com/swagger-api/swagger-core/wiki/Annotations`.

Having learned the basics of Swagger, it is time for us to move on and build a simple example to get a feel of the real-life use of Swagger in a JAX-RS application. As always, this example uses the Jersey implementation of JAX-RS.

Specifying dependency to Swagger

To use Swagger in your Jersey 2 application, specify the dependency to `swagger-jersey2-jaxrs` jar. If you use Maven for building the source, dependency to the `swagger-core` library will look like the following:

```
<dependency>
    <groupId>com.wordnik</groupId>
    <artifactId>swagger-jersey2-jaxrs</artifactId>
    <version>1.5.1-M1</version>
    <!—use the appropriate version here,
    1.5.x supports Swagger 2.0 spec -->
</dependency>
```

 You should be careful while choosing the `swagger-core` version for your product. Note that `swagger-core` 1.3 produces the Swagger 1.2 definitions, whereas `swagger-core` 1.5 produces the Swagger 2.0 definitions.

The next step is to hook the Swagger provider components into your Jersey application. This is done by configuring the Jersey servlet (`org.glassfish.jersey.servlet.ServletContainer`) in `web.xml` as shown here:

```
<servlet>
    <servlet-name>jersey</servlet-name>
    <servlet-class>
        org.glassfish.jersey.servlet.ServletContainer
    </servlet-class>
```

```
        <init-param>
            <param-name>jersey.config.server.provider.packages
            </param-name>
            <param-value>
                com.wordnik.swagger.jaxrs.json,
                com.packtpub.rest.ch7.swagger
            </param-value>
        </init-param>
        <load-on-startup>1</load-on-startup>
    </servlet>
        <servlet-mapping>
            <servlet-name>jersey</servlet-name>
            <url-pattern>/webresources/*</url-pattern>
        </servlet-mapping>
```

To enable the Swagger documentation features, it is necessary to load the Swagger framework provider classes from the package, `com.wordnik.swagger.jaxrs.` `listing`. The package names of the JAX-RS resource classes and provider components are configured as the value for the `jersey.config.server.provider.packages` `init` parameter. The Jersey framework scans through the configured packages for identifying the resource classes and provider components during the deployment of the application. Map the Jersey servlet to a request URI so that it responds to the REST resource calls that match the URI.

If you prefer not to use `web.xml`, you can also use the custom application subclass for (programmatically) specifying all the configuration entries discussed here. To try this option, refer to `https://github.com/swagger-api/swagger-core/wiki/` `Swagger-Core-JAX-RS-Project-Setup`.

Configuring the Swagger definition

After specifying the Swagger provider components, the next step is to configure and initialize the Swagger definition. This is done by configuring the `com.wordnik.` `swagger.jersey.config.JerseyJaxrsConfig` servlet in `web.xml` as follows:

```
    <servlet>
        <servlet-name>Jersey2Config</servlet-name>
        <servlet-class>
            com.wordnik.swagger.jersey.config.JerseyJaxrsConfig
        </servlet-class>
        <init-param>
            <param-name>api.version</param-name>
            <param-value>1.0.0</param-value>
        </init-param>
```

```
      <init-param>
          <param-name>swagger.api.basepath</param-name>
          <param-value>
              http://localhost:8080/hrapp/webresources
          </param-value>
      </init-param>
      <load-on-startup>1</load-on-startup>
  </servlet>
```

Here is a brief overview of the initialization parameters used for `JerseyJaxrsConfig`:

- `api.version`: This parameter specifies the API version for your application
- `swagger.api.basepath`: This parameter specifies the base path for your application

With this step, we have finished all configuration entries for using Swagger in a JAX-RS (Jersey 2 implementation) application. In the next section, we will see how to use the Swagger metadata annotation on a JAX-RS resource class for describing the resources and operations.

Adding Swagger annotations on a JAX-RS resource class

Let's revisit the DepartmentResource class used in the previous sections. In this example, we will enhance the DepartmentResource class by adding the Swagger annotations discussed earlier. We use @Api to mark DepartmentResource as the Swagger resource. The @ApiOperation annotation describes the operation exposed by the DepartmentResource class.

```
import com.wordnik.swagger.annotations.Api;
import com.wordnik.swagger.annotations.ApiOperation;
import com.wordnik.swagger.annotations.ApiParam;
import com.wordnik.swagger.annotations.ApiResponse;
import com.wordnik.swagger.annotations.ApiResponses;
//Other imports are removed for brevity

@Stateless
@Path("departments")
@Api(value = "/departments", description = "Get departments
    details")
public class DepartmentResource  {
```

```
@ApiOperation(value = "Find department by id",
    notes = "Specify a valid department id",
    response = Department.class)
@ApiResponses(value = {
    @ApiResponse(code = 200, message = "successful operation"),
    @ApiResponse(code = 404, message = "Department not found")
})
@GET
@Path("{id}")
@Produces("application/json")
public Department findDepartment(
    @ApiParam(value = "The department id", required = true)
    @PathParam("id") Integer id){
        return findDepartmentEntity(id);
    }

//Rest of the codes are removed for brevity


}
```

To view the Swagger documentation, build the source and deploy it to the server. Once the application is deployed, you can navigate to `http://<host>:<port>/<application-name>/<application-path>/swagger.json` to view the Swagger resource listing in the JSON format. The Swagger URL for this example will look like the following: `http://localhost:8080/hrapp/webresource/swagger.json`.

The following sample Swagger representation is for the `DepartmentResource` class discussed in this section:

```
{
  "swagger": "2.0",
  "info": {
    "version": "1.0.0",
    "title": ""
  },
  "host": "localhost:8080",
  "basePath": "/hrapp/webresources",
  "schemes": [
    "http"
  ],
  "paths": {
    "/departments/{id}": {
      "get": {
        "tags": [
```

```
              "user"
          ],
          "summary": "Find department by id",
          "description": "",
          "operationId": "findDepartment",
          "produces": [
            "application/json"
          ],
          "parameters": [
            {
              "name": "id",
              "in": "path",
              "description": "The department id",
              "required": true,
              "type": "integer",
              "format": "int32"
            }
          ],
          "responses": {
            "200": {
              "description": "successful operation",
            },
            "404": {
              "description": "Department not found"
            }
          }
        }
      }
    }
  },
  "definitions": {
    "Department": {
      "properties": {
        "departmentId": {
          "type": "integer",
          "format": "int32"
        },
        "departmentName": {
          "type": "string"
        },
        "_persistence_shouldRefreshFetchGroup": {
          "type": "boolean"
        }
      }
    }
  }
}
```

As mentioned at the beginning of this section, the Swagger 2.0 release supports the YAML representation of the APIs. You can access the YAML representation by navigating to `swagger.yaml`. For instance, in the preceding example, the following URI gives you the YAML file: `http://<host>:<port>/<application-name>/<application-path>/swagger.yaml`.

 The complete source code for this example is available at the Packt website. You can download the example from the Packt website link that we mentioned at the beginning of this book in the *Preface* section. In the downloaded source code, see the `rest-chapter7-service-doctools/rest-chapter7-jaxrs2swagger` project.

Generating Java client from Swagger

The Swagger framework is packaged with the Swagger code generation tool as well (`swagger-codegen-cli`), which allows you to generate client libraries by parsing the Swagger documentation file. You can download the `swagger-codegen-cli.jar` file from the Maven central repository by searching for `swagger-codegen-cli` in `http://search.maven.org`. Alternatively, you can clone the `https://github.com/swagger-api/swagger-codegen` Git repository and build the source locally by executing `mvn install`.

Once you have `swagger-codegen-cli.jar` locally available, run the following command to generate the Java client for the REST API described in Swagger:

```
java -jar swagger-codegen-cli.jar generate
-i <Input-URI-or-File-location-for-swagger.json>
-l <client-language-to-generate>
-o <output-directory>
```

The following example illustrates the use of this tool:

```
java -jar swagger-codegen-cli-2.1.0-M2.jar generate
-i http://localhost:8080/hrapp/webresources/swagger.json
-l java
-o generated-sources/java
```

When you run this tool, it scans through the RESTful web API description, available at `http://localhost:8080/hrapp/webresources/swagger.json`, and generates a Java client source in the `generated-sources/java` folder.

Note that the Swagger code generation process uses the mustache templates for generating the client source. If you are not happy with the generated source, Swagger lets you specify your own mustache template files. Use the `-t` flag to specify your template folder. To learn more, refer to the `README.md` file at `https://github.com/swagger-api/swagger-codegen`.

A glance at the market adoption of Swagger

The great strength of Swagger is its powerful API platform that satisfies the client, documentation, and server needs. The Swagger UI framework serves as the documentation and testing utility. Its support for different languages and matured tooling support have really grabbed the attention of many API vendors, and it seems to be the one with the most traction in the community today.

Swagger is built using Scala. This means that when you package your application, you need to have the entire Scala runtime in your build, which may considerably increase the size of your deployable artifact (the EAR or WAR file). That said, however, Swagger is improving with each release. For example, the Swagger 2.0 release allows you to use YAML for describing APIs. So, keep a watch on this framework.

Revisiting the features offered in WADL, RAML, and Swagger

The following table summarizes the discussion that we have had so far on the WADL, RAML, and Swagger tools:

Features	WADL	RAML	Swagger
Release date	2009	2013	2011
File format	XML	RAML	JSON/YAML
Open source	Yes	Yes	Yes
Commercial offering	No	Yes	Yes
Language support	Java	JS, Java, Node, PHP, Python, and Ruby	Clojure, Go, JS, Java, .Net, Node, PHP, Python, Ruby, and Scala
Authentication	No	Basic, Digest, OAuth 1, and OAuth 2	Basic, API Key, and OAuth 2
API console	No	Yes	Yes

Features	WADL	RAML	Swagger
Code generation for server (Java)	No	Yes	Yes
Code generation for client (Java)	Yes	Yes	Yes

Summary

A number of RESTful web API metadata standards have emerged in the recent past. The objective of this chapter is to introduce you to some of the popular RESTful web API documentation tools, namely WADL, RAML, and Swagger. This chapter is not meant for making any recommendation on choosing a documentation solution for your RESTful web application, but to help you understand the API documentation tools and their offerings in general. To choose the right solution for your organization, you should start by looking at client applications that access the APIs and their usage pattern, and then choose a tool that makes the API consumption easier, which may eventually improve the adoption of APIs by the customers.

The next chapter summarizes the best practices and coding guidelines that developers will find useful when building RESTful web service applications. This chapter is very important for you as a developer and it is worth spending time on each item that we discuss.

8
RESTful API Design Guidelines

REST is a software architectural style, not a specification, for building scalable web services. Since RESTful web services do not have any strict specifications for designing and building APIs, you may find many interpretations for how the RESTful web API should work.

In this chapter, you will learn standards, best practices, conventions, and tips and tricks that you can apply to your RESTful web service applications today. Some of the important topics discussed in this chapter are as follows:

- Naming RESTful web resources
- Implementing partial response
- Paging resource collection
- Using HATEOAS in response representation
- Versioning RESTful web APIs
- Caching RESTful web API results
- Microservice architecture style for RESTful web applications
- Using Open Data Protocol with RESTful web APIs

Let's start by discussing the guidelines for identifying resources in a problem domain.

Identifying resources in a problem domain

The basic steps that you may need to take while building a RESTful web API for a specific problem domain are as follows:

1. Identify all possible objects in the problem domain. This can be done by identifying all nouns in the problem domain. For example, if you are building an application to manage employees in a department, the obvious nouns are department and employee.

2. The next step is to identify the objects that can be manipulated using the CRUD operations. These objects can be classified as resources. Note that you should be careful while choosing resources. Based on the usage pattern, you can classify resources as top-level and nested resources (which are the children of a top-level resource). Also, there is no need to expose all resources for use by the client; expose only those resources that are required for implementing the business use case.

Transforming operations to HTTP methods

Once you have identified all the resources, as the next step, you may want to map the operations defined on the resources to the appropriate HTTP methods.

The most commonly used HTTP methods (verbs) in RESTful web APIs are POST, GET, PUT, and DELETE. Note that there is no one-to-one mapping between the CRUD operations defined on the resources and the HTTP methods.

 An operation is called **idempotent** if multiple identical requests produce the same result. Similarly, an idempotent RESTful web API will always produce the same result on the server irrespective of how many times the request is executed with the same parameters; however, the response may change between requests. The HTTP methods – GET, HEAD, PUT, and DELETE – are all idempotent, while POST is not.

Here are some tips for identifying the most appropriate HTTP method for the operations that you want to perform on the resources:

- GET: You can use this method for reading a representation of a resource from the server. According to the HTTP specification, GET is a safe operation, which means that it is only intended for retrieving data, not for making any state changes. As this is an idempotent operation, multiple identical GET requests will behave in the same manner.

A GET method can return the 200 OK HTTP response code on the successful retrieval of resources. If there is any error, it can return an appropriate status code such as 404 NOT FOUND or 400 BAD REQUEST.

- DELETE: You can use this method for deleting resources. On successful deletion, DELETE can return the 200 OK status code. According to the HTTP specification, DELETE is an idempotent operation. Note that when you call DELETE on the same resource for the second time, the server may return the 404 NOT FOUND status code since it was already deleted, which is different from the response for the first request. The change in response for the second call is perfectly valid here. However, multiple DELETE calls on the same resource produce the same result (state) on the server.

- PUT: According to the HTTP specification, this method is idempotent. When a client invokes the PUT method on a resource, the resource available at the given URL is completely replaced with the resource representation sent by the client. When a client uses the PUT request on a resource, it has to send all the available properties of the resource to the server, not just the partial data that was modified within the request.

> You can use PUT to create or update a resource if all attributes of the resource are available with the client. This makes sure that the server state does not change with multiple PUT requests. On the other hand, if you send partial resource content in a PUT request multiple times, there are chances that some other clients might have updated some attributes that are not present in your request. In such cases, the server cannot guarantee that the state of the resource on the server will remain identical when the same request is repeated, which breaks the idempotency rule.

- POST: This method is not idempotent. This method enables you to use the POST method to create or update resources when you do not know all the available attributes of a resource. For example, consider a scenario where the identifier field for an entity resource is generated at the server when the entity is persisted in the data store. You can use the POST method for creating such resources as the client does not have an identifier attribute while issuing the request. Here is a simplified example that illustrates this scenario. In this example, the employeeID attribute is generated on the server:

```
POST /hrapp/api/employees HTTP/1.1
Host: packtpub.com
{employee entity resource in JSON}
```

On successful creation of resource, it is recommended to return the status of 201 Created and the location of the newly created resource. This allows the client to access the newly created resource later (with server generated attributes). The sample response for the preceding example will look like as follows:

```
201 Created
Location: /hrapp/api/employees/1001
```

Understanding the difference between PUT and POST

A common question that you will encounter while designing a RESTful web API is when to use the PUT and POST methods? Here is the simplified answer:

You can use PUT for creating or updating a resource when the client has the full resource content available. In this case, all values are with the client, and the server does not generate a value for any of the fields.

You will use POST for creating or updating a resource if the client has only partial resource content available. Note that you are losing the idempotency support with POST. An idempotent method means that you can call the same API multiple times without changing the state. This is not true for the POST method; each POST method call may result in a server state change. PUT is idempotent, and POST is not. If you have strong customer demands, you can support both methods and let the client choose the suitable one on the basis of the use case.

Naming RESTful web resources

Resources are a fundamental concept in a RESTful web service. A resource represents an entity that is accessible via the URI that you provide. The URI, which refers to a resource (which is known as a RESTful web API), should have a logically meaningful name. Having meaningful names improves the intuitiveness of the APIs, and therefore, their usability. Some of the widely followed recommendations for naming resources are shown here:

- It is recommended to use nouns to name both resources and path segments that will appear in the resource URI. You should avoid using verbs for naming resources and resource path segments. Using nouns to name a resource improves the readability of the corresponding RESTful web API, particularly when you are planning to release the API over the Internet for the mass public.

- You should always use plural nouns to refer to a collection of resources. Make sure that you are not mixing up singular and plural nouns while forming the REST URIs. For instance, to get all departments, the resource URI must look like /departments.

  If you want to read a specific department from the collection, the URI becomes /departments/{id}. Following the convention, the URI for reading the details of the HR department identified by id=10 should look like /departments/10.

  The following table illustrates how you can map the HTTP methods (verbs) to the operations defined for the departments' resources:

Resource	GET	POST	PUT	DELETE
/departments	Get all departments	Create a new department	Bulk update on departments	Delete all departments
/departments/10	Get the HR department with id=10	Not allowed	Update the HR department	Delete the HR department

- While naming resources, favor more concrete names over generic names. For instance, when reading all programmers' details of a software firm, it is preferable to have a resource URI of the form /programmers (which tells about the type of resource), over the much generic form /employees. This improves the intuitiveness of the APIs by clearly communicating the type of resources that it deals with.

- Keep the resource names that appear in the URI in the lowercase to improve the readability of the resulting resource URI.

- Resource names may include hyphens; avoid using underscores and other punctuation.

- If the entity resource is represented in the JSON format, field names used in the resource must conform to the following guidelines:
    - Use meaningful names for the properties
    - Follow camel-cased naming convention: the first letter of the name is in lowercase, for example, departmentName
    - The first character must be a letter, an underscore (_), or a dollar sign ($), and the subsequent characters can be letters, digits, underscores, and/or dollar signs
    - Avoid using the reserved JavaScript keywords

- If a resource is related to another resource(s), use a subresource to refer to the child resource. You can use the path parameter in the URI to connect a subresource to its base resource. For instance, the resource URI path to get all employees belonging to the HR department (with `id=10`) will look like `/departments/10/employees`. To get the details of `employee` with `id=200` in the HR department, you can use the following URI: `/departments/10/employees/200`. To learn how to implement subresources using JAX-RS, refer back to the *Understanding subresources and subresource locators in JAX-RS* section in *Chapter 4, Advanced Features in the JAX-RS API.*

The resource path URI may contain plural nouns representing a collection of resources, followed by a singular resource identifier to return a specific resource item from the collection. This pattern can repeat in the URI, allowing you to drill down a collection for reading a specific item. For instance, the following URI represents an employee resource identified by `id=200` within the HR department: `/departments/hr/employees/200`.

Although the HTTP protocol does not place any limit on the length of the resource URI, it is recommended not to exceed 2000 characters because of the restriction set by many popular browsers.

Fine-grained and coarse-grained resource APIs

While building a RESTful web API, you should try avoiding the chattiness of APIs. On the other hand, APIs should not be overly coarse-grained as well. Highly coarse-grained APIs become too complex to use because the response representation may contain a lot of information, all of which may not be used by a majority of your API clients.

Let's take an example to understand the difference between fine-grained and coarse-grained approaches for building APIs. Suppose that you are building a very fine-grained API to read the employee details as follows:

- **API to read employee name:** GET `/employees/10/name`
- **API to read employee address1:** GET `/employees/10/address1`
- **API to read employee address2:** GET `/employees/10/address2`
- **API to read employee e-mail:** GET `/employees/10/email`

It is obvious that a majority of your clients may need all the preceding details to work on an employee resource. As a result, clients may end up making four different remote API calls to get all the required details of an employee resource. This is very expensive in terms of the network (resource) usage and CPU cycles. A possible solution to this scenario of converting all these fine-grained APIs into a coarse-grained API that returns all the required details as part of a single API call is `GET /employees/10.`

On the other hand, highly coarse-grained APIs may not fit all use cases. Suppose that you built a highly coarse-grained API that returns an employee resource along with the associated department, `/employees/{id}`. If not many consumers use the department details present in the employee resource, it simply makes the API complex to use and does not add any value for the consumers.

A better solution to this scenario is to build two separate fine-grained APIs, one for reading employee details and the other for reading the department details as shown here:

- **API to read individual employee details**: `GET /employees/10`
- **API to read department of an employee**: `GET /employees/10/departments`

To summarize this discussion, always look at the usage pattern of the APIs and the consumer requirements before deciding on the granularity of the APIs. Although very fine-grained APIs may not be an efficient solution for many use cases, it is perfectly valid to have fine-grained inner interfaces (not exposed for public) if this improves the modularity of the application.

Using header parameter for content negotiation

It is recommended to have an appropriate header parameter in the client request and in the server response to indicate how the entity body is serialized when transmitted over a wire.

- `Accept`: This request header field defines a list of acceptable response formats for the response, for example, `Accept: application/json,application/xml`

    The `javax.ws.rs.client.WebTarget` class allows you to specify the `Accept` header via the `request()` method for a JAX-RS client application

- `Content-Type`: This header field defines the type of the request or response message body content, for example, `Content-Type: text/plain; charset=UTF-8`

 Note that when you use the `@javax.ws.rs.Produces` annotation, the JAX-RS runtime sets the content type automatically.

Multilingual RESTful web API resources

If your RESTful web API needs to return the resource representations in different languages depending upon the client locale, use the content negotiation offering in HTTP:

- Clients can use the `Accept-Language` request header to specify language preferences.
- While generating a response, the server is expected to translate the messages into the language supported by the client. The server can use the `Content-Language` entity-header field to describe the natural language(s) of the intended audience.

Representing date and time in RESTful web resources

Here is a list of recommendations when you have the date (and time) fields in the RESTful web API resources:

- ISO 8601 is the International Standard for the representation of dates and times. It is recommended to use the **ISO-8601** format for representing the date and time in your RESTful web APIs. Here is an example for the ISO-8601 date and time: `YYYY-MM-DDThh:mm:ss.sTZD` (for example, `2015-06-16T11:20:30.45+01:00`)
- The API that you build must be capable of accepting any time zone set by the client.
- While storing the date and time fields present in the resource representation in the database, use **Coordinated Universal Time (UTC)**. UTC is guaranteed to be consistent.

- While retuning the date and time fields in response to an API call, use the UTC time zone. The client can easily convert the date field present in the resource into the desired local time by using an appropriate UTC offset.

Implementing partial response

Partial response refers to an optimization technique offered by the RESTful web APIs to return only the information (fields) required by the client. In this mechanism, the client sends the required field names as the query parameters for an API to the server, and the server trims down the default response content by removing the fields that are not required by the client. In the following example, the `select` query parameter is used for selecting fields that would be transferred over the wire:

```
/employees/1234?select=firstName,lastName,email
```

The Jersey framework supports the partial response feature via `org.glassfish.jersey.message.filtering.SelectableEntityFilteringFeature`. To enable this feature, you just need to register `SelectableEntityFilteringFeature` in the application. The client can use the `select` query parameter to select the fields that would be transferred over the wire, as illustrated in the following example:

```
GET employees/1234?select=email,department.departmentName HTTP/1.1
```

To learn more about this feature, see the Jersey example available at `https://github.com/jersey/jersey/tree/2.18/examples/entity-filtering-selectable`.

Implementing partial update

When a client changes only one part of the resource, you can optimize the entire update process by allowing the client to send only the modified part to the server, thereby saving the bandwidth and server resources. **RFC 5789** proposes a solution for this use case via a new HTTP method called PATCH. To learn more about this RFC, visit `https://tools.ietf.org/html/rfc5789`. Note that PATCH is not yet officially a part of HTTP/1.1. However, the HTTP protocol allows both the client and the server to implement any new method. Leveraging this flexibility, many vendors have started supporting the HTTP PATCH method.

The PATCH method takes the following form:

```
PATCH /departments/10 HTTP/1.1
[Description of changes]
```

The [Description of changes] section, in the preceding PATCH method, contains instructions describing how a resource currently residing on the origin server should be modified in order to reflect the changes performed by the client. **RFC 6902** defines a JSON document structure for expressing the sequence of changes performed on the resource by the client. Note that you can also have the XML structure for describing the changes performed on the XML representation of the resource. We are not covering the XML-based description in this book, because most of the RESTful web APIs currently use the JSON format for representing resources. You can learn more about RFC 6902 at https://tools.ietf.org/html/rfc6902. The PATCH operations supported by JSON PATCH are add, remove, replace, move, copy, and test.

The following example illustrates how you can use JSON PATCH for describing changes performed by a client on a department resource.

As the first step, the client retrieves the department resource from the server that looks like the following:

```
{"departmentId":10, "departmentName":"Administration",
  "managerId":200, "comments":"Administrative works" }
```

The client then performs the following modifications on the department resource:

- Modifies the manager by setting managerId to 300
- Adds a new locationId=1200 value to the department resource
- Removes the comments attribute

The JSON PATCH request body containing the preceding changes will look like the following:

```
PATCH /departments/10 HTTP/1.1
[
  { "op": "replace", "path": "/managerId", "value": 300 },
  { "op": "add", "path": "/locationId", "value": 1200 },
  { "op": "remove", "path": "/comments" }
]
```

The server applies the data manipulation instructions present in the incoming JSON PATCH document and modifies the original resource to reflect the changes performed by the client. After applying the modifications, the department resource on the server will look like the following:

```
{"departmentId":10, "departmentName":"Administration",
  "managerId":300, locationId=1200}
```

Currently, neither JAX-RS 2 nor Jersey support PATCH out of the box. However, JAX-RS allows you to add support for the new HTTP methods via the `javax.ws.rs.HttpMethod` annotation. To learn how to enable complete support for the HTTP PATCH method in your JAX-RS application, refer to the *Appendix, Useful Features and Techniques*, section of this book.

Returning modified resources to the caller

In a typical REST request-response model, an API client reads a resource from the server, makes some modifications, and sends the modified resource back to the server to save the changes via the PUT, POST, or PATCH operations as appropriate. While persisting changes, there are chances that the server may modify some of the fields, such as the version field and the modification date. In such cases, it makes sense to return the modified resource representation back to the client in order to keep both the client and the server in sync. The following example returns the modified Department entity back to the caller:

```
@POST
@Path("{id}")
public Department editDepartment(@PathParam("id") Short id,
  Department entity) {
  Department modifiedEntity=editDepartmentEntity(entity);
  return modifiedEntity;
}
```

If you are using the POST operation for creating a resource, you can use the HTTP 201 status code in the response, indicating the status of operation, and include a Location header that points to the URL of the new resource. Here is an example:

```
import javax.ws.rs.core.Response;
import javax.ws.rs.core.UriInfo;
import javax.ws.rs.core.Context;

@POST
public Response createDepartment(Department entity,
    @Context UriInfo uriInfo) {
    Integer deptId=createDepartmentEntity(entity);
    //Builds a URI for the newly created resource
    UriBuilder builder = uriInfo.getAbsolutePathBuilder();
    builder.path(deptId.toString());
    return Response.created(builder.build()).build();
}
```

Paging resource collection

It is not considered a good practice to return all resources that you may have in the database (or in any other data source) to a client in response to a GET API call. A very common approach for limiting the resource collection returned by an API is to allow the client to specify the offset and the page size for the collection. For example, the API that allows the client to specify the offset and the limit for the resource collection as the query parameters is /departments?offset=1&limit=20.

The following code snippet demonstrates how you can build a JAX-RS resource method that takes the offset and the page size (limit) sent by the client via query parameters:

```
@GET
@Produces("application/json")
public List<Department> findDepartments(@QueryParam("offset")
@DefaultValue("0") Integer offset, @QueryParam("limit")
    @DefaultValue("20") Integer limit) {
    //Complete method implementation is not shown for brevity
    return findDepartmentEntitiesInRange(offset, limit);
}
```

The preceding example is the simplest solution for paging a resource collection. You can improve this solution by including additional attributes in the resulting collection resource representation as follows:

- hasMore: This attribute indicates whether the collection has more elements to be retrieved
- limit: This attribute indicates the limit used by the server while querying the collection; this scenario arises if the limit is missing in the client request
- count: This attribute indicates the total number of elements in the collection
- totalSize: This attribute indicates the number of elements on the server that match the criteria used for reading the collection
- links: This attribute contains links to the next and the previous sets

The following example illustrates the resource collection returned by the server with the additional pagination attribute that we discussed:

```
{
    "departments": [{
        "departmentId": "11",
        "departmentName": "HR"
    }, {
```

```
        "departmentId": "12",
        "departmentName": "IT"
    },...
    ],
    "hasMore": true,
    "count": 10,
    "totalSize": 25,
    "links": [
        {"rel":"self",
        "href":"/hrapp/api/departments?offset=10&limit=10"},
        {"rel":"prev",
        "href":"/hrapp/api/departments?offset=0&limit=10"},
        {"rel":"next",
        "href":"/hrapp/api/departments?offset=20&limit=10"}
    ]
}
```

Implementing search and sort operations

Allowing a client to perform the search and sort operations on a resource collection is very essential to improve the market adoption of your APIs. As there is no existing standard for passing sort criteria or search conditions, various API vendors follow different patterns. A very common approach is to pass the search and sort criteria as the query parameters to the server.

The following example illustrates how you can pass the search criteria as the query parameters to the server:

```
/employees?departmentName=hr&salary>500000
```

The query parameters present in the preceding resource request URI can be used by the RESTful API implementation to find out the employee resources belonging to the HR department whose annual salary is greater than 500000.

Similarly, to read the collection of resources in a sorted order, you can pass the sort criteria as the query parameter to the API. The following example uses the sort keyword as the query parameter to indicate the beginning of fields in the URI for sorting, followed by the asc or desc keyword, indicating the sort order:

```
/employees?sort=firstName:asc,lastName:asc
```

If you have complex search conditions that cannot be easily represented as the request parameter in the URI, you can consider moving the search conditions into the request body and use the POST method for issuing the search. Here is an example:

```
POST   employees/searches HTTP/1.1
Host: packtpub.com
Accept: application/json
Content-Type: application/json
{
  "criteria": [{
    "firstName": "A";
    "operator": "startswith"
  }],
  "sort": [{"firstName":"asc","lastName":"asc" }
}
```

Using HATEOAS in response representation

Hypertext as the Engine of Application State (HATEOAS) refers to the use of hypermedia links in the resource representations. This architectural style lets the clients dynamically navigate to the desired resource by traversing the hypermedia links present in the response body. There is no universally accepted single format for representing links between two resources in JSON. This section shows some of the popular standards for defining links between resources.

Hypertext Application Language

The **Hypermedia API Language (HAL)** is a promising proposal that sets the conventions for expressing hypermedia controls (such as links) with JSON or XML. Currently, this proposal is in the draft stage. It mainly describes two concepts for linking resources:

- **Embedded resources**: This concept provides a way to embed another resource within the current one. In the JSON format, you will use the _ embedded attribute to indicate the embedded resource.

- **Links**: This concept provides links to associated resources. In the JSON format, you will use the _links attribute to link resources.

Here is the link to this proposal: `http://tools.ietf.org/html/draft-kelly-json-hal-06`. It defines the following properties for each resource link:

- `href`: This property indicates the URI to the target resource representation
- `template`: This property would be true if the URI value for `href` has any path variable inside it (template).
- `title`: This property is used for labeling the URI
- `hreflang`: This property specifies the language for the target resource
- `title`: This property is used for documentation purposes
- `name`: This property is used for uniquely identifying a link

The following example demonstrates how you can use the HAL format for describing the department resource containing hyperlinks to the associated employee resources. This example uses the JSON HAL for representing resources, which is represented using the `application/hal+json` media type.

```
GET /departments/10 HTTP/1.1
Host: packtpub.com
Accept: application/hal+json

HTTP/1.1 200 OK
Content-Type: application/hal+json

{
  "_links": {
    "self": { "href": "/departments/10" },
    "employees": { "href": "/departments/10/employees" },
    "employee": { "href": "/employees/{id}", "templated": true  }
  },
  "_embedded": {
    "manager": {
      "_links": { "self": { "href": "/employees/1700" } },
      "firstName": "Chinmay",
      "lastName": "Jobinesh",
      "employeeId": "1700",

    }
  },
  "departmentId": 10,
  "departmentName": "Administration"
}
```

RFC 5988 – Web Linking

RFC 5988 offers a framework for building links that define the relation between resources on the web. Although this specification defines the properties for the links, it does not define how the links as a whole should be represented in an HTTP message. However, it defines the guidelines for specifying the Link HTTP header. The syntax set for links in the HTTP headers in this specification may supplement the JSON resources as well. Each link in RFC 5988 may contain the following properties:

- **Target URI**: Each link should contain a target **Internationalized Resource Identifiers (IRIs)**. This property is represented by the href attribute. In case you are not familiar with IRI, it is the same as URI in function. However, IRI extends upon URI by using the universal character set, whereas URI is limited to ASCII characters.

- **Link relation type**: The link relation type describes how the current context (source) is related to the target resource. This is represented by the rel attribute.

- **Attributes for target IRI**: The attributes for a link include hreflang, media, title, title*, and type, as well as any extension link parameters.

You can learn more about RFC 5988 (Web Linking) at http://tools.ietf.org/html/rfc5988.

The following example demonstrates how you can use the Link entity-header fields for describing a relationship between two resources. This example defines the relation between the department (identified by id=10) and the employee resources:

```
GET /departments/10 HTTP/1.1
Host: packtpub.com
Accept: application/json

HTTP/1.1 200 OK
Content-Type: application/json
Link: <http://www.packtpub.com/departments/10>; rel="self";
  type="application/json"; title="Self Link"
Link: <http://www.packtpub.com/departments/10/employees>;
  rel="employees"; type="application/json"; title="Employees"
Link: <http://www.packtpub.com/employees/1700>; rel="manager";
  type="application/json"; title="Manager"
{"departmentId": 10, "departmentName": "Administration",
  "locationId": 1700}
```

Note that the syntax set for links in the HTTP headers can also be leveraged for adding the entity links within the resource body. For example, the department response entity in the preceding example can be modified to include the entity links as follows:

```
{
   "departmentId": 10,
   "departmentName": "Administration",
   "locationId": 1700
   "links": {
     { "rel"="self", "href": "/departments/10",
       type="application/json" },
     { "rel"="employees", "href": "/departments/10/employees",
       type="application/json" },
     { "rel"="manager","href": "/employees/1700",
       type="application/json" }
   }
}
```

A detailed discussion on resource link formats falls outside the scope of this book. However, the short but fruitful discussion that we had on HAL and RFC 5988 will definitely help you quickly learn any other resource linking schemes. Here is a quick summary of a few other popular formats available today for formatting resource links:

- **Collection+JSON**: This format is a JSON-based hypermedia type for describing a collection of resources represented in JSON. You can learn more about this type at `http://amundsen.com/media-types/collection/format`.

- **JSON Schema**: This format is a JSON-based format for defining the structure of the JSON data. As part of this definition, it provides a method for extracting the link relations from one resource to another. To learn more about JSON Schema, go to `http://tools.ietf.org/html/draft-zyp-json-schema-04`.

- **JSON for Linking Data (JSON-LD)**: This format is a lightweight Linked Data format. To learn more about JSON-LD, go to `http://json-ld.org/`.

Although RFC 5988 standardizes the syntax for the `Link` headers to link web resources, many API vendors do not prefer using the `Link` headers for linking resources. One of the reasons for not using the `Link` header is because this approach does not really work when the API returns the collection of resources. This is due to the fact that it is not easy for a client to accurately identify the `Link` header for a specific resource item present in the collection. Many API vendors prefer to place the links in the entity body as it is more convenient for a client to process.

Note that there is no clear consensus among various resource linking schemes that we have today on how the links should be formatted within resource representations. You can choose a format that meets your requirements and stick to it. Also, you may want to document all the APIs clearly, indicating the type of format used for generating the resource links, which will help your API consumers.

Choosing between absolute URI and relative URI for resource links

Many API vendors prefer to use absolute URI (`http://api.packtpub.com/hrapp/departments/10/employees`) over relative URI(`/departments/10/employees`) for links present in the resource representations. The absolute URI helps client to access the target resource easily, without worrying about how to construct the full URI.

Once you decide on the format for representing hypermedia links, the next step is to choose the right tool for implementing it in the application. Here is a quick summary of the JAX-RS and Jersey framework offerings for generating the HTTP links for your REST resource representations:

- `javax.ws.rs.core.Link`: You can use the `Link` utility class offered by JAX-RS 2.0 for generating the HTTP links (based on RFC 5988)

- `@org.glassfish.jersey.linking.InjectLink`: The `@InjectLink` annotation can be applied on the resource entity class fields to declaratively generate the HTTP links linking the web resources

To learn how to use the `javax.ws.rs.core.Link` and `org.glassfish.jersey.linking.InjectLink` APIs for generating resource links, refer to the *Building Hypermedia as the Engine of Application State (HATEOAS) APIs* section in *Chapter 5, Introducing the Jersey Framework Extensions*.

Versioning RESTful web APIs

You should always version the RESTful web APIs. Versioning of APIs helps you to roll out new releases without affecting the existing customer base as you can continue to offer the old API versions for a certain period of time. Later, a customer can move on to a new version if he/she prefers to do so.

You can version RESTful web APIs in many ways. Three popular techniques for versioning RESTful web APIs are given in this section.

Including the version in resource URI – the URI versioning

In the URI versioning approach, the version is appended along with the URI. An example is as follows:

```
GET /api/v1/departments HTTP/1.1
```

A sample RESTful web API implementation that takes a version identifier as part of the resource URI will look like the following:

```
//Imports are removed for brevity
@Path("v1/departments")
public class DepartmentResourceV1{
    @GET
    @Produces("application/json")
    public List<Department> findDepartmentsInRange(
        @QueryParam("offset") @DefaultValue("1") Integer offset,
        @QueryParam("limit") @DefaultValue("20") Integer limit) {

        return findAllDepartmentEntities(offset, limit);
    }
    //Other methods are removed for brevity
}
```

With this approach, if you want to upgrade the version for a resource, you will have to build a new resource class that takes the latest API version as the path parameter. To avoid code duplication, you can subclass the existing resource class and override only the modified resource methods, as shown here:

```
//Imports are removed for brevity
@Path("v2/departments")
public class DepartmentResourceV2 extends DepartmentResourceV1{
    @GET
    @Produces("application/json")
    @Override
    public List<Department> findDepartmentsInRange(
        @QueryParam("offset") @DefaultValue("1") Integer offset,
        @QueryParam("limit") @DefaultValue("20") Integer limit) {

        return findAllDepartmentEntities(offset, limit);
    }
    //Other methods are removed for brevity
}
```

Many big social sites (Twitter, Facebook, and so on) use the URI versioning approach for versioning the APIs.

Conceptually, this is the simplest solution for API versioning. However, there are certain drawbacks associated with this approach:

- As the resource URI changes with each release, client applications may have to change all the existing URI references in order to migrate to a new release. The impact may be minimal if all the resource URIs are localized and stored in a configuration file.

- This approach may disrupt the concept of HATEOAS.

- Since the URI path for an API gets updated for each change in the REST resource class, you may experience a large URI footprint over a period of time. This may result in a code maintenance issue for both the client and the server.

- If the URI is versioned, the cache may contain multiple copies of each resource, one for every version of the API.

Including the version in a custom HTTP request header – HTTP header versioning

The HTTP header versioning approach uses a custom header field to hold the API version. While requesting for a resource, the client sets the version in the header along with other information (if any). The server can be built to use the version information sent by the client in order to identify the correct version of the resource.

The following example uses a custom header to specify the API version that the client is looking for:

```
GET /api/departments HTTP/1.1
api-version: 1.0
```

The API implementation can read the request header via @javax.ws.rs. HeaderParam.

```
//Other imports are omitted for brevity
import javax.ws.rs.HeaderParam;
@GET
@Produces("application/json")
public List<Department> findAllDepartments(
    @HeaderParam("api-version") String version){
    //Method body is omitted for brevity
}
```

Including the version in a HTTP Accept header – the media type versioning

The media type versioning approach adds the version information to the media content type. You can do this by introducing custom vendor media types that hold the version information along with the media type details. The version information in the `Accept` header takes the following form:

```
Accept: application/vnd.{app_name}.{version}+{response_type}
```

The `vnd` part that you see in the `Accept` header is based on **RFC 6838**. The `vnd` keyword indicates the custom vendor-specific media types. More details are available at `https://tools.ietf.org/html/rfc6838`.

When you use this approach for versioning APIs, the client has to specify the version in the HTTP `Accept` header, as shown in the following example:

```
GET /api/v1/departments
Accept: application/vnd.packtpubapi.v1+json
```

A sample RESTful web API implementation that uses the media type versioning approach is shown here for your reference:

```java
@Path("departments")
@Produces({"application/json", "application/vnd.packtpub.v1+json"})
@Consumes({"application/json", "application/vnd.packtpub.v1+json"})
public class DepartmentResource{
    //The following method is a modified implementation
    //to read the list of employees, so the version number has been
    //incremented
    @GET
    @Produces({"application/vnd.packtpub.v2+json"})
    public List<Department> findDepartmentsInRangeV2(
        @QueryParam("offset") @DefaultValue("1") Integer offset,
        @QueryParam("limit") @DefaultValue("20") Integer limit) {
        return findDepartmentEntitiesWithDetails(offset, limit);
    }

    @GET
    public List<Department> findDepartmentsInRangeV1(
        @QueryParam("offset") @DefaultValue("1") Integer offset,
        @QueryParam("limit") @DefaultValue("20") Integer limit){
        return findDepartmentEntities(offset, limit);
    }

}
```

The preceding implementation has two methods annotated with different media type versions. At runtime, the Jersey framework automatically picks up a method to serve a request on the basis of the media type version information present in the Accept header parameter.

Many new API vendors have started supporting this approach. For example, GitHub uses the Accept header approach for versioning its APIs.

Although this approach works for many of the common use cases, there are challenges associated with the caching of results returned by these kinds of APIs. Many user agents do not consider the Accept header while reading the cached contents. For instance, when using the same URI for multiple versions of APIs, there are chances of caching proxies to return wrong representations from the cache. Although you can configure caching proxies to consider the Accept headers along with the URI, doing so may add complexity to your network configuration.

Hybrid approach for versioning APIs

Some API vendors choose a combination of URI versioning and HTTP header versioning approaches, where the major version information is kept along with the URI and the minor version information for subresources is stored in the custom header field. In this case, the major version information indicates the structural stability of the API as a whole, while the minor versions indicate smaller changes at the implementation level.

To summarize the discussion, there is no wrong and right approach for versioning APIs. You can choose one of the options that we have discussed here for your application as long as it meets your application's needs.

Caching RESTful web API results

The ability to cache and reuse previously retrieved resources is essential for improving the performance of a REST application. The HTTP/1.1 protocol specification provides a number of features to facilitate the caching of network resources. These offerings can be leveraged for improving the performance of the RESTful web APIs accessed over the HTTP protocol.

HTTP Cache-Control directive

The HTTP `Cache-Control` directive defines the HTTP response caching policies. You can use it for enabling the caching of the RESTful web API results for a specified interval. Here is a quick summary of the important HTTP `Cache-Control` directives:

HTTP Cache-Control directive	Description
Public	In this directive, public resources can be cached by the client and all intermediate public proxies.
private	In this directive, private resources can be cached only by the client.
max-age	This directive specifies how long a resource cached on the client is valid (measured in seconds).
smax-age	This property specifies the maximum age for a shared cache such as proxy cache (for example, content delivery network).
no-cache	This directive indicates that the resource should not be cached.
no-store	This directive indicates that the cached resource should not be stored on disk; however, it can be cached in-memory.
must-revalidate	This directive indicates that once the cache expires, the cache must revalidate the resource with the origin server even if the client is willing to work on the stale resource.

JAX-RS allows you to specify the `Cache-Control` directives on the `javax.ws.rs.core.Response` object via the `javax.ws.rs.core.CacheControl` class. To learn how to use the `CacheControl` class in your JAX-RS resource class, refer to the *Using Cache-Control directives to manage the HTTP cache* section in *Chapter 4, Advanced Features in the JAX-RS API*.

HTTP conditional requests

The conditional requests feature offered by HTTP allows the clients to ask the server whether it has an updated copy of the resource by including some extra header parameters in the request. The server will return the resource back to the client only if the resource that the client is having is not up to date.

Conditional requests can be implemented either by comparing the hash value of resource contents (via the ETag header) or by checking the time at which the resource is modified (via the Last-Modified header). Here is the quick summary of the request and response header parameters used in conditional requests:

- ETag: When requesting for a resource, the client adds an ETag header containing a hash or checksum of the resource that the client has received from the server for the last request. This hash value should change whenever the resource representation changes on the server. This allows the server to identify whether the client-cached contents of the resource are different from the actual content at the server.

- Last-Modified: This header works similar to ETag, except that it uses the timestamp for validating the cache. While generating a response, the server generates the Last-Modified header for the resource and passes it to the client. Subsequent requests from the client can send this timestamp information to the server via the If-Modified-Since request header, which tells the server not to send the resource again if it has not been changed.

> You can use the mentioned conditional approach while modifying a resource as well. This will help you ensure that the update is not happening against a stale instance of the resource. Your RESTful web API can be designed to throw 412 Precondition Failed if the ETag header sent by the client does not match the ETag header generated on the server using the latest contents.

To enable conditional requests, JAX-RS offers APIs such as javax.ws.rs.core.EntityTag and javax.ws.rs.core.Request::evaluatePreconditions(), the former to generate ETag and the later to evaluate the preconditions present in the request such as If-Modified-Since and If-None-Match. To learn the usage of the ETag and Last-Modified headers in a JAX-RS application, you can refer to the *Conditional request processing with the Last-Modified HTTP response header* and *Conditional request processing with the ETag HTTP response header* section in *Chapter 4, Advanced Features in the JAX-RS API.*

Using HTTP status codes in RESTful web APIs

Currently, there are over 75 status codes to report the statuses of various operations. The HTTP status codes are classified into the following five categories:

- `1xx Informational`: This code indicates informational messages
- `2xx Successful`: This code indicates the successful processing of the requests
- `3xx Redirection`: This code indicates that an action needs to be taken by the client to complete the request
- `4xx Client error`: This code indicates a client error
- `5xx Server error`: This code indicates a server failure in fulfilling the request

It is always recommended to return the appropriate status codes in response to a RESTful web API call. The status code present in the response helps the client take an appropriate action, depending upon the status of the operation. The following table summarizes the commonly used HTTP status codes to describe the status of a RESTful web API call:

Commonly used HTTP status codes	Description
200 OK	This status indicates a successful GET, PUT, PATCH, or DELETE operation. This status can be used for POST if an existing resource has been updated.
201 Created	This status is generated in response to a POST operation that creates a new resource.
204 No Content	This code tells that the server has processed the request but not returned any content. For example, this can be used with the PUT, POST, GET, or DELETE operations if they do not result in any result body.
304 Not Modified	This code tells the client that it can use the cached resource that was retrieved in the previous call. This code is typically used with the GET operation.
400 Bad Request	This code indicates that the request sent by the client was invalid (client error) and could not be served. The exact error should be explained in the response entity body payload.

Commonly used HTTP status codes	Description
`401  Unauthorized`	This code indicates that the REST API call requires user authentication. The client can take the necessary steps for authentication based on this response status.
`403  Forbidden`	This code indicates that the caller (even after authentication) does not have access to the requested resource.
`404  Not Found`	This code indicates that the requested resource is not found at this moment but may be available again in the future.
`405  Method Not Allowed`	This code indicates that the HTTP method requested by the caller is not supported by the resource.
`406  Not Acceptable`	This code indicates that the server does not support the required representation. For example, this can be used in response to the `GET`, `PUT`, or `POST` operations if the underlying REST API does not support the representation of the resource that the client is asking for.
`409  Conflict`	This code indicates that the request could not be completed due to some general conflict with the current state of the resource. This response code makes sense where the caller is capable of resolving the conflict by looking at the error details present in the response body and resubmitting the request. For example, this code can be used in response to `PUT`, `POST`, and `DELETE` if the client sends an outdated resource object to the server or if the operation results in the duplication of resources.
`410  Gone`	This code indicates that the resource identified by this URI is no longer available. Upon receiving a `410` status code, the caller should not request the resource again in the future.
`415  Unsupported Media Type`	This code indicates that the entity media type present in the request (`PUT` or `POST`) is not supported by the server.

Commonly used HTTP status codes	Description
422 Unprocessable Entity	This code indicates that the server cannot process the entity present in the request body. Typically, this happens due to semantic errors such as validation errors.
429 Too Many Requests	This code indicates that the client has sent too many requests in a given time, which results in the rejection of requests due to rate limiting. Note that rate limiting is used for controlling the rate of traffic sent or received by a network interface controller.
500 Internal Server Error	This code indicates that the server encountered an unexpected error scenario while processing the request.

When an operation fails on a resource, the RESTful web API should provide a useful error message to the caller. As a best practice, it is recommended to copy the detailed exception messages into the response body so that the client can take appropriate actions. By default, all JAX-RS containers intercept all exceptions thrown during the processing of the REST APIs and process them in their own way. However, you can provide your own `javax.ws.rs.ext.ExceptionMapper` to override the default exception handling offered by the JAX-RS runtime. We have discussed this topic in detail under the *Mapping exceptions to a response message using ExceptionMapper* section in *Chapter 4, Advanced Features in the JAX-RS API*. The following code snippet illustrates how you can build an `ExceptionMapper` provider for handling `javax.validation.ValidationException`. The `ValidationException` errors are typically thrown by the framework when the bean validation rules that you set on the model class fails.

```
//Imports are removed for brevity
@Provider
// A provider that maps Java exceptions to a Response
public class ValidationExceptionMapper implements
ExceptionMapper<ValidationException> {

    // Map validation exception to a Response
    @Override
    public Response toResponse(ValidationException exception) {
        //Set 400 Bad Request status and error message entity
        if (exception instanceof ConstraintViolationException) {
            return buildResponse(unwrapException((
                ConstraintViolationException) exception),
                MediaType.TEXT_PLAIN, Status.BAD_REQUEST);
```

```
        }else{
        return buildResponse(unwrapException(exception),
            MediaType.TEXT_PLAIN, Status.BAD_REQUEST);
        }
    }
    //Build response obj containing error message as entity
    protected Response buildResponse(Object entity,
        String mediaType,
        Status status) {
        ResponseBuilder builder = Response.status(status).
            entity(entity);
        builder.type(MediaType.TEXT_PLAIN);
        builder.header("validation-Error", "true");
        return builder.build();
    }
    //unwrapException() method definition is removed for brevity
}
```

> The complete source code for this example is available at the
> Packt website. You can download the example from the Packt
> website link mentioned at the beginning of this book in the
> *Preface* section. In the downloaded source code, see the Java
> source file called com.packtpub.rest.ch8.service.
> exception.ValidationExceptionMapper, available in the
> rest-chapter8-jaxrs/rest-chapter8-service project.

Overriding HTTP methods

Due to security reasons, some corporate firewalls (HTTP proxies) support only
the POST and GET methods. This restriction forces a REST API client to use only
those HTTP methods that are allowed through the firewall. RESTful web API
implementations can work around this restriction by letting the client override the
HTTP method via the custom X-HTTP-Method-Override HTTP header. The REST
API client can specify an X-HTTP-Method-Override request header with a string
value containing either PUT, PATCH, or DELETE. When the server gets the request,
the server replaces the POST method call with the method string value set for
X-HTTP-Method-Override.

JAX-RS allows you to implement this behavior via prematching
`javax.ws.rs.container.ContainerRequestFilter`. To learn more about
`ContainerRequestFilter`, refer to the *Understanding filters and interceptors
in JAX-RS* section in *Chapter 4, Advanced Features in the JAX-RS API*.

```
//Other imports are omitted for brevity
import javax.ws.rs.container.PreMatching;
@Provider
@PreMatching
// A provider impl for handling the X-Http-Method-Override header
public class HttpOverride implements ContainerRequestFilter {

    public void filter(ContainerRequestContext ctx) {
        String method = ctx.getHeaderString
            ("X-Http-Method-Override");
        //override header should only be accepted on POST
        if (method != null
            && ctx.getMethod().equals("POST"))
        //Set the method to the X-HTTP-Method-Override header value
            ctx.setMethod(method);
    }
}
```

Documenting RESTful web APIs

Good API documentation improves the market adoption of APIs. The API
documentation should be both human and machine readable. There are many tools
available today for documenting RESTful web APIs. Some of the popular RESTful
web API documentation tools are listed here for your quick reference:

- **WADL**: This tool is an XML description of HTTP-based web applications
  such as RESTful web services. Not many vendors use WADL nowadays
  due to the emergence of more developer-friendly API documentation tools
  such as Swagger, RAML, and API Blueprint. To learn more about the WADL
  specification, visit `http://www.w3.org/Submission/wadl`.

- **RAML**: This tool provides both human- and machine-readable formats
  (YAML) for describing APIs. This is relatively new in the market and is
  well supported by the active open source community. To learn more about
  RAML, visit the official site at `http://raml.org`.

- **Swagger**: This tool allows you to define APIs either in YAML or JSON and is
  backed up by a large open source community. More details can be found at
  `http://swagger.io`.

- **API Blueprint**: This tool provides a documentation-oriented web API description language that uses the markdown format for describing the APIs. It is backed by Apiary and a large open source community. To learn more, visit the official site at `https://apiblueprint.org`.

We discussed WADL, RAML, and Swagger in detail in *Chapter 7, The Description and Discovery of RESTful Web Services*.

Asynchronous execution of RESTful web APIs

If your RESTful web API takes a considerable amount of time for finishing the job and the users cannot wait for the API to finish, you may want to consider using the asynchronous mode of execution.

The asynchronous RESTful web API works as explained here. The client calls the asynchronous RESTful API as any other API:

```
POST /employees HTTP/1.1
[{"departmentId": 10, "departmentName": "IT"},
{"departmentId": 20, "departmentName": "HR"},...]
```

The asynchronous API that is responsible for handling the preceding request accepts the request and returns the `202 Accepted` status to the caller without keeping the caller waiting for the request to finish. The response also can have a temporary resource inside the `Location` header, which can be used by the client to query the status of the process. Here is an example of the response generated by the server:

```
HTTP/1.1 202 Accepted
Location: /queue/job1234
```

The JAX-RS 2.0 specification allows you to build asynchronous APIs via the following two classes:

- `javax.ws.rs.container.AsyncResponse`: This interface gives you a means for asynchronous server-side response processing

- `@javax.ws.rs.container.Suspended`: This annotation is used for injecting a suspended `AsyncResponse` object into a parameter of an invoked JAX-RS resource

To learn how to build an asynchronous RESTful web API with the JAX-RS APIs, refer to the *Asynchronous RESTful web services* section in *Chapter 4, Advanced Features in the JAX-RS API*.

Microservice architecture style for RESTful web applications

Microservice is an architectural style for implementing a single application as a suite of small services. Each service can be deployed and managed separately. This is an emerging software architectural style adopted by many enterprises today in order to meet the rapidly evolving business needs. To follow this pattern for your JAX-RS application, you may want to break down the top-level monolithic JAX-RS resources into separate modules, where each module contains the logically related JAX-RS resource classes. Each module is deployed as a self-contained WAR file. Services communicate with each other via synchronous protocols such as REST over HTTP or asynchronous protocols such as messaging queue. If the performance is really a concern, you can consider using binary protocols, such as Thrift or Avro, for enabling the communication between services. The following diagram demonstrates how you can breakdown the human resource services application of an organization into multiple microservices. It also illustrates the interaction between various microservices.

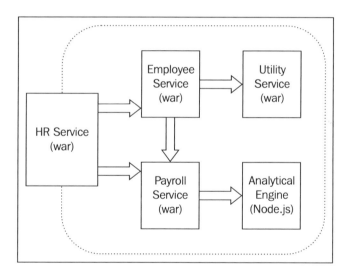

Some of the advantages of the microservice architecture are as follows:

- A small, modular, and easily manageable code base
- Each service can be deployed, managed, and tuned separately
- The ability to use the most appropriate technology stack (polyglot programming model) for individual services
- Improved resilience for the entire application
- Individual modules can be redeployed without affecting the entire application

Using Open Data Protocol with RESTful web APIs

REST is an architecture style for sending messages back and forth from the client to the server over HTTP. The REST architectural style does not define any standard for querying and updating data. **Open Data Protocol (OData)** defines a web protocol for querying and updating data via RESTful web APIs uniformly. Many companies, including Microsoft, IBM, and SAP, support OData today, and it is governed by **Organization for the Advancement of Structured Information Standards (OASIS)**. Currently, the latest release of OData is Version 4.0.

A quick look at OData

OData provides you with a uniform way of describing the data and the data model. This helps you to consume the REST APIs from various vendors uniformly. Let's take a quick look at some of the core features offered in OData with some examples.

URI convention for OData-based REST APIs

The OData specification defines a set of recommendations for forming the URIs that identify OData-based REST APIs. The URI for an OData service may take up to three parts, as follows:

- **Service root**: This part identifies the root of an OData service
- **Resource path**: This part identifies the resources exposed by an OData service
- **Query string options**: This part identifies the query options (built-in or custom) for the resource

Here is an example:

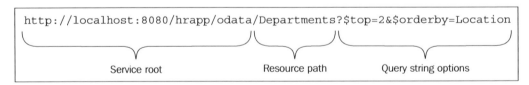

Reading resources

Resources from OData RESTful APIs are accessible via the HTTP GET request. For instance, the following GET request retrieves the Departments entity collection from the OData REST API server as follows:

```
GET http://localhost:8080/hrapp/odata/Departments HTTP/1.1
```

The result that you may get from the OData REST API server in response to the preceding call will be structured in accordance with the OData protocol specification. This keeps the client code simple and reusable.

To read the individual resource element, you can pass the unique identifier for the resource, as shown in the following code snippet. This example reads the details of department with the given ID:

```
GET http://localhost:8080/hrapp/odata/Departments(10) HTTP/1.1.
```

Querying data

OData supports various kinds of query options as query parameters. For instance, $orderby can be used for sorting the query results. Here is an example:

```
GET http://localhost:8080/hrapp/odata/Departments?$orderby=
    DepartmentName HTTP/1.1
```

Similarly, you can use the $select option for limiting the attributes on the entity resources returned by a REST API. Here is an example:

```
GET http://localhost:8080/hrapp/odata/Departments?
$orderby=DepartmentName&$select=DepartmentName,ManagerId HTTP/1.1
```

Some of the frequently used query options are listed in the following table:

Query Option	Description	Example
$filter	This option allows the client to filter a collection of resources.	/Employees? $filter=FirstName eq 'Jobinesh'
$expand	This option includes the specified (child) resource in line with the retrieved resources.	/Departments(10)?$expand= Employees

Query Option	Description	Example
`$select`	This option includes the supplied attributes alone in the resulting entity.	`/Departments?$select=Name, LocationId`
`$orderby`	This option sorts the query result by one or more attributes.	`Departments?$orderby= DepartmentName desc`
`$top`	This option returns only the specified number of items (from the top) in the result collection.	`Departments?$top=10`
`$skip`	This option indicates how many items need to be skipped from the top while returning the result.	`Departments?$skip=10`
`$count`	This option indicates the total number of items in the result.	`Departments/$count`

Modifying data

The updatable OData services provide a standardized interface for performing the following operations on entities exposed via the OData services:

- `Create`: This operation is performed via HTTP POST
- `Update`: This operation is performed via HTTP PUT or HTTP PATCH
- `Delete`: This operation is performed via HTTP DELETE

Relationship operations

OData supports the linking of related resources. Relationships from one entity to another are represented as navigation properties. The following API reads employees in the HR department:

```
http://localhost:8080/hrapp/odata/Departments("HR")/
   EmployeeDetails
```

The OData service even allows you to add, update, and remove a relation via navigation properties. The following example shows how you can use the navigation properties to link the employee with the id value of 1700 to the IT department:

```
POST odata/Departments('IT')/Employees/$ref
OData-Version: 4.0
Content-Type: application/json;odata.metadata=minimal
Accept: application/json
{
  "@odata.id": "odata/Employees(1700)"
}
```

Many API vendors have started considering OData for standardizing their REST APIs, particularly with the release of OData Version 4.0. A detailed discussion of OData is beyond the scope of this book. To learn more about OData, visit the official documentation page available at http://www.odata.org/documentation.

To learn how to transform the **Java Persistence API (JPA)** entities into OData REST APIs, refer to the *Transforming the JPA model in to OData-enabled RESTful web services* section in *Appendix, Useful Features and Techniques*, of this book.

Summary

This chapter summarized the design guidelines, best practices, and coding tips that developers will find useful when building RESTful web services. You can freely refer to this chapter while working with the JAX-RS and Jersey frameworks.

This chapter started with tips for designing and developing scalable RESTful web APIs and moved from the design guidelines to REST API optimization techniques, such as caching, partial representation, partial update, and asynchronous API calls. It then moved on to discuss the microservice architectural style and its relevance. The chapter concluded by discussing OData in short and its usage. By now, you must have learned how to build scalable and well-performing RESTful applications by using the JAX-RS and Jersey APIs.

With this chapter, we finish our journey of RESTful Java web services. We began with the theory of REST, continued with the JAX-RS APIs and the Jersey framework, and completed our study with topics on security, API documentation, and design guidelines. We hope that you enjoyed reading this book.

Useful Features and Techniques

This appendix discusses various useful features and techniques that we deferred while discussing specific topics in this book. Make sure that you read the first three chapters of this book before you start reading this appendix. The following topics are discussed in this appendix:

- Tools for building a JAX-RS application

- The integration testing of JAX-RS resources with Arquillian

- Implementing PATCH support in JAX-RS resources

- Using third-party entity provider frameworks with Jersey

- Transforming a JPA model into OData enabled RESTful web services

- The packaging and deploying of JAX-RS applications

Tools for building a JAX-RS application

The JAX-RS examples discussed in this book are built using the following software and tools:

- **Java SE Development Kit 8 (JDK 8) or newer**: You can download the latest JDK from `http://www.oracle.com/technetwork/java/javase/downloads/index.html`. After downloading the appropriate release of JDK, you can navigate to the **Installation Instructions** section on the download page for detailed instructions of installing JDK in your computer.

- **NetBeans IDE 8.0.2 (with Java EE bundle) or newer**: NetBeans IDE helps you to quickly develop JAX-RS web applications. You can download the latest NetBeans IDE from `https://netbeans.org/downloads`. In the download page, choose either the **Java EE** or **All** download bundles because many of the examples discussed in this book are based on Java EE features.

  Detailed instructions for setting up NetBeans IDE are available at `https://netbeans.org/community/releases/80/install.html`.

- **GlassFish server 4.1 or newer**: GlassFish is an open source application server project for the Java EE platform. The NetBeans Java EE download bundle comes with an integrated GlassFish server, which is good enough for you to run all the examples discussed in this book.

  Alternatively, you can download the latest release of the GlassFish server from `https://glassfish.java.net/download.html` and wire it with NetBeans. The `README.txt` file in the downloaded zip file contains instructions for installing the GlassFish server.

- **Apache Maven 3.2.3 or newer**: Apache Maven is a build tool used in Java applications to compile source files, execute unit tests, and generate deployable artifacts. The NetBeans IDE standard installation comes with an integrated Maven installation by default.

  Alternatively, you can configure NetBeans to use an external Maven installation for building the source. To download Maven, visit `https://maven.apache.org` and navigate to the **Download** section. You will find the installation instructions under the **Installation Instructions** section on the download page itself. To point the NetBeans IDE to use an external maven installation, choose the **Tools | Options** menu item and in the **Java** tab, choose the **Maven** tab. In the Maven page, make sure that **External Maven Home** points to your Maven install folder.

- **Oracle Database Express Edition 11g release 2 or newer**: Oracle Database Express Edition is a lightweight RDBMS, based on the Oracle Database. We use this database to build the examples discussed in this book. To directly download Oracle Database Express Edition 11g Release 2, go to `http://www.oracle.com/technetwork/database/database-technologies/express-edition/downloads/index.html`. Alternatively, you can visit the Oracle Technology Network site: `http://www.oracle.com/technetwork/index.html`, and then navigate to the menu options **Downloads | Database | Oracle Database 11g Express Edition** to reach the download page.

If you want, you can use any lightweight database, such as Apache Derby or db4o, instead of the Oracle database to try out the examples that we discussed in this book. However, in such a case, all the examples that you would download from the Packt site need to be reconfigured to fit into the database that you choose.

- **Oracle Database JDBC Driver (ojdbc7.jar or newer)**: The JDBC driver is a software library that lets Java applications interact with a database. You can download the latest JDBC driver from `http://www.oracle.com/technetwork/database/features/jdbc/jdbc-drivers-12c-download-1958347.html`.

 To learn how to use NetBeans IDE for building JAX-RS web applications, refer to the *Building a simple RESTful web service application using NetBeans IDE*, section in *Chapter 3, Introducing the JAX-RS API*.

Integration testing of JAX-RS resources with Arquillian

Integration testing tests the interactions between the individual software components in a system. It helps you uncover faults with the integrated components of a system earlier in the lifecycle. In this section, we will learn how to develop and run integration tests for a JAX-RS web application.

A typical JAX-RS web application is comprised of various software components, such as databases, the persistence layer, business service implementation, and the client interface layer. Integration tests that you write for a JAX-RS application should test the interaction between all these components when putting them together to build the complete application.

 Unit testing versus integration testing:

A unit test is typically a test written by developers to verify a relatively small piece of code and it should not depend upon any other components or external resources, such as a database. They are narrow in scope.

An integration test verifies that different pieces of the system work together when they are put together to build a complete system. These tests typically require external resources like database instances or third party APIs.

JBoss Arquillian is a powerful tool for integration testing of Java EE applications. With Arquillian, you do not need to take care of setting up the environment, including the container for running integration tests. Arquillian lets you set up the container in three modes, as explained next:

- **Remote**: A remote container runs in a separate JVM

- **Managed**: A managed container is functionally the same as a remote container, except that its lifecycle (starting and stopping) is managed by Arquillian

- **Embedded**: An embedded container resides in the same JVM as your test case

A container can be any of the following types:

- **Servlet container**: Examples of a servlet container are Tomcat and Jetty

- **Full-fledged Java EE application server**: Examples of a full-fledged Java EE application server are JBoss AS, GlassFish, and WebLogic

- **Java SE Contexts and Dependency Injection(CDI) environment**: Examples of Java SE contexts and dependency injection (CDI) environment are OpenEJB and Weld SE

Let's learn how to use Arquillian for building integration tests for a JAX-RS application. The following diagram illustrates the high-level architecture of the application that we use in this example:

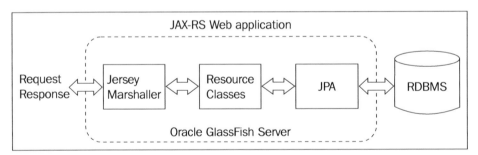

This example exposes stateless session beans as RESTful web resources, and uses **Java Persistence API (JPA)** for database access. We will use Maven for building this example. In reality you can use Arquillian with your favorite build tools, such as Ant, Maven, or Gradle.

The following discussion assumes that you have already created a Maven based JAX-RS application. The source structure may look as follows:

```
-src/
    -main/
      -java/ [Contains all application Java source files]
      -resources/ [Contains all application configuration files]
      -webapp/ [Contains all web files]
    -test/
      -java/ [Contains all test Java source files]
      -resources/ [Contains all test configuration files here]
-pom.xml [The Maven build file]
```

If you are not sure how to build Maven based JAX-RS applications, refer to the *Building a simple RESTful web service application using NetBeans IDE* section, in *Chapter 3, Introducing the JAX-RS API*.

Now, we will look at the steps for adding Arquillian to a Maven based JAX-RS application.

Adding Arquillian dependencies to the Maven-based project

The Arquillian dependency entries in your `pom.xml` file may look like the following:

```
<dependency>
   <groupId>junit</groupId>
   <artifactId>junit</artifactId>
   <version>4.11</version>
   <scope>test</scope>
</dependency>
<dependency>
   <groupId>org.jboss.arquillian.junit</groupId>
   <artifactId>arquillian-junit-container</artifactId>
   <scope>test</scope>
</dependency>
<dependency>
   <groupId>org.jboss.arquillian.container</groupId>
   <artifactId>arquillian-glassfish-managed-3.1</artifactId>
   <version>1.0.0.Final-SNAPSHOT</version>
   <scope>test</scope>
</dependency>
<dependency>
   <groupId>org.glassfish.jersey.containers</groupId>
```

```
        <artifactId>jersey-container-servlet-core</artifactId>
        <version>2.0</version>
        <type>jar</type>
        <scope>provided</scope>
    </dependency>
```

To use the latest release of Arquillian, point your Maven to use repository hosted on `repository.jboss.org`. A quick summary of the dependencies set for Arquillian are as follows:

- **junit and arquillian-junit-container**: These are dependencies for the JUnit and Arquillian JUnit extensions, respectively.

- **arquillian-glassfish-managed**: This represents the managed GlassFish server instance for running the integrations tests.

- **jersey-container-servlet-core**: This dependency is used for Jersey implementation of JAX-RS API.

 The minimum recommended versions of Java and JUnit for using Arquillian are Java 1.6 and JUnit 4.8, respectively.

Configuring the container for running tests

Arquillian uses `arquillian.xml` to locate and communicate with the container. Typically this file is placed in the `src/test/resources` folder. The following `arquillian.xml` file demonstrates entries for connecting to a locally installed GlassFish server, which we use in this example:

```xml
<?xml version="1.0"?>
<arquillian xmlns:xsi="http://www.w3.org/2001/XMLSchema-instance"
            xmlns="http://jboss.org/schema/arquillian"
            xsi:schemaLocation="http://jboss.org/schema/arquillian
                http://jboss.org/schema/arquillian/
                arquillian_1_0.xsd">
    <container qualifier="glassfish" default="true">
        <configuration>
            <property name="glassFishHome">
             D:\glassfish-4.1
            </property>
            <property name="adminHost">localhost</property>
            <property name="adminPort">4848</property>
            <property name="adminUser">admin</property>
            <property name="adminPassword">admin</property>
        </configuration>
    </container>
</arquillian>
```

Adding Arquillian test classes to the project

Once you have the basic infrastructure ready for running tests, you can start building test cases. Add your test classes to the `src/test` folder in the Maven project structure. The following annotations will help you avail of Arquillian features in your test classes:

- Annotate the class with the `@org.junit.runner.RunWith(Arquillian.class)` annotation. This tells JUnit to invoke Arquillian for running tests.

- Designate a `public static` method to return a deployable archive by annotating it with the `@org.jboss.arquillian.container.test.api.Deployment` annotation. This method should return a `org.jboss.shrinkwrap.api.ShrinkWrap.ShrinkWrap` archive. ShrinkWrap is an easy way to create deployable archives in Java, and Arquillian uses this API to build minimal deployable artifacts for running tests. You can learn more about `ShrinkWrap` at `http://arquillian.org/guides/shrinkwrap_introduction`.

- Annotate all the methods that need to be tested with `@org.junit.Test`.

Following is an Arquillian test class example for your quick reference. This class performs integration tests on the department resource:

```
//Other imports are removed for brevity
import org.junit.Test;
import org.jboss.arquillian.container.test.api.Deployment;
import org.jboss.arquillian.junit.Arquillian;
import org.jboss.arquillian.junit.InSequence;
import org.jboss.shrinkwrap.api.ShrinkWrap;
import org.jboss.shrinkwrap.api.spec.WebArchive;

@RunWith(Arquillian.class)
public class DepartmentResourceTest {

    public DepartmentResourceTest() {
    }

    //This method returns minimal files that needs to be deployed
    //for running integration test
    //@Deployment(testable=true) : Runs within container(default)
    //@Deployment(testable=false) : Runs outside of container
    @Deployment(testable=true)
    public static WebArchive createDeployment() {
        return ShrinkWrap
                .create(WebArchive.class, "arquilian-demo-test.war")
```

```
                        .addClasses(Department.class,ApplicationConfig.class,
                             JPAResource.class,
                             DepartmentResource.class)
                        .addAsWebInfResource("test-web.xml",
                                      "web.xml")
                        .addAsResource("test-persistence.xml",
                                     "META-INF/persistence.xml");
    }

    //Method to be tested
    @Test
    @InSequence(1)
    public void testAddDeptResource() {
        WebTarget target = ClientBuilder.newClient()
                .target(
        "http://localhost:8080/arquilian-demo-test/api/departments");
        // Crate a new dept.
        Department dept = new Department();
        dept.setDepartmentId(new Short((short) 10));
        dept.setDepartmentName("HR");
        Department  deptResult = target.request("application/json").
                    post(Entity.json(dept), Department.class);

        assertEquals("HR", deptResult.getDepartmentName());
    }

    //Rest of the methods are removed for brevity
}
```

If you have used JUnit before the preceding test class implementation, it may look familiar to you, except for a couple of methods and APIs:

- The `createDeployment()` method used in this example generates a web archive and deploys it to the container. You do not need to build and deploy an entire application for testing a specific API. The `ShrinkWrap` class exposes APIs to create WebArchive. You can use the `addClasses()` method on the WebArchive to add only the required classes in the web archive file.

- Use the `WebArchive::addAsWebInfResource()` API to specify different configuration files for testing. For instance, in the preceding example's API, call `WebArchive::addAsWebInfResource("test-web.xml", "web.xml")` adds `test-web.xml` to the web archive in the place of `web.xml`. This feature allows you to specify a different set of deployment descriptors and configuration files for the purpose of testing. All the test related resources, such as deployment descriptors and configuration files, are stored in the `src/test/resources` folder.

The complete source code for this example is available in the Packt website. You can download the example from the Packt website link that we mentioned at the beginning of this book, in the *Preface* section. In the downloaded source code, see the `rest-appendix-arquillian` project to a get a feel of end to end implementation.

Running Arquillian tests

Once all the necessary settings and test classes are ready, you can run the Arquillian tests. This process is just like running any unit tests in your project. For example, with Maven, you can use the following command:

```
mvn test
```

Arquillian takes the following steps to run tests:

1. When the test is run, the `@org.junit.runner.RunWith(Arquillian.class)` annotation present on the test class tells JUnit to invoke Arquillian for running the tests, instead of the default runner built into JUnit.

2. Arquillian then looks for a `public static` method annotated with the `@org.jboss.arquillian.container.test.api.Deployment` annotation in the test class to retrieve the deployable archive.

3. In the next step, Arquillian contacts the container configured in `arquillian.xml` and deploys the archive to the container.

4. All methods annotated with `@org.junit.Test` are run now.

In-depth coverage of Arquillian is beyond the scope of this book. To learn more on Arquillian, visit `http://arquillian.org`.

Jersey framework comes with built-in support for unit testing the JAX-RS server-side components. However this lacks many features as compared to Arquillian and is not an ideal tool for performing full fledged integration tests on Java EE components. You can learn more about the Jersey test framework at `https://jersey.java.net/documentation/latest/test-framework.html`.

Implementing PATCH support in JAX-RS resources

When a client changes only one part of the resource, you can optimize the entire update process by allowing the client to send only the modified part to the server and thereby saving the bandwidth and server resources. RFC 5789 proposes a solution for this use case via a new HTTP method, PATCH. We have already covered the theoretical concepts behind the PATCH method in *Chapter 8, RESTful API Design Guidelines*, under the *Implementing partial update* section. In this section, we will see how to actually implement the PATCH method in your JAX-RS application.

Defining the @PATCH annotation

JAX-RS allows you to define annotations to represent any custom or non-standard HTTP methods by annotating them with `javax.ws.rs.HttpMethod`. We will use this feature to define the @PATCH annotation, which can be used later to designate resource class methods for responding to HTTP PATCH method calls. Following is an example:

```
import javax.ws.rs.HttpMethod;
import javax.ws.rs.NameBinding;
//Other imports are removed for brevity
@Target({ElementType.METHOD, ElementType.TYPE})
@Retention(RetentionPolicy.RUNTIME)
@HttpMethod("PATCH")
@Documented
@NameBinding
public @interface PATCH {
}
```

Defining a resource method to handle HTTP PATCH requests

As we discussed at the beginning of this section, a PATCH request sends only the modified fields to the server, along with the type of operations performed on each modified field.

The following example illustrates a PATCH request for a department resource:

```
PATCH /departments/10 HTTP/1.1
[
  { "op": "replace", "path": "/managerId", "value": 300 },
```

```
    { "op": "add", "path": "/locationId", "value": 1200 }
]
```

JAX-RS does not support a PATCH method by default. However, this does not prevent you from supporting PATCH in your application. Following are the steps that you need to take:

1. The resource method that you define should have logic to read the partial changes sent by the client.

2. The next step is to construct the resource entity representation out of the partial representation.

3. The last step is to save the changes.

The following code snippet demonstrates how you can implement a partial update for the Department resource. This example uses the json-patch library available in GitHub (https://github.com/fge/json-patch) to read the partial updates present in the request payload and build an entity out of it:

```java
//Other imports are removed for brevity
import com.fasterxml.jackson.databind.JsonNode;
import com.fasterxml.jackson.databind.ObjectMapper;
import com.github.fge.jsonpatch.JsonPatch;
import javax.ws.rs.Path;
import javax.ws.rs.PathParam;
import javax.ws.rs.Produces;
import javax.ws.rs.WebApplicationException;
import javax.ws.rs.core.Response;
import javax.ws.rs.core.Response.Status;

@Path("departments")
public class DepartmentResource{

@PATCH
@Path("{id}")
@Consumes({"application/json-patch+json"})
public Response patch(@PathParam("id") Short id,
    String deptUpdatesInJSON) {
  // get the dept from DB
  Department dept = findDepartmentEntityFromDB(id);

  try {
    if (dept != null) {
      //The mapper provides
      //functionality for converting between Java objects
```

```
    //and matching JSON constructs.
    ObjectMapper mapper = new ObjectMapper();

    // convert JSON string to a Java class
    //JsonPatch is here https://github.com/fge/json-patch
    JsonPatch patch = mapper.readValue(deptUpdatesInJSON,
                JsonPatch.class);
    // convert Dept from DB to a JSON object
    JsonNode deptJson = mapper.valueToTree(dept);
    // apply patch on latest Dept read from DB
    JsonNode patched = patch.apply(deptJson);
    // convert the patched object to Dept to store
    dept = mapper.readValue(patched.toString(),
                Department.class);
    // save the patched department object
    saveEntity(dept);
}else{
            //Dept obj for the patch sent by client is
            //not found in DB
            return Response.serverError().
                status(Status.NOT_FOUND).build();

    }
} catch (Exception ex) {
    throw new WebApplicationException(ex);
}
return Response.ok().build();
}
//Other methods are removed for brevity


}
```

> The complete source code for this example is available in the Packt
> website. You can download the example from the Packt website link
> that we mentioned at the beginning of this book, in the *Preface* section.
> In the downloaded source code, see the rest-appendix-patch-
> demo project to get a feel of the sample PATCH implementation that
> we discussed in this section.

You can use REST API testing tools, such as the Postman REST client or the SoapUI, to quickly test the PATCH implementation that we built. The sample PATCH API call may look like the following:

```
PATCH /rest-appendix-patch-demo/webresources/departments/10 HTTP/1.1
Host: localhost:8080
Content-Type: application/json-patch+json
Cache-Control: no-cache


[ { "op": "replace", "path": "/departmentName", "value": "IT"},
  { "op": "add", "path": "/locationId", "value": 1200 } ]
```

Using third-party entity provider frameworks with Jersey

We discussed about various frameworks for JSON processing (and binding) in *Chapter 2*, *Java APIs for JSON Processing*. In this section, we will see how to tell JAX-RS runtime to use a different entity provider (also known as binding framework) framework instead of the default one provided by the container.

When you deploy the JAX-RS 2.0 application on theWebLogic or GlassFish server, runtime automatically adds MOXy as the JSON binding framework for your application. Note that MOXy is EclipseLink's object-to-XML and object-to-JSON mapping provider. However, you can override the default JSON processor framework offered by runtime (Jersey) with the one that you may prefer for your application.

The following example overrides the default JSON framework used in the Jersey implementation with Jackson (https://github.com/FasterXML/jackson):

1. The first step is to add dependency to the JSON processor framework that you want to use. For instance, to use Jackson, you need to add jackson-jaxrs-json-provider and jackson-databind jars to the application.

2. Jersey allows you to disable the MOXy JSON framework by setting the jersey.config.disableMoxyJson configuration property to true. You can do this by overriding javax.ws.rs.core.Applicatio::getProperties(). This is shown in the code snippet given towards the end of this section.

3. Next, is to register the Provider class. You can register the provider class as a singleton as this provider does not hold any state.

The following code snippet shows a configuration that you will need to make in the `Application` subclass to use `JacksonJsonProvider` as the JSON binding framework:

```java
//Other imports are omitted for brevity
import javax.ws.rs.core.Application;
import javax.ws.rs.ext.Provider;
import com.fasterxml.jackson.jaxrs.json.JacksonJsonProvider;

@javax.ws.rs.ApplicationPath("webresources")
public class HRApplication extends Application {

    @Override
    public Set<Class<?>> getClasses() {
        Set<Class<?>> resources = new java.util.HashSet<>();
        resources.add(HRService.class);
        return resources;
    }

    @Override
    public Set<Object> getSingletons() {
        Set<Object> set = new HashSet<>();
        // Register JacksonJsonProvider as a singleton
        // to allow reuse of ObjectMapper:
        set.add(
            new com.fasterxml.jackson.jaxrs.json.
            JacksonJsonProvider());
        return set;
    }

    @Override
    public Map<String, Object> getProperties() {
        Map<String, Object> map = new HashMap<>();
        //Disables configuration of MOXy Json feature.
        map.put("jersey.config.disableMoxyJson.server", true);
        return map;
    }
}
```

Transforming the JPA model in to OData-enabled RESTful web services

Open Data Protocol (**OData**) is an open protocol for the web. We discussed the advantages of using OData with RESTful web APIs under the *Using Open Data Protocol with RESTful web APIs* section in *Chapter 8, RESTful API Design Guidelines*. In this section, we will see how to build OData services for the **Java Persistence API (JPA)** model.

Apache Olingo is an open source Java library that implements OData protocol. You can use the Apache Olingo framework to enable OData services for your JPA model. At the time of writing this book, the latest release of Olingo was based on the OData Version 2.0 specifications, and the support for OData Version 4.0 was underway.

With the Olingo framework, you can easily transform your JPA models into OData services using the OData JPA Processor Library.

High level steps for enabling OData 2 services for your JPA model are listed as follows:

1. Build a web project to hold the RESTful web API components.

2. Generate JPA entities as appropriate.

   The next step is to configure the application to use the Apache Olingo framework for generating OData services for the JPA model.

3. Add dependency to the Olingo OData Library (Java) and the OData JPA Processor Library. The complete list of jars is listed at `http://olingo.apache.org/doc/odata2/tutorials/CreateWebApp.html`.

4. Add a service factory implementation that provides a means for initializing the OData JPA Processors and data model provider (JPA entity). You can do this by adding a class that extends `org.apache.olingo.odata2.jpa.processor.api.ODataJPAServiceFactory`, as shown in the following:

```
//Imports are removed for brevity
public class ODataJPAServiceFactoryImpl extends
    ODataJPAServiceFactory {
  //HR-PU is the persistence unit
  //configured in persistence.xml for the JPA model
    final String PUNIT_NAME = "HR-PU";
  @Override
```

```
public ODataJPAContext initializeODataJPAContext()
    throws ODataJPARuntimeException {
  ODataJPAContext oDataJPAContext =
      getODataJPAContext();
  oDataJPAContext.setEntityManagerFactory(
  JPAEntityManagerFactory
  .getEntityManagerFactory(PUNIT_NAME));
    oDataJPAContext.setPersistenceUnitName(PUNIT_NAME);
return oDataJPAContext;
  }
  //Other methods are removed for brevity
}
```

5. Configure the web application by adding `CXFNonSpringJaxrsServlet` to `web.xml`. This servlet manages OData features for your JPA model. Specify the service factory implementation class that you created in the last step as one of the `init` parameters for this servlet. The `web.xml` configuration may look like the following lines:

```xml
<servlet>
    <servlet-name>ODataEnabledJPAServlet</servlet-name>
    <servlet-class>
      org.apache.cxf.jaxrs.servlet.CXFNonSpringJaxrsServlet
    </servlet-class>
    <init-param>
      <param-name>javax.ws.rs.Application</param-name>
      <param-value>
        org.apache.olingo.odata2.core.rest.app.ODataApplication
      </param-value>
    </init-param>
    <init-param>
      <param-name>org.apache.olingo.odata2.service.factory</param-
name>
      <param-value>com.packtpub.odata.ODataJPAServiceFactoryImpl</
param-value>
    </init-param>
    <load-on-startup>1</load-on-startup>
</servlet>
<servlet-mapping>
  <servlet-name>ODataEnabledJPAServlet</servlet-name>
  <url-pattern>/odata/*</url-pattern>
</servlet-mapping>
```

Now you can build the application and deploy it to a JAX-RS container, such as the GlassFish server. The Olingo framework will automatically convert all the JPA entities into OData services. You can access the APIs via standard OData clients. To test the deployment, try accessing the OData service as follows: `http://localhost:8080/<appname>/odata`.

You can go through the tutorial to learn how to build a Java client for OData services at `https://olingo.apache.org/doc/odata2/tutorials/OlingoV2BasicClientSample.html`.

> The complete source code for this example is available in the Packt website. You can download the example from the Packt website link that we mentioned at the beginning of this book, in the *Preface* section. In the downloaded source code, see the `rest-appendix-odata/rest-appendix-odata-service` project.

Packaging and deploying JAX-RS applications

There are multiple ways to configure, package, and deploy a JAX-RS application. While configuring an application, you can use an annotation-based approach (for the Servlet 3.x based container) and thereby avoid deployment descriptors such as `web.xml`. Alternatively, you can use a mix of both approaches, which uses both annotations and `web.xml`. This section describes the various configurations and packaging models followed for a JAX-RS web service application.

The JAX-RS specification states that a RESTful web service must be packaged as part of a web application if you want to run it in a container (web server or application server). Following this rule, any JAX-RS application that you want to deploy on a server must be packaged in a **Web Application Archive (WAR)** file. If the web service is implemented using an EJB, it must be packaged and deployed within a WAR file. The application classes are packaged in `WEB-INF/classes` or `WEB-INF/lib` and all the dependent library jars are packaged in `WEB-INF/lib`. You can configure a JAX-RS application in following ways:

- Using the `javax.ws.rs.core.Application` subclass, without `web.xml`
- Using the `Application` subclass and `web.xml`
- Using `web.xml`, without the `Application` subclass

Let's take a closer look at all these packaging models. The following discussion presumes the Jersey framework as the JAX-RS implementation. Though the basic packaging model is the same across all JAX-RS implementations, the exact value for certain metadata fields used in deployment descriptors, such as the servlet class, may change with each implementation. Please refer to the product documentation if you are using a different JAX-RS implementation.

Packaging JAX-RS applications with an Application subclass

The servlet 3.0 specification allows you to build a web application without `web.xml`. You will annotate the component as appropriate without describing them in web. xml. JAX-RS also follows the same model and allows you to annotate components for supplying metadata required by the runtime and thereby avoiding deployment descriptors, such as `web.xml`, for holding the metadata.

In this packaging model, you will define a class that extends `javax.ws.rs.core.Application`. Your subclass will have entries for all root resources and providers, such as filters, interceptors, message body reader/writers, and feature classes that are used in the application. Additionally, this class can return a map of custom application-wide properties. You can use the `@javax.ws.rs.ApplicationPath` annotation on the subclass to configure the context path for the RESTful web service.

The following is an example of a class that extends `javax.ws.rs.core.Application`. This class configures all the REST resources, message body reader, writer, filters, and interceptors that are used in the application:

```
//Other imports are removed for brevity
import javax.ws.rs.core.Application;

@javax.ws.rs.ApplicationPath("webresources")
public class HRApplication extends Application {
    //Get a set of root resource, provider and feature classes.
    @Override
    public Set<Class<?>> getClasses() {
        Set<Class<?>> resources = new java.util.HashSet<>();
        //Configure resource classes
        resources.add(HRResource.class);
        //Message body writer
        resources.add(CSVMessageBodyWriter.class);
        //Filters and interceptors
        resources.add(CORSResponseFilter.class);
        resources.add(ZippedWriterInterceptor.class);
        return resources;
```

```
    }
//Get a map of custom application-wide properties
 @Override
 public Map<String, Object> getProperties() {
     return super.getProperties();
 }
//Get Singletons instances of set of root resource,
 //provider and feature classes
 @Override
 public Set<Object> getSingletons() {
     return super.getSingletons();
 }
}
```

The default implementations of `getClasses()` and `getSingletons()` return empty sets, which tells runtime to add all resource and provider classes that are identified via annotations. While deploying the application, the JAX-RS runtime scans the deployed artifacts for the REST resource classes (identified by the `@Path` annotation) and providers (identified by the `@Provider` annotation), and automatically discovers and registers all components before the activation of the application.

This packaging model assumes that the application is not bundled with any `web.xml` file. This model leverages the pluggability mechanism offered by the servlet 3.x framework to enable portability between containers. You cannot follow this model if you are deploying the application into servlet 2.x based containers.

If you would like to have a `web.xml` file for the application, then follow the steps given in the next section, for configuring the applications with a servlet, which will show you how to update a `web.xml` file with entries for the JAX-RS servlet.

Packaging the JAX-RS applications with web.xml and an Application subclass

Sometimes, you may want to use both `Application` subclass and `web.xml` for your JAX-RS application. This deployment model will be the best fit for the following scenarios, where you will use `web.xml` to configure the following:

- To configure security for the application
- To specify some context parameters for the application
- To configure some container-specific parameters for the application

Depending on the capabilities of the target server, configuration entries in `web.xml` varies. This will be explained in the following sections.

Configuring web.xml for a servlet 2.x container

The following example illustrates the `web.xml` entries that you make for packaging a JAX-RS application, which contains both the `Application` subclass and `web.xml`. This example uses `com.packtpub.rest.ch4.service.HRApplication` as the application subclass. The following `web.xml` shows configuration entries that you may need to add for deploying into a servlet 2.x container. If there are multiple application subclasses, then you will need to configure them separately:

```
<web-app ... >
    <servlet>
        <servlet-name>jaxrs.servlet</servlet-name>

        <!—- Set this to fully qualified name of the
        Servlet offered by the JAX-RS runtime -->
        <servlet-class>
        org.glassfish.jersey.servlet.ServletContainer
        </servlet-class>

        <!-- Set this element to define the class that
        extends the javax.ws.rs.core.Application -->
        <init-param>
            <param-name>javax.ws.rs.Application</param-name>
            <param-value>
             com.packtpub.rest.ch4.service.HRApplication
            </param-value>
        </init-param>
        <!--Use init params as appropriate-->
        <load-on-startup>1</load-on-startup>
    </servlet>
    <servlet-mapping>
        <servlet-name>jaxrs.servlet</servlet-name>
        <url-pattern>/webresources/*</url-pattern>
    </servlet-mapping>
</web-app>
```

Configuring web.xml for a Servlet 3.x container

If you are deploying the application on a servlet 3.x container, then the configuration entries are much simpler. In this case, you just need to mention the servlet name and servlet mapping, as follows (for each application subclass bundled in the application). Runtime will automatically add the servlet class and assign it to the name that you'd specified:

```
<web-app ...
    <servlet>
```

```
    <!-- Set this element to the fully qualified
    name of the class that extends javax.ws.rs.core.Application
    -->
     <servlet-name>
      com.packtpub.rest.ch4.service.HRApplication
     </servlet-name>
    <!-- servlet-class and init-param are not needed -->
  </servlet>
  <servlet-mapping>
     <servlet-name>
      com.packtpub.rest.ch4.service.HRApplication
     </servlet-name>
     <url-pattern>/webresources/*</url-pattern>
  </servlet-mapping>
</web-app>
```

Packaging the JAX-RS applications with web.xml and without an Application subclass

In some cases, your JAX-RS application will not have any Application subclass apart from web.xml. Though this scenario is rare, the framework supports such a packaging model.

Configuring web.xml for the servlet 2.x container

If the JAX-RS application does not have an Application subclass in the project, then you need to specify a fully qualified servlet class that is used by the JAX-RS runtime, and a servlet-mapping entry in web.xml. You can also specify the package where the runtime should scan though to find the JAX-RS components, such as class resources, filters, interceptors, and so on.

The following example shows the configuration entries that you may need to make in web.xml to deploy a JAX-RS application without the Application subclass on the servlet 2.0 based container:

```
<web-app>
    <servlet>
        <servlet-name>jaxrs.servlet</servlet-name>
        <servlet-class>
         org.glassfish.jersey.servlet.ServletContainer
        </servlet-class>
        <!-- Register resources and providers
         under com.packtpub.rest -->
```

```
    <init-param>
        <param-name>
         jersey.config.server.provider.packages</param-name>
        <param-value>com.packtpub.rest</param-value>
    </init-param>

    <!—
     Register custom providers
     (not needed if they are in com.packtpub.rest)   -->
    <init-param>
        <param-name>
         jersey.config.server.provider.classnames</param-name>
        <param-value>
         com.packtpub.rest.filetr.SecurityRequestFilter;
         com.packtpub.rest.filetr.Logger
        </param-value>
    </init-param>
</servlet>
<servlet-mapping>
    <servlet-name>jaxrs.servlet</servlet-name>
    <url-pattern>/webresources/*</url-pattern>
</servlet-mapping>

</web-app>
```

Configuring web.xml for the servlet 3.x container

The following `web.xml` shows the configurations to deploy a JAX-RS application on the servlet 3.0 container. In this case, we are adding only the mapping entry, not the corresponding servlet class. The container is responsible for adding the corresponding servlet class automatically, for the `javax.ws.rs.core.Application` servlet name. The following `web.xml` demonstrates this configuration:

```
<web-app ...>
    <servlet>
        <servlet-name>javax.ws.rs.core.Application</servlet-name>
    </servlet>
    <servlet-mapping>
        <servlet-name>javax.ws.rs.core.Application</servlet-name>
        <url-pattern>/webresources/*</url-pattern>
    </servlet-mapping>
</web-app>
```

Note that in the preceding case, runtime will automatically detect and register JAX-RS components (by scanning through the annotations).

Summary

In this appendix, we discussed the tools needed for building a JAX-RS application, integration testing JAX-RS applications with Arquillian, and adding the PATCH support for JAX-RS resources. We also discussed an example showing how to convert JPA models into OData enabled RESTful web services. We ended our discussions by taking a look at the various packaging and deployment models for JAX-RS applications.

Index

Symbols

1xx Informational status code series
100 Continue 10
101 Switching Protocols 11
102 Processing 11
about 10
2xx Success status code series
102 Processing 11
200 OK 11
201 Created 11
204 No Content 11
3xx Redirection status code series
304 Not Modified 11
about 11
4xx Client Error status code series
400 Bad Request 11
401 Unauthorized 11
403 Forbidden 11
404 Not Found 11
405 Method Not Allowed 12
408 Request Timeout 12
409 Conflict 12
about 11
5xx Server Error status code series
500 Internal Server Error 12
about 12
@BeanParam annotation 80, 81
@Consumes annotation 69, 70
@Context annotation 79, 80
@CookieParam annotation 77
@DefaultValue annotation 78
@DELETE annotation 72
@Encoded annotation 81

@FormParam annotation 77, 78
@GET annotation 71
@HEAD annotation 72
@HeaderParam annotation 76
@InjectLinks
used, for building HTTP link headers 173
used, for grouping multiple links 172, 173
@javax.ws.rs.NameBinding annotation 148
@MatrixParam annotation 75, 76
@OPTIONS annotation 73
@PATCH annotation
defining 300
@Path annotation
about 66
specifying, on resource class 66
specifying, on resource class method 66
values, restricting for path variables with
    regular expressions 68
variables, specifying URI path template 67
@PathParam annotation 73, 74
@POST annotation 72
@Produces annotation 69
@PUT annotation 71
@QueryParam annotation 74, 75

A

access token URI 207
additional metadata
returning, with responses 82
Apache CXF
URL 64
Apache Maven
URL 292

Apache Olingo 305
Apache Oltu
  reference link 218
API Blueprint
  about 27
  URL 284
application development
  reference link 7
Application subclass
  JAX-RS applications, packaging
    with 308, 309
arguments, wadl2java
  -a 232
  -c customization 232
  -o outputDir 232
  -p package 232
  -s jaxrs20 233
  outputfile.wadl 233
Arquillian
  about 294
  URL 299
Arquillian dependencies
  adding, to Maven based project 295, 296
Arquillian test classes
  adding, to project 297, 298
Arquillian tests
  running 299
asynchronous RESTful web services
  about 126-128
  invoking, on client 129, 130
AsyncResponse instance
  about 127
  cancel() method 127
  register() method 127
  resume() method 127
  setTimeout() method 127
attribute definitions, in constraint
    annotation
  groups 116
  message 116
  payload 116
authentication 192
authorization 192
authorization flow, OAuth 2.0 212, 213
authorization server 211
authorization URI 207

B

basic authentication
  JAX-RS application, configuring for 198-200
  JAX-RS clients, building with 194-197
  JAX-RS services, securing with 197, 198
Bean Validation
  about 113
  constraints 113-115
  URL 118

C

Cache-Control directives
  about 132
  max-age 133
  must-revalidate 133
  no-cache 132
  no-store 133
  no-transform 133
  private 132
  proxy-revalidate 133
  public 132
  s-maxage 133
  URL 133
chunked input
  reading, Jersey client API used 181
chunked output
  generating, Jersey APIs used 178
classes and interfaces, @Context annotation
  javax.servlet.http.HttpServletRequest 80
  javax.servlet.http.HttpServletResponse 80
  javax.servlet.ServletConfig 80
  javax.servlet.ServletContext 80
  javax.ws.rs.core.Application 79
  javax.ws.rs.core.HttpHeaders 80
  javax.ws.rs.core.Request 79
  javax.ws.rs.core.SecurityContext 80
  javax.ws.rs.core.UriInfo 79
  javax.ws.rs.ext.ContextResolver<T> 80
  javax.ws.rs.ext.Providers 80
client APIs
  JAX-RS client API dependency,
    specifying 99
  REST APIs, calling with JAX-RS
    client 99-101
  used, for accessing REST APIs 101, 102

used, for accessing RESTful web services 98
client (consumer) 205, 211
coarse-grained resource APIs
 naming 260, 261
Collection+JSON format
 URL 271
command-line interface (CLI)
 about 239
 URLs 239-241
comma-separated values (CSV) 45
Common Object Request Broker
 Architecture (CORBA) 25
Concise Binary Object Representation
 (CBOR) 45
conditional data update, in RESTFul
 web services 138
 Etag of resource, comparing 138
 last modified date of resource,
  comparing 138
container modes, Arquillian
 embedded 294
 managed 294
 remote 294
ContainerRequestFilters
 about 140
 postmatching 140
 postmatching server-side request
  message filters 140
 prematching 140
 prematching server-side request
  message filters 142
container types, Arquillian
 full-fledged Java EE application server 294
 Java SE Contexts and Dependency
  Injection(CDI) environment 294
 servlet container 294
Content Negotiation 100
content types
 representing, HTTP header fields used 9
Context and Dependency Injection (CDI)
 URL 107
Coordinated Universal Time (UTC) 262
core architectural elements, RESTful system
 about 14
 generic interaction semantics, for REST
  resources 16, 17

Hypermedia as the Engine of Application
 State (HATEOAS) 25
 representation of resources 16
 resources 14
 URI 15
Cross Origin Resource Sharing (CORS) 143
custom entity provider
 building 120
 CSV representation,
  marshalling to Java objects with
  MessageBodyReader 124-126
 Java objects, marshalling to CSV
  representation with
  MessageBodyWriter 121-123
custom request-response message formats
 supporting 118-120
custom validation constraints
 building 116, 117

D

data binding rules, JAX-RS
 about 83
 JAXB, used for managing request
  and response entity body
  mapping 84-87
 path variable, mapping with Java types 83
 request and response entity body,
  mapping with Java types 84
data types, JSON
 array 31
 Boolean 31
 null 31
 number 31
 object 31
 string 31
dependencies
 specifying, for Jersey 156
 specifying, for using Jersey declarative
  linking 169
dependencies, Arquillian
 arquillian-glassfish-managed 296
 jersey-container-servlet-core 296
 junit and arquillian-junit-container 296
dependencies, for JSR 353 - Java API
 URL 34

dependencies, Gson APIs
URL 53
dependencies, Jackson2 APIs
URL 46
digest authentication realm,
GlassFish server
reference link 202
Document Object Model (DOM) 34

E

EclipseLink MOXy 87
elements, WADL
<method> 226
<request> 227
<resource> 226
<resources> 226
<response> 227
entity filtering offerings, Jersey framework
reference link 222
Entity tags (ETag)
about 136
URL 136
ETag HTTP response header 136
exception handling, in JAX-RS
about 107
error reporting, application exceptions
used 110, 111
error reporting, ResponseBuilder
used 107, 108
error reporting, WebApplicationException
used 108-110
exceptions, mapping to response message
with ExceptionMapper 111, 112
Expires HTTP header 131
Expression Language (EL) 171

F

filters and interceptors, in JAX-RS
about 139
applying dynamically, on REST
resources 150
applying selectively, on REST
resources 148-150
order of execution, managing 148

request and response message
bodies, modifying with JAX-RS
interceptors 146
request and response parameters,
modifying with JAX-RS filters 140
fine-grained resource APIs
naming 260, 261
fluent APIs
URL 98
formats, for specifying JSON REST API
hypermedia links
JSON Hypermedia API Language
(HAL) 165
RFC 5988 (Web Linking) 164, 165

G

generic interaction semantics,
REST resources
about 16
HTTP DELETE method 23
HTTP GET method 18
HTTP POST method 21
HTTP PUT method 22
GlassFish
URL 201
GlassFish server
groups, defining in 201, 202
URL 292
users, defining in 201, 202
GlassFish server administration guide
reference link 202
grant types, OAuth 2.0
about 213
authorization code 213
client credential 214
implicit 213
resource owner password credentials 213
groups
defining, in GlassFish server 201, 202
Gson
URL 60
Gson API
URL 60
used, for processing JSON 53
Gson streaming APIs
JSON data, reading with 57, 58

JSON data, writing with 59, 60
JSON, processing with 57

H

HATEOAS APIs
  building 163, 164
header parameter
  Accept 261
  Content-Type 262
  using, for content negotiation 261
**high-level architectural view, RESTful
    system 3, 4**
Home Documents
  URL 165
HTTP 4
HTTP/0.9 4
HTTP/1.0 4
HTTP/1.1 4
HTTP/2 4
HTTP basic authentication
  about 192-194
  reference link 197
HTTP Cache-Control directives
  max-age 277
  must-revalidate 277
  no-cache 277
  no-store 277
  private 277
  public 277
  smax-age 277
**HTTP cache, managing in RESTful
    web service**
  about 131
  Cache-Control directives, using 132-134
  conditional data update 138, 139
  ETag HTTP response header, conditional
    request processing with 136, 137
  Expires header, using 131, 132
  Last-Modified HTTP response header,
    conditional request processing
    with 134, 135
HTTP conditional requests
  about 278
  ETag 278
  Last-Modified 278
HTTP digest authentication 202, 203

HTTP header fields
  used, for representing content types 9
HTTP link headers
  building, @InjectLinks used 173
HTTP methods
  about 234
  DELETE 257
  GET 256
  operations, transforming to 256, 257
  overriding 282
  POST 257
  PUT 257
  query parameters 234
  request data 234
HTTP request headers
  URL 100
HTTP request methods
  about 8
  CONNECT 8
  DELETE 8
  GET 8
  HEAD 8
  OPTIONS 8
  PATCH 8
  POST 8
  PUT 8
  TRACE 8
HTTP request-response model 5-7
HTTP status codes
  200 OK 279
  201 Created 279
  204 No Content 279
  304 Not Modified 279
  400 Bad Request 279
  401 Unauthorized 280
  403 Forbidden 280
  404 Not Found 280
  406 Not Acceptable 280
  409 Conflict 280
  410 Gone 280
  415 Unsupported Media Type 280
  422 Unprocessable Entity 281
  429 Too Many Requests 281
  500 Internal Server Error 281
  about 10
  categories 279

HTTP status codes, IANA
  URL 12
HTTP status codes series
  1xx Informational 10
  2xx Success 11
  3xx Redirection 11
  4xx Client Error 11
  5xx Server Error 12
HTTP versions 4
Hypermedia API Language (HAL)
  about 268
  embedded resources 268
  links 268
  RFC 5988 270, 271
  URL 269
Hypertext as the Engine of Application
    State (HATEOAS)
  Hypermedia API Language (HAL) 268
  using, in response representation 268
Hypertext Transfer Protocol. See HTTP

I

idempotent 256
input validation 224
integration test 293
integration testing of JAX-RS resources,
    with Arquillian
  about 293, 294
  Arquillian dependencies, adding to
    Maven based project 295, 296
  Arquillian test classes, adding to
    project 297, 298
  container, configuring for running tests 296
Internationalized Resource Identifiers (IRIs)
    164, 270
Internet Assigned Numbers Authority
    (IANA)
  URL 10
ISO-8601 format 262

J

Jackson
  URL 53, 303
Jackson API
  used, for processing JSON 45

Jackson streaming APIs
  used, for generating JSON 52
  used, for parsing JSON data 50
Jackson tree model APIs
  used, for querying data 47, 48
  used, for updating data 47, 48
Java API for JSON Processing 34
Java Architecture for XML Binding.
    See JAXB
Java Bean Validation 112
Java client
  generating, from Swagger 251, 252
  generating, from WADL 232
  URL 232
Java client, for OData services
  URL, for tutorials 307
Java Persistence API (JPA)
  about 93, 289
  URL 93
Java Persistence API model. See JPA model
Java Platform Enterprise Edition
    (Java EE) 27
Java Remote Method Invocation
    (Java RMI) 25
JavaScript Object Notation for Linked Data
  URL 165
JavaScript Object Notation (JSON) 10
Java SE Development Kit 8 (JDK 8)
  URL, for downloading 291
Java Specification Request (JSR) 34
JavaTM API for JSON Binding (JSON-B) 37
Java tools and frameworks
  used, for building RESTful web services 27
javax.annotation.security annotations
  used, for controlling access with
    Jersey framework 220, 221
javax.json.JsonArrayBuilder builder
    class 39
javax.json.JsonObjectBuilder builder
    class 39
javax.ws.rs.ext.MessageBodyReader<T>
    provider
  isReadable() method 124
  readFrom() method 124
javax.ws.rs.ext.MessageBodyWriter<T>
  about 120
  getSize() method 121

isWriteable() method 121
writeTo() method 121
JAXB
  used, for managing request and response
    entity body mapping 85
JAXB annotations
  @javax.xml.bind.annotation.Xml
    AccessorType 85
  @javax.xml.bind.annotation.Xml
    RootElement 85
  @javax.xml.bind.XmlElement 85
  @javax.xml.bind.XmlTransient 85
JAX-RS
  @PathParam, using 83
  @QueryParam, using 83
  annotations 64
  data binding rules 83
  exception handling 107
  filters and interceptors 139
  generating, from RAML 239, 240
  generating, from RAML via CLI 241
  implementations 64
  overview 63
  RAML, generating from 236-238
  resource lifecycle 151-153
  subresources 104, 105
  subresources locators 105-107
  Swagger, generating from 244-246
  URL 232
  used, for building RESTful web service 87
  WADL, generating 228-231
JAX-RS annotations
  for accessing request parameters 73
  for defining RESTful resource 65
  for processing HTTP request methods 70
  for specifying dependence of JAX-RS
    API 65
  for specifying request-response media
    types 68
  URL 65
  using, for building RESTful web services 65
JAX-RS annotations, for accessing request
    parameters
  about 73
  @BeanParam 80
  @Context 79
  @CookieParam 77

@DefaultValue 78
@Encoded 81
@FormParam 77
@HeaderParam 76
@MatrixParam 75, 76
@PathParam 73, 74
@QueryParam 75
JAX-RS annotations, for processing HTTP
    request methods
  @DELETE 72
  @GET 71
  @HEAD 72
  @OPTIONS 73
  @POST 72
  @PUT 71
  about 70
JAX-RS annotations, for specifying
    request-response media types
  @Consumes 69, 70
  @Produces 69
  about 68
JAX-RS APIs
  used, for building entity body
    links 166, 167
  used, for building header links 168
JAX-RS applications
  configuring, for basic
    authentication 198-200
  deploying 307, 308
  packaging 307, 308
  packaging, with Application
    subclass 308, 309
  validations 112
JAX-RS applications, packing with web.xml
    and Application subclass
  about 309
  web.xml, configuring for Servlet 2.x
    container 310
  web.xml, configuring for Servlet 3.x
    container 310
JAX-RS applications, packing with web.xml
    and without Application subclass
  about 311
  web.xml, configuring for Servlet 2.x
    container 311
  web.xml, configuring for Servlet 3.x
    container 312

JAX-RS clients
building, with basic authentication 194-197
JAX-RS implementations
Apache CXF 64
Jersey RESTful web service framework 64
RESTEasy 64
Restlet 64
jaxrs-raml-maven-plugin
URL 236
JAX-RS resources
configuring, programmatically during
deployment 157-159
modifying, during deployment 160
PATCH support, implementing in 300
static resource configurations 160
JAX-RS services
securing, with basic authentication 197, 198
Jersey
dependencies, specifying for 156
role-based entity data filtering,
using 222-224
third-party entity provider frameworks,
using with 303
Jersey annotations
used, for building links 169
Jersey APIs
used, for building OAuth 1.0 client 206
used, for building OAuth 2.0 client 214-218
used, for generating chunked output 178
used, for monitoring RESTful web
services 189
used, for reading binary large objects 174
used, for writing binary large objects 174
Jersey client API
used, for reading chunked input 181
Jersey declarative linking feature
enabling, for application 169
Jersey example
URL 263
Jersey framework
about 299
URL 299
Jersey model processor
about 160
working 160
Jersey modules
reference link 156

Jersey RESTful web service framework
URL 64
Jersey server-side configuration
properties 187, 188
Jersey User Guide
reference link 189
JPA model
about 294, 305
transforming, into OData enabled RESTful
web services 305-307
JSON
about 29
data types 31
generating, Jackson streaming APIs
used 52
processing, Jackson API used 45
processing, with Gson API 53
processing, with Gson Streaming APIs 57
JSON data
parsing, Jackson streaming APIs used 50
processing 32, 33
reading, with Gson streaming APIs 57, 58
syntax 30
writing, with Gson streaming APIs 59, 60
JSON for Linking Data (JSON-LD format)
URL 271
JSON Hypermedia API Language (HAL)
about 165
link relation 165
reference link 165
target URI 165
type 165
json-patch library
URL 301
**JSON, processing with Gson object
model APIs**
about 54
JSON representation, generating from
object model 56
object model, generating from JSON
representation 54, 55
parameterized Java collection, generating
from JSON representation 55, 56
**JSON, processing with Jackson data
binding APIs**
about 48

full Jackson data binding, with
  specialized objects 49
simple Jackson data binding, with
  generalized objects 48
**JSON, processing with Jackson
  streaming APIs 50**
**JSON, processing with Jackson tree
  model APIs 46**
**JSON, processing with JSR 353 object
  model APIs**
about 34
JSON representation, generating from
  object model 39, 40
object model, generating from JSON
  representation 35-38
**JSON, processing with JSR 353
  streaming APIs**
about 41
streaming APIs, used for generating
  JSON data 44, 45
streaming APIs, used for parsing JSON
  data 41, 44
JSON Schema
URL 165
JSR 353
about 34
using 34
JSR 367 37

L

Last-Modified HTTP header 134
line of business (LOB) 13
links
adding, to resource representation 170, 171
building, Jersey annotations used 169

M

MediaType class
URL 70
MessageBodyReader provider 124
MessageBodyWriter provider 121
URL 121
methods, for processing JSON
data binding API 46
streaming API 46
tree model APIs 46

microservice architecture
advantages 285
for RESTful web application 285
ModelProcessor
methods 161-163
used, for modifying JAX-RS resources
  during deployment 160
modified resources
returning, to caller 265
**multilingual RESTful web API
  resources 262**
multiple links
grouping, @InjectLinks used 172, 173

N

NetBeans IDE
URL 292
used, for building RESTful web service
  application 88-92

O

OAuth
used, for securing RESTful web
  services 203
OAuth 1.0 client
building, Jersey APIs used 206
OAuth 1.0 protected resource
accessing 207-210
OAuth 1.0 protocol
about 204
example 204, 205
reference link 206
OAuth 2.0
about 210
authorization flow 212, 213
grant types 213, 214
improvements 210
reference link 214
roles, defining in authorization process 211
OAuth 2.0 client
building, Jersey APIs used 214-218
OAuth 2.0 protected Google APIs
reference link 215
object model 33
object model APIs, JSR 353
URL 35

OData enabled RESTful web services
JPA model, transforming into 305-307
Olingo OData Library (Java)
URL 305
Open Data Protocol (OData)
about 286
data, modifying 288
data, querying 287, 288
relationship operations 288, 289
resources, reading 287
URI convention 286
URL 289
using, with RESTful web APIs 286
Oracle Database Express Edition 11g
Release 2
URL 292
Oracle Database JDBC Driver
URL, for downloading 293
Oracle XE
HR sample schema , URL 93
Organization for the Advancement of
Structured Information Standards
(OASIS) 286

P

partial response
implementing 263
partial update
implementing 263, 264
PATCH support
implementing, in JAX-RS resources 300
Plain Old Java Object (POJO) 48
Play 28
POST 258
Postman
about 97
URL 97
postmatching server-side request
message filters 140
prematching server-side request
message filters 142
primitive Java types
URL 83
PrintInc 204
problem domain
resource, identifying 256

programming models, for processing JSON
object model 33
streaming model 33
Project Object Model (POM) 65, 156
protected resource 205
PUT 258

Q

query options
$count 288
$expand 287
$filter 287
$orderby 288
$select 288
$skip 288
$top 288

R

RAML
about 233, 283
features 252
for JAX-RS, URL 236
generating, from JAX-RS 236, 237
generating, from JAX-RS via CLI 239
JAX-RS, generating from 239, 240
market adoption 241
structure overview 234, 235
URL 283
raml-jaxrs-maven-plugin
URL 239
README.md file
URL 252
Representational State Transfer. *See* **REST**
request and response message bodies,
modifying with JAX-RS interceptors
request message body interceptors,
implementing 146, 147
response message body interceptors,
implementing 147, 148
request and response parameters,
modifying with JAX-RS filters
client-side request message filters,
implementing 144, 145
client-side response message filters,
implementing 145

server-side request message filters,
    implementing 140
server-side response message filters,
    implementing 143
request token URI 207
resource collection
  count attribute 266
  hasMore attribute 266
  limit attribute 266
  links attribute 266
  paging 266
  totalSize attribute 266
ResourceConfig class
  reference link 160
resource lifecycle, JAX-RS 151-153
resource method
  defining, for handling HTTP PATCH
    requests 300-303
resource owner 205, 211
resource server 211
REST 1, 255
REST architectural style
  about 1, 2
  reference link 1
RESTful system
  cacheable 2
  client-server 2
  code on demand 2
  core architectural elements 14
  high-level architectural view 3, 4
  layered system 2
  stateless 2
  uniform interface 2
RESTful web API documentation tools
  about 283
  API Blueprint 284
  RAML 283
  Swagger 283
  WADL 283
RESTful web API results
  caching 276
  HTTP Cache-Control directive 277
  HTTP conditional requests 277
RESTful web APIs
  asynchronous execution 284
  documenting 283
  HTTP header versioning 274

HTTP status codes, using 279-282
media type versioning 275, 276
microservice architecture style 285
Open Data Protocol (OData), using 286
URI versioning 273
URI versioning, drawbacks 274
versioning 272
versioning, hybrid approach 276
RESTful web application
  basePath property 243
  consumes property 243
  definitions property 243
  externalDocs property 243
  host property 243
  info property 243
  parameters property 243
  paths property 243
  produces property 243
  responses property 243
  schemes property 243
  securityDefinitions property 243
  security property 243
  swagger property 243
RESTful web resources
  date, representing 262
  naming 258-260
  time, representing 262
RESTful web service
  about 13, 226
  accessing, with client APIs 98
  building, for reading images 177
  building, for storing images 174, 175
  building, Java tools and frameworks
    used 27
  building, with JAX-RS 87
  discovery 26, 27
  evolution 12-14
  monitoring, Jersey APIs used 189
  securing, with OAuth 203
  Server Sent Event, supporting in 182-186
RESTful web service accesses
  authorizing, via security APIs 218
RESTful web service, building
  CRUD operations, adding on REST
    resource class 93-98
  environment, setting up 87, 88
  JAX-RS, using 87

NetBeans IDE, using 88-92
Restlet
  URL 64
REST resource class
  CRUD operations, adding 93-98
RESTX 27
RFC 5789
  URL 263
RFC 5988
  about 270
  attributes for target IRI 270
  collection+JSON format 271
  JSON for Linking Data (JSON-LD
    format 271
  JSON Schema 271
  link relation type 270
  target URI 270
  URL 270
RFC 5988 (Web Linking)
  about 164
  attributes, for target IRI 165
  link relation type 165
  target URI 164
RFC 6838
  about 275
  URL 275
RFC 6902
  about 264
  URL 264
role-based entity data filtering, Jersey
  using 222-224
root resource class 104

S

sample JSON document file
  used, for representing employee objects 32
search operation
  implementing 267
Secure Socket Layer (SSL) 201, 202
security 191
security APIs
  RESTful web service accesses,
    authorizing via 218
SecurityContext APIs
  reference link 219

RESTful web service accesses,
  authorizing via 219
SecurityContext, methods
  getAuthenticationScheme() 219
  getUserPrincipal() 219
  isSecure() 219
  isUserInRole(String role) 219
security, elements
  authentication 192
  authorization 192
security, Java web application
  reference link 201
Server Sent Event (SSE)
  supporting, in RESTful web
    services 182-186
server (service provider) 205
Service-Oriented Architecture (SOA) 13
ShrinkWrap
  about 297
  URL 297
Simple Object Access Protocol (SOAP) 12
sort operations
  implementing 267
Spark 27
SSL configuration, on Jersey client
  reference link 202
Streaming API for XML (StAX) 41
streaming APIs, JSR 353
  URL 41
streaming model 33
structure overview, RAML
  about 234
  basic information 234
  HTTP methods 234
  resources and nested resources 234
  response 235
  security 234
subresource locators, JAX-RS 105-107
subresources, JAX-RS 104, 105
Swagger
  about 27, 242
  annotation, adding on JAX-RS resource
    class 248-251
  annotations 245
  annotations, URL 246
  API overview 244
  client 242

definition, configuring 247, 248
dependency, specifying 246, 247
features 252
generating, from JAX-RS 244-246
Java client, generating from 251, 252
market adoption 252
server 242
structure overview 242, 243
URL 247, 283
user interface 242
Swagger 2.0
  URL 244
Swagger projects
  swagger-codegen 244
  swagger-core 244
  swagger-editor 244
  swagger-spec 244
  swagger-ui 244
  URL 244

T

third-party entity provider frameworks
  using, with Jersey 303
token types, JsonParser
  URL 52
tools, for building JAX-RS application
  Apache Maven 3.2.3 292
  GlassFish server 4.1 292
  Java SE Development Kit 8 (JDK 8) 291
  NetBeans IDE 8.0.2 292
  Oracle Database Express Edition 11g
    release 2 292
  Oracle Database JDBC Driver 293
Transport Layer Security (TLS) 201, 202

U

Uniform Resource Identifier (URI)
  about 7
  URL 8
Uniform Resource Locator (URL) 7
unit test 293
Universal Character Set (UCS) 164
**URI convention, for OData-based
    REST APIs**
  about 286

query string options 286
resource path 286
service root 286
uriParameters property 234
URL specification
  URL 82
users
  defining, in GlassFish server 201, 202

V

validations, in JAX-RS applications
  about 112
  Bean Validation 113
  Bean Validation, failing 118
  custom validation constraints,
    building 115-117

W

WADL
  about 27, 226, 283
  features 252
  generating, from JAX-RS 228-231
  Java client, generating 232
  market adoption 233
  specification, URL 227
  structure overview 226, 227
  URL 283
Web Application Archive (WAR) 307
Web Application Description Language.
    See **WADL**
web services
  authenticating 192
  securing 192
**Web Services Description Language
    (WSDL) 12**
World Wide Web Consortium (W3C) 226
World Wide Web (WWW) 3
WSDL 2.0 27

Y

Yaml Ain't Markup Language (YAML)
  about 233
  URL 233

Thank you for buying
RESTful Java Web Services
Second Edition

About Packt Publishing

Packt, pronounced 'packed', published its first book, *Mastering phpMyAdmin for Effective MySQL Management*, in April 2004, and subsequently continued to specialize in publishing highly focused books on specific technologies and solutions.

Our books and publications share the experiences of your fellow IT professionals in adapting and customizing today's systems, applications, and frameworks. Our solution-based books give you the knowledge and power to customize the software and technologies you're using to get the job done. Packt books are more specific and less general than the IT books you have seen in the past. Our unique business model allows us to bring you more focused information, giving you more of what you need to know, and less of what you don't.

Packt is a modern yet unique publishing company that focuses on producing quality, cutting-edge books for communities of developers, administrators, and newbies alike. For more information, please visit our website at www.packtpub.com.

About Packt Open Source

In 2010, Packt launched two new brands, Packt Open Source and Packt Enterprise, in order to continue its focus on specialization. This book is part of the Packt Open Source brand, home to books published on software built around open source licenses, and offering information to anybody from advanced developers to budding web designers. The Open Source brand also runs Packt's Open Source Royalty Scheme, by which Packt gives a royalty to each open source project about whose software a book is sold.

Writing for Packt

We welcome all inquiries from people who are interested in authoring. Book proposals should be sent to author@packtpub.com. If your book idea is still at an early stage and you would like to discuss it first before writing a formal book proposal, then please contact us; one of our commissioning editors will get in touch with you.

We're not just looking for published authors; if you have strong technical skills but no writing experience, our experienced editors can help you develop a writing career, or simply get some additional reward for your expertise.

RESTful Java Patterns and Best Practices

ISBN: 978-1-78328-796-3   Paperback: 152 pages

Learn best practices to efficiently build scalable, reliable, and maintainable high performance RESTful services

1. Learn how to build RESTful services with JAX-RS 2.0.

2. Efficiently use the techniques outlined to build reliable and highly available applications based on REST.

3. Compare REST API from Twitter, GitHub, Facebook and others in a conversational and easy-to-follow style.

RESTful Java Web Services Security

ISBN: 978-1-78398-010-9   Paperback: 144 pages

Secure your RESTful applications against common vulnerabilities

1. Learn how to use, configure, and set up tools for applications that use RESTful web services to prevent misuse of resources.

2. Get to know and fix the most common vulnerabilities of RESTful web services APIs.

3. A step-by-step guide portraying the importance of securing a RESTful web service with simple examples applied to real-world scenarios.

Please check **www.PacktPub.com** for information on our titles

Developing RESTful Web Services with Jersey 2.0

ISBN: 978-1-78328-829-8   Paperback: 98 pages

Create RESTful web services smoothly using the robust Jersey 2.0 and JAX-RS APIs

1. Understand and implement the Jersey and JAX-RS APIs with ease.

2. Construct top-notch server and client side web services.

3. Learn about Server sent events, for showing real-time data.

Developing RESTful Services with JAX-RS 2.0, WebSockets, and JSON

ISBN: 978-1-78217-812-5   Paperback: 128 pages

A complete and practical guide to building RESTful Web Services with the latest Java EE7 API

1. Learning about different client/server communication models including but not limited to client polling, Server-Sent Events and WebSockets.

2. Efficiently use WebSockets, Server-Sent Events, and JSON in Java EE applications.

3. Learn about JAX-RS 2.0 new features and enhancements.

Please check **www.PacktPub.com** for information on our titles

Made in the USA
Lexington, KY
10 February 2017